Living and Dying with Cancer

Living and Dying with Cancer is a powerful and moving account of the experiences of those affected by one of the most common causes of death in the Western world. Through a series of individual narratives based on extensive interviews carried out by the author, the book explores the impact that being diagnosed with cancer has on those with the disease and the people around them. It follows the different trajectories of the disease from the very first symptoms, through treatment to death and shows how the experience of the disease and even the way it develops is affected by the social context of the people involved, as well as their own physical and psychological characteristics. This book will be an invaluable resource not only for social scientists and health professionals but also for those coming to terms with the impact of cancer on their own lives.

ANGELA ARMSTRONG-COSTER is a Lecturer in the Division of Social Sciences, University of Southampton, with interests in palliative care, death and dying and narrative research. She is also a regular contributor to the media in these areas.

Living and Dying with Cancer

Angela Armstrong-Coster

CAMBRIDGE
UNIVERSITY PRESS

04-67

PUBLISHED BY THE PRESS SYNDICATE OF THE UNIVERSITY OF CAMBRIDGE
The Pitt Building, Trumpington Street, Cambridge, United Kingdom

CAMBRIDGE UNIVERSITY PRESS
The Edinburgh Building, Cambridge, CB2 2RU, UK
40 West 20th Street, New York, NY 10011–4211, USA
477 Williamstown Road, Port Melbourne, VIC 3207, Australia
Ruiz de Alarcón 13, 28014 Madrid, Spain
Dock House, The Waterfront, Cape Town 8001, South Africa

http://www.cambridge.org

© Angela Armstrong-Coster 2004

First published 2004

Printed in the United Kingdom at the University Press, Cambridge

Typeface Plantin 10/12 pt.   *System* LaTeX 2$_\varepsilon$ [TB]

A catalogue record for this book is available from the British Library

Library of Congress Cataloguing in Publication Data
Armstrong-Coster, Angela.
Living and dying with cancer / Angela Armstrong-Coster.
    p. cm.
Includes bibliographical references and index.
ISBN   0521 83765 0 – ISBN 0 521 54667 2 (pbk.)
1. Cancer – Patients – Interviews.   2. Cancer – Psychological aspects.
3. Death – Psychological aspects.   I. Title.
RC262.A756   2004
362.196′994 – dc22   2003065617

ISBN 0 521 83765 0 hardback
ISBN 0 521 54667 2 paperback

This book is dedicated
with love to my father, Ronnie Armstrong, who
   taught me so much
and to
all the individuals who participated in the research,
   many of whom you will meet in the pages of this
   book.

Death is no enemy of life; it restores our sense of the value of living. Illness restores the sense of proportion that is lost when we take life for granted. To learn about value and proportion, we need to honor illness, and ultimately to honor death.

Arthur W. Frank, *At the Will of the Body* (1991: 120)

. . . my *life* counts; its termination, its being-no-more, my *death*, is no more a senseless, absurd, unjustifiable occurrence: not that sinking into the emptiness of non-existence it once was – that vanishing which changes nothing in the world. Through making myself for-the-other, I make myself for-myself, I pour meaning into my being-in-the world. I refuse the world the licence to disdain and dismiss my presence; I force the world to note, and to dread in advance my passing away, and to bewail it when it comes. [his italics]

Zygmunt Bauman, *Mortality, Immortality
and Other Life Strategies* (1992: 202)

Contents

Tables

Preface: Opening the silence

Dying is a period of life, fraught with complex issues which can occasion a depth of feeling impossible to quantify. This, in part, may be why details about the actual minutiae of dying, a devastating experience, are not usually made public knowledge. The actuality of serving what is left of a life, of continuing to survive in what to many becomes an enforced and unspeakable existence, is not often aired before the public. The pain is quite simply too much to be transmitted (Frank, 1995). Consequently, there is a dearth of valid, truthful experiential accounts of dying which warrants immediate attention. My respondents allowed me a brief glimpse into that most awful of experiences.

To give these previously silent voices a space in which they may be heard, to open up this silence, I decided that this book would be narrative driven. I was aware of the value of the stories and the responsibility of presenting the information ethically. Having grasped something of their pain and appreciated the urgent need for these stories to be made public, my objective was to act as transmitter of what I heard. This book is primarily concerned with presenting and analysing the respondents' view, the stories which they told me. It makes no claim to be generalisable. It quite simply attempts to present a series of accounts from individuals of what it was like for them to be dying from cancer. As with all individuals, their reactions were based on their interpretations (Hammersley and Atkinson, 1996) of their experiences, so it would be foolish to claim that any one reaction held validity over another or that anyone else, given the same variables, would act in the same way.

My problem was that the data required was, even by the standards of those not dying, of an exceptionally sensitive nature. I needed a tool that could respond effectively and appropriately. Indeed, I was aware that some of the issues arising during the interviews could focus directly on thoughts which some may have had difficulty countenancing even when in good health. This difficulty was compounded by the fact that I knew I would be retrieving it from individuals who would probably be at their most vulnerable, both physically and psychologically.

Having weighed the prospective difficulties of longitudinal interviewing against the potential benefits and, in spite of knowing that it would add years to this study, I specifically chose to do just that, as it would allow me to monitor the physical and social changes which occurred to the respondents as their dying journeys progressed.

This decision was greatly influenced by the knowledge that working with vulnerable people would call for trust, which could only be earned over a period of time. The interviews began, continued and, as I hoped, our relationships matured sufficiently to foster the disclosure of the more sensitive 'private' accounts (Cornwell, 1984).

The decision of whether to participate in the research was left to the respondents, who received the information sheets and consent forms, approved by the relevant Research Ethics committees, from their medical staff. At no stage did I actively recruit any particular respondent or refuse any individual who volunteered themselves.

Although I am in no way medically trained, I have had previous experience of working as a volunteer in hospices. I was pleased then, when two hospices, including one where I had previously worked, were kind enough to allow me to carry out my observations there.

At the beginning of each initial interview, every respondent was given and read what I refer to as Pre-interview Information. This explained to them, amongst other facts, that I would endeavour to ensure that they would receive anonymity and complete confidentiality at all times, that they might terminate their inclusion in the research whenever they wished and that I was not a counsellor nor medically trained but a social science researcher. All of these interviews, which were taped, were open; the content and issues under discussion being determined by the respondents with minimal intrusion or prompts by me and then only in an attempt to facilitate a more coherent articulation of the subject under discussion.

When I arranged the initial interviews, I left it up to the individuals concerned whether we would be alone or have a supporter present. Some, like Clive, I saw alone; others like Gita's family, I saw as a complete unit. I also interviewed several professionals and this proved invaluable in educating me on the substantive detail that has informed the background to this work.

All the respondents were given different names, allocated after some reflection, with consideration to names that might have been popular around the time and place where they were born. I have also altered some minor details of their lives, to protect their anonymity further.

The main participants in this study fell into three groups: respondents who had cancer, supporters of these respondents and individuals who had been recently bereaved. To allow development of their stories, I have used extensive quotations and examples from a small subset of these respondents but my comments and analysis apply equally to many more.

During the study I encountered several unexpected and difficult problems. Amongst other factors, these concerned respondents who did not conform to their anticipated trajectory, either by fortunately outliving their prognosis or by, regrettably, dying prematurely. I found the problem of premature death especially demanding to deal with. It was difficult to recruit respondents for the study, as I was seeking volunteers who were facing very real physical and psychological issues. When a respondent agreed to be interviewed, I had to establish contact speedily as the very reason I was interested in them, their status of being terminally ill, might in itself preclude them from taking part.

It is difficult to determine which part of the fieldwork I found most challenging; however, having to learn to temper, and at times quell, my natural inclination to 'cheer people up' by presenting an alternative perspective to a problem they felt was insurmountable, was very demanding.

The prolonged periods spent in my 'volunteer' observer role within the hospices were difficult, too. As it is emotionally draining work, regular volunteers there usually work one shift every two weeks. My need for this research was to observe the evolving dying trajectories of several patients, so I needed to spend concentrated periods of duty there. This inevitably led to my relationships with the patients and their families becoming closer, which introduced its own problems. I clearly remember my shock when, on reporting for duty on the Care Floor one evening, I asked after one young patient, who had been vigorously alive just the evening before, and was casually told 'Oh, he's just been taken to have his eyes removed'. He had, of course, died before becoming a donor! That same difficult evening two patients asked me to help speed their dying.

Counter to the reaction of many others to people who are dying, I always perceived my respondents to be very much alive, possibly because, in our interviews there was frequently more laughter than tears. In understanding that this laughter probably functioned as a valve to release heightened emotions, I feel strongly that dying does not diminish a sense of humour but rather serves to stress the vital side of life so that all its aspects are appreciated.

Acknowledgements

A few moments before she died, a hospice patient explained to me that in giving a person your time you were really giving them a part of your life. It is important therefore that I acknowledge the contributions and support given by my friends and colleagues during the composition of this book. I am especially indebted to Joan Busfield who gave generously and unstintingly of her time supervising much of my PhD, which has formed the nucleus of the text. The support I received from the sociology staff at the University of Essex was remarkable; my special thanks go to Elizabeth Francis (now at LSE), Jeff Geiger, Ken Plummer, Colin Samson and John Scott. My thanks also to Ian Craib, who gave me the freedom to pursue my research but who has since, sadly, died.

My colleagues in the University of Southampton have also helped through the various drafts of this book: David Colombi, Lena Dominelli, Peter Ford and Tom Strickland, all read selections of drafts and contributed constructively. My gratitude is also due to Glennys Howarth for her erudite comments and to Steven Jackson who always found time to help me. The anonymous reviewers from Cambridge University Press also merit special mention for their most valuable comments on the manuscript. To Sarah Caro, commissioning editor, my thanks for her sense of humour and her sensitive handling of this, my first book.

I would like to thank my friends and family for their valued support and practical help. Peta Allen was so kind in helping with the proof reading, Celia Witney, who was always there for me during my fieldwork and writing up, my mother and my sister Anne-Marie, who encouraged me to believe that I could do it, and Chris Coster, whose very real practical and technical support coupled with his patience to support me throughout. Put simply, without his help, the research for this book would not have happened. My children deserve special thanks too, Louise, Eve and Mikes, thank you for putting up with me throughout and distracting me from the difficult nature of death with your many problems!

The research for my PhD was, in part, contributed to by the Fuller Foundation at the University of Essex. I would also like to thank the

University of Southampton who kindly freed me from some of my commitments, in order to focus on turning what began as a PhD thesis into this book. I would like to thank those involved in the publication of the journal *Mortality* (www.teandf.co.uk/journals/titles.13576275.html) especially David Field and Peter Jupp, for all their support and also kindly allowing me to reproduce part of my article which appeared there.

This book could not, of course, have been written without the help of the individuals who were the respondents in the research. Their participation was entirely voluntary, as they believed their contributions would be of use to others, and so they gave the most precious gift they could – their time. Sadly, virtually all of them have died but I would like to thank their families who encouraged them in their desire to help and welcomed me into their homes at that most difficult of times. To the directors of the three anonymous hospices who allowed me access to their patients and to conduct my observations, my thanks to you and your staff; you know who you are.

Introduction

No matter where we are in life, we are seldom prepared for death. Over the course of writing this book, I did not ever meet with anyone who, before their diagnosis, had ever seriously contemplated the idea of dying. Thirty-six-year-old Louise had not ever imagined herself having cancer. She told me how, when she was a medical undergraduate, a lecturer informed her class that demographically it was probable that in y number of years, x number of them would be dead. She explained to me:

We laughed; we thought it was so funny. Quite a few laughed, others shivered. I know at least one has died in an accident, two of us have cancer, various other things have happened, nervous breakdowns, divorces and we have not hit forty yet. No one expects it at their doorstep and we all feel immune from it. Up until it happens to you it is the truth, it always was someone else. Who expects to have a life threatening illness in their thirties?

Confrontation with potentially fatal diseases focuses the mind; it provides an opportunity for values to be reassessed. Priorities are examined and many re-evaluate their commitments and relationships.

The people I met whilst conducting my research were very much individuals. They differed in their reactions to, for example, finding their first symptoms; they responded differently when learning their diagnosis; how they chose to spend the time leading up to their deaths was different too. There were, however, also similarities; their altruistic tendency to defend others from the harsh truth of their actual experience; their increased appreciation of life; their propensity to maximise their capacity to endure and to minimise reports of their physical pain.

In spite of being individuals, we are social beings who live out our lives in the company of others. Long before Auguste Comte ever conceived of sociology as a discipline, John Donne profoundly observed that 'No man is an island, entire of itself'. As well as being individuals, we are social beings and this book explores not only how the respondents experienced their dying but also the impact they and their experiences had on those around them.

The individuals to whom you will be introduced during the course of reading this book were shocked by their diagnosis, traumatised by this confrontation with their own mortality. However, they hoped for, and indeed deserved, standards of excellence in how their treatment would be managed. Sadly, however, this was not always the case. Ben and Eilish were bewildered by how a series of calamitous human errors resulted in his tragic diagnosis and they found themselves pitched into a political battle between the two senior consultants who were to manage his treatment. On learning her diagnosis, Louise, herself a doctor and mother of two, very young children, was shocked at the callous manner in which her ex-colleague broke the news of her diagnosis, asking her 'What are you crying for?' Rose struggled to contain her emotions when, as the result of a casual question from a radiographer, she discovered that her breast cancer had invaded her brain.

Ben, Louise and Rose lived out their lives in mainstream society. They were people like us. However, the voices of individuals who are dying have seldom been heard. This book aims to open that silence.

The substantive body of this book is the narrative section, which is presented through the framework of four separate stages that combine to form the coherent dying journey. These individual stages can, of course, be explored in isolation as discrete and separate periods, some of which might be experienced also by those who are fortunate enough to recover from their cancer. This narrative is grounded primarily in longitudinal, in-depth interviews held with patients and their carers throughout their dying journey. The accounts are augmented, when appropriate, with field-notes and a brief selection of supplementary studies. Although commentary is provided to highlight motifs and point out themes of particular relevance, the primary intent has been to give voice to those individuals who were in the process of experiencing their dying.

In the many conversations I enjoyed with the respondents, I had a heightened awareness of how they all unconsciously compartmentalised the events they encountered as they progressed through their illness trajectories. Although they did not consciously prompt me into organising their temporal framework into the model I eventually applied, I was, probably not surprisingly, influenced by how they themselves perceived the events to fall. These can be summarised in the four stages I outline below in Table 1.

Although time is an abstract concept into which individuals are socialised (Zerubavel, 1981), those living in contemporary Western life have come to regard it as almost tangible and use it as a form of currency. This can be illustrated by examining how the respondents experienced, especially, the period around the detection and diagnosis of their cancer.

Table 1 *The four stages common to those who are dying from cancer*

Departure	The time of detecting initial symptoms and learning their diagnosis
Exploration	The time of tests and treatment
Anticipation	The time of remission and fear of recurrence
Destination	The time when the imminence of death could not be denied

Stage one charts the events that occurred between the discovery of the symptom(s) and the cancer diagnosis, exploring how those involved first became aware of illness indicators. I examine how contacts were initiated with general practitioners and then consider the earliest meetings with consultants and detail some of the problems that were encountered. The anxiety generated whilst waiting for the results of the medical tests is discussed before I investigate the individuals' immediate reactions on learning their diagnosis.

The individuals with whom I spoke related to that first stage of their illness as though it was as physically real and firmly fixed as a cliff, a boundary marker that explicitly marks the clear division between land and sea. They now thought of specific events in their lives as occurring either before or after their cancer diagnosis. The detection and diagnosis of their cancer marked a 'Departure' away from the life they had previously lived in mainstream society and marked the beginning of their journey.

The second stage investigates the events between individuals learning of their cancer diagnosis and settling into their treatment regime. During this difficult time, many struggled to accept the fact of their cancer and to deal with the subsequent changes practically, emotionally and socially. The reality of their illness was, for some, reinforced tangibly as the treatment wrought physical side effects, which had to be confronted and managed: their principal reaction seemed to have been one of complete uncertainty and fear. They had left their familiar mode and temporal pace of life behind and were now attempting to 'Explore' and negotiate strange terrain in a time structure that was both unfamiliar and disturbing to them. Still absorbing the shock of their diagnosis, they followed the maps offered by medical science and made their initial connections in the hope that they were not lost. This was not only a time when they were expected to adapt to the requirements and routines of the medical domain but was also when they first began to notice a change in established social relationships.

The third and penultimate stage following the medical treatment appeared for many to be the most difficult. This part examines how the respondents made sense of the liminal time they spent between their remission and the recurrence of their cancer. This was a period when they not only worked hard to maintain a grip on 'normal' life but also struggled with the sense that they had to live up to the heroic role others unwittingly imposed. In many ways, this was the most testing of times, a period marked by gruelling psychological swings between hope and dread.

At this time, their social, and for some, physical identities had already undergone change and they worked to re-establish their previous social status. They craved recognition of their return to mainstream society but this was not always guaranteed. This was a time when they desperately hoped that their cancer would succumb to the treatment but feared it would not. It was a time of 'Anticipation'. As the captain of a ship, trapped within an ice field, might present a confident face to the passengers on board, so too did the respondents present a positive front to those for whom they cared whilst, in reaction to their inner anxiety, they attempted to pre-empt possible symptoms of their cancer's return by monitoring all and every corporeal change.

Stage four, the final stage, investigates the period around death. By the time the respondents moved into this stage, they were aware that they were dying, they knew for certain that the ultimate 'Destination' of their journey was death – a premature death. Some contributed to how their death would be managed, for example, by making known their wishes about where the death should occur. Death was now advancing steadily and as its threat became imminent, those who cared for them drew physically closer, valuing the scarce time that remained and guarding it jealously. Those who were still able, both supporters and the individual who would shortly die, worked together to effect as good a death as possible. For many, however, the difficulties of this challenging time were compounded by their lack of familiarity with how dying occurs. This sometimes resulted in a situation where the person who was dying continued to struggle, even in extremis, to maintain control over the event, in their altruistic efforts to protect those for whom they cared.

Beginning with a narrative drawn directly from an interview held with a respondent, just five days before she died, this final stage primarily utilises conversations with the bereaved, who relate how the deaths were experienced by the dying person. To substantiate these accounts, a series of case studies are presented, based on observations in hospices.

The conclusion considers how the individuals you will have met in this book managed the various challenges they encountered during their illness. It explores the role of the everyday dying hero, consolidating Seale's work in *Constructing Death* (1998). It further examines some of the strategies individuals employ to enhance their own remaining time and to ease close relationships that have come under enormous stress.

Table 2 *Characteristics common to the contemporary dying hero*

Defend or protect others	The respondents all worked on both practical and social levels in their endeavour to defend those for whom they cared from the harsh realities of the experience.
Increased appreciation of life	The respondents all had a heightened emotional appreciation of what they had previously taken for granted.
Endurance of illness	The respondents all tended to endure the psychological and physical aspects of their illness, all of them making practical and emotional efforts to conceal their pain from those for whom they cared.

The degree to which the respondents were socially embedded, enmeshed within their social groups, significantly influenced how they interpreted and managed what was left of their lives. Thus, they handled the various challenges they encountered, interpreting and experiencing the events that they met on an individual level and, therefore, often reacting to them in quite disparate ways. There were however, some specific behaviour patterns to which they did all appear to conform.

The respondents pro-actively engaged in plans designed to diminish something of the practical and emotional difficulties that they believed their illness and dying brought to others. To this end, some made practical provision, for example, negotiating how young children would be cared for after death and organising their own funeral arrangements.

The interviewees, independently of each other, took time to stress how, since becoming ill, they had all learned an increased appreciation of issues, which they had previously considered mundane. They now understood and realised with increasing pleasure the value which underlay the simple things in life, one even commenting on how she had been '. . . woken up to the millions of miracles happening . . . not major ones like stopping wars but the milk being delivered on time . . .'

Despite the horrendous psychological pressures and physical agonies which they endured, in preference to causing those they loved the grief that they knew their death would bring, all preferred to cling on to their lives. Experiencing the physical pain was something only they could do and they often chose to keep the full extent of this suffering private, rather than make it known.

All the respondents in this study, however unconsciously, altruistically attempted to protect those for whom they cared from the pain that they knew their dying would cause.

To summarise, there are three features common to how they managed their illness, set out in Table 2.

For the respondents, dying had become a frightening probability, but they needed to maintain their place in society during the long journey. This book tells us something about how individuals, who had a life threatening disease, lived up to their deaths.

To put their experiences in context, it seems sensible to begin by addressing issues of mortality, exploring how current cultural responses have evolved and shape how death is managed.

1 Mortality in modern culture

Dying is not what it used to be. Temporal changes have seen a movement away from a time when dying was often rapid to a time when a lingering trajectory is increasingly becoming the norm (McKeown, 1976; Ariès, 1974; Walter, 1994). We have shifted away from an era when individuals died secure and confident in their unshakeable belief in an after life to an era when dying is perceived to be an inner journey of the psyche (Kubler-Ross, 1995). We have moved away from a period when death was experienced as part of life to a period when fighting death has turned into the meaning of life (Bauman, 1992).

How have social scientists responded to these transformations in the management of dying and death? Lagging behind the exciting and rapidly accelerating developments in technology, only a few psychological and sociological theories or models (Freud, 1959; Gorer, 1965) were in evidence before, even as recently as the late 1960s.

It may be because of the difficulty many find in countenancing their own mortality that, except for work on demographic aspects, social scientific research concerning death was, until the late 1960s, largely focused on the survivors of death, the bereaved, rather than on those who were themselves dying. Death up to this time was presented almost entirely as though the chief protagonist was the mourner and not the individual most concerned: the person who was dying. Death implied bereavement and not dying; it was about those who survived death. With few, notable, but highly influential exceptions (Kubler-Ross, 1995; Glaser and Strauss, 1964), what work has been contributed tends, for the most part, to be theoretically based. This paucity in sound, empirically sourced work is one which needs to be redressed as present-day mainstream perceptions of dying are influenced less and less by direct personal experience with individuals who are dying, but increasingly by the opinion makers, the academics who formulate theory which is in turn disseminated by the media (Freimuth et al., 1989; Armstrong-Coster, 2001).

Mellor (1993) considers why death remains excluded from mainstream sociology and suggests how this might be remedied. First, he contends,

7

along with others, that death in high modernity has become sequestrated from the public arena. Second, he analyses the privatisation and sub-jectivisation of death, a phenomenon that, he argues, has been fed, for example, by Kubler-Ross's stage model, which focuses on how death is managed at an individual rather than collective level. Third, he argues that, because sociology as a discipline is so engaged with the project of modernity, it too has sequestered issues of dying and death. He suggests that:

> ... an adequate integration of death into sociological theory can be achieved only by a partial reorientation of sociology, since sociology itself has been inextricably bound up with the project of modernity. While sociology remains so closely tied to such a project, modernity's systematic sequestration of considerations of mortality will continue to be reflected in sociological theory and practice. (1993: 12)

This point demands a radical revision of the discipline of sociology. Mellor does not call for a total reversal of interest from issues of life to those concerning death; rather he appeals for an integration of both life and death into sociology's core. Should this fail to occur, he argues, then death will continue to be sequestrated both by mainstream society and also by sociologists.

Also promulgated by the media, the seductive philosophies and ethos of the new Hospice Movement, a phenomenon infused with the heartening message of 'good death', have now spread, stretching beyond the confines of the Hospice itself and having informed, have gone on to persuade and pervade general public opinion. The importance of the new Hospice Movement and its philosophies has been and continues to be central to how public attitude to dying and death is shaped.

These two sources then, academia and the media that feeds off it, now inform and educate public opinion on death related issues.

What is the current public stance on issues of mortality? The position of mainstream attitudes has been hotly contested over the years. The United Kingdom is a society that continues to be charged with being 'death denying'. The extent to which this is true has long been at the heart of sociological debate on death (Parsons and Lidz, 1967; Parsons, 1978; Kellehear, 1984; Walter, 1991) but, so far, there has been no satisfactory resolution to that proposition.

What is clear, however, is that the dominance of science has greatly contributed to enhanced standards of living, to a consequent rise in the population (McKeown, 1976) and change in the causes of mortality (Busfield, 2000). We are part of a society living longer and dying more slowly than ever before. The dramatic drop in mortality from infectious illnesses amongst the young means that, increasingly, non-infectious fatal diseases now tend to strike the elderly (Busfield (2000) cites heart diseases, respiratory diseases and cancers specifically). This change in how individuals die has been further affected by the fact that, because of significant advances in medication, death is more inclined to occur after a prolonged period of chronic, rather than, acute illness and, as a result, dying became colonised by the medics (Zola, 1972; Illich, 1976). Consequently, individuals who were dying were subjected to 'shutting away' (Ariès, 1974, 1981), 'cutting off' (Illich, 1976) and 'exiling' (Elias, 1985) from mainstream society.

Countering these pessimistic charges, however, are two facts, which have combined to influence how individuals who are dying are managed. The first is that increasing medical advances together with the initiation, development and growth of specialist Palliative Care services mean that there are more individuals who are living in the midst of prolonged dying trajectories than ever before (Young and Cullen, 1996). The needs of these individuals are at last receiving attention and are in the process of being evaluated and addressed at government policy level.

The second point, perhaps influenced by the first, is that there has been a reversal of clinical opinion. Before 1970, clinicians were reluctant to inform patients of what was viewed, in their opinion, as a dismal prognosis. However, more recently there has been a movement away from that to a position in which people who are dying, as autonomous individuals, are now kept openly informed of their situation (Seale, 1998).

When framed within a society that has embraced the growth of the new Hospice Movement, these two facts render it implausible that death-related concerns continue to be denied but, instead, suggest that they are becoming increasingly aired.

How have these changes come about? Reviewing any development which has evolved over time is difficult: a lens which is appropriate for life in the United Kingdom of the twenty-first century may, with hindsight, judge prejudicially and perhaps harshly, the less advanced conditions of earlier times. However, whichever meter is applied to evaluate the conditions prevalent in the United Kingdom following the Second World War and leading up to the early 1970s, it is indisputable that individuals who were dying were, during those times, considered the 'failures' of modern medical science and found themselves marginalised (Thomas, 1980).

Clark's (1999) authoritative study of the history of the hospice movement (1948–1967) sheds some light on what it was like to die in the United Kingdom in that era. He frames it against the background of the newly developing National Health Service (NHS), a service whose 'intensely modernising ethic . . . entailed a deep ideological suspicion of charity and which made cure and rehabilitation its clinical goals'

(1999: 226–7). The medical focus was, at that time, on those who could be cured rather than those who could not.

Illustrating something of the plight of those who were dying at that time, Clark draws on an article written in 1948 by W. N. Leak that appeared in *The Practitioner*. Leak argued that a most difficult situation had arisen because 'relatives are not available or willing' to care for the dying at home (1948: 80). Before the Second World War, the decision about where to die rested on the goodwill of a supportive family or in the gift of charitable endeavours. Even those fortunate enough to have relatives disposed to meet the difficult task of nursing them at home were frequently not in receipt of adequate medical care. This situation was aggravated by the fact that, as Leak observed: 'Medical treatment can almost be written in one word – morphine' (1948: 85). Individuals dying slowly in the late 1940s were left in the charge of their relatives and doctors whose knowledge of medication and inclination to prescribe it was often tempered by their own personal beliefs.

For those who were dying without families, other than finding a bed in one of the few charitable homes or religious hospices in existence in this era, the only alternative left was to seek accommodation in hospital. The problem, however, was, as we have already learned, that hospitals were, and still are, institutions whose priority is to provide cure and not nurse the chronically ill: although the physical trajectory of the individuals who were dying was monitored, once considered past cure, they were no longer of interest or concern to the experts. Control and choice were removed from them in favour of the work of the medical teams primarily concerned with patients considered to have some prospect of survival.

This situation was paralleled in the United States, where Sudnow (1967) argued that, at that time (the 1960s), human dignity in hospital was sacrificed in favour of bureaucratic efficiency. Indeed, so far were people who were dying removed from normal ward management that, when a death occurred, other than the basic nursing offices being observed, it was virtually ignored. Individuals who were dying were considered an embarrassment and death was understood principally in negative terms (Thomas, 1980).

It was in an attempt to resolve the problems imposed on the dying by this cultural climate that seeds were germinated which were to become influential in the rooting and consequent flowering of the new Hospice Movement. At this time, individuals who were dying were sequestered and separated, held at a physical remove from mainstream society and psychologically distanced from the staff caring for them (Gorer, 1965). Such situations prompted Swiss physician, Elisabeth Kubler-Ross, to write in 1969 how, at that time in the United States, people who were dying were:

... treated like a thing. He [sic] is no longer a person. Decisions are made often without taking his opinion. If he tries to rebel he will be sedated ... He may cry out for rest, peace, dignity but he will get infusions, transfusions, a heart machine or a tracheostomy. (1995: 8)

Concurrent with the work of Kubler-Ross and also based in the United States, was other interesting research being carried out by Glaser and Strauss (1965). These two pieces of research, together with the work of Herman Feifel (1959) in the United States and of John Bowlby (1961) and Colin Murray Parkes (1972) in the United Kingdom, set the stage for what Walter (1994: 1) describes as the 'revival of death' and culminated in the social phenomenon we now know as the new Hospice Movement.

How did this come about? In 1969, Kubler-Ross published her influential empirical study *On Death and Dying* (1995), which propagated the idea that there was something good and spiritually enriching about dying. This treatise captured a little of the spirit of these increasingly secular times, advocating a promotion of the spiritual in favour of the religious. Her thesis remains one of the most influential ever within the dying and death field (Field, 1984, 1996; Walter, 1994) and the ethos behind her stage theory, the drive towards a good death, continues to dominate hospice philosophy (Germain, 1980; McNamara, Waddell *et al.*, 1994). Her work is held to be responsible for placing the dying back into the public arena (Walter, 1994).

The second formative contribution to changes in attitude to individuals who are dying and the rise of the new Hospice Movement came also from research conducted in the United States by Glaser and Strauss. In 1965, they published *Awareness of Dying*, another empirical study that focused on how patients learned that they were dying. Arguing that an individual's awareness of their prognosis might colour their dying trajectory, Glaser and Strauss classified the patient's knowledge of their situation as falling into one of four different states and argued that an individual's dying trajectory could be significantly affected by the extent of their knowledge of their prognosis.

Glaser and Strauss's work was hailed as pioneering, sparked shifts in attitudes amongst medical opinion (Seale, 1998) and proved vital in furthering honest communication between the participants involved in the dying trajectory. This facilitated open and frank dialogue between individuals who were dying and their supporters.

It is important to remember though, that although the changes driven by these two pieces of research (Kubler-Ross and Glaser and Strauss) were in themselves significant, they were, arguably more importantly, also to prove formative to the moulding and shaping of what has come to be known today as the new Hospice Movement.

We have already explored something of the background that underlies its development and highlighted how the limited financial resources of the developing and increasingly complex NHS were targeted at those with hope of a cure rather than people who were dying. Clark observes that, as a result, there was '. . . no strategic or operational guidance on terminal care and no systematic commitment to the subject as a clinical issue' (1999: 227).

Although hospices originated in the Middle Ages and survived in Ireland where they are still in operation, they did not exist in the United Kingdom or elsewhere in the form recognised today until Cicely Saunders revived them. Witnessing how a friend, (David Tasma) was treated while he was dying in hospital, Saunders left her job as a social worker and, though initially training as a nurse, completed a full medical training. On becoming a doctor, she determined that, as tribute to her friend, she would establish a special place where individuals who were dying would be enabled to live out their last days in the way that they wished. To fund this grand scheme she mounted a prolonged public campaign and her ambition, finally realised, took tangible form in the shape of St Christopher's in London, the inaugural contemporary hospice, officially opened in 1967. The hospice philosophy, in direct opposition to the goals of curative medicine, was to value and celebrate life, facilitating as much richness in the physical, emotional and social lives of the patients as possible, right up until the moment of death, which, it was planned, would occur naturally and unaided (McNamara, Waddell et al., 1994; Hart, Sainsbury et al., 1998). In part, this aim was bolstered and achieved by Saunders' pioneering pain control methods, which served as the basis for contemporary palliative medicine. This nursing of the suffering body was further strengthened by the provision of holistic care. Saunders recognised that physical pain was often heightened or stimulated by non-biological factors and argued that, since much of the pain involved in dying was psychological, those needs, too, should be met. She used the expression 'total pain' (Saunders and Baines, 1983) to refer to the physical, psychological, social and spiritual problems which individuals might encounter when dying. In summary, then, whilst the goal of mainstream medicine is to cure, the intention of the hospice movement is to palliate symptoms holistically in an endeavour to ensure a good death.

In tandem with the development and subsequent boom of the new Hospice Movement, there has been a blossoming of growth in research and publications about dying: not only from academics but increasingly too from the caring professions and the medically affiliated disciplines which have experience of working directly with individuals who are dying. Valuable contributions are now being made by clinicians, counsellors, social workers and the veritable plethora of eclectic specialists: the subject of dying and death, after all, spans an enormous field which has until recently lain fallow. Encouragingly, these emergent and useful contributions have been met with an increase in the number of publications targeted at cancer care providers. The number of conferences organised around the theme of dying, too, is growing steadily albeit slowly and innovations in the NHS have called for the development of professionally accredited courses on the subject of Palliative Care.

These welcome developments in research and teachings based on dying mean that the present-day United Kingdom is now in a position where it is equipped to respond to these demands. Advanced and specialist knowledge has been generated and is now available in the form of literature such as Walter's *The Revival of Death* (1994), *Death and Bereavement Across Cultures* (Murray Parkes *et al.*, 1997), *Death, Gender and Ethnicity* (Field *et al.*, 1997) and Seale's *Constructing Death* (1998). The United Kingdom can now even boast its own *British Encyclopaedia of Death and Dying* (Howarth and Leamon, 2001) available as a general guide to matters appertaining to death.

Unfortunately, still to be filled adequately is the depressingly yawning chasm in the provision of empirical work based on dying as reported by the individuals who are most concerned, those who are dying. Lawton (2000) is restricted in her admirable anthropological research, confining her study to those who were actually at the end-stage of their illness and making use of hospice facilities. Costain Schou and Hewison's (1999) *Experiencing Cancer: Quality of Life in Treatment* presents empirical data, narratives garnered from individuals who had only recently been diagnosed with cancer. This book focuses, for the most part, on the social processes involved during the initial medical care which is encountered in cancer but it confines itself solely to the temporal period between diagnosis and treatment. It does not engage with, for example, the existential concerns.

We are all mortal: one day we will die. Ernest Becker observed that our '. . . body is a material fleshy casing that is alien . . . in many ways – the strangest and most repugnant way being that it aches and bleeds and will decay and die' (1973: 26). The paradox is that whilst we have been gifted with intellects capable of soaring above and beyond the boundaries of nature (Becker, 1973), as animals we are hopelessly locked within it.

To develop something of an understanding into what it is like to die in present day society, I conducted ethnographic research which involved my spending extended periods of time working with, and interviewing, people who were dying as well as those who cared for them. Although I interviewed over thirty individuals many times over the course of a six-year period, the experiences of the twelve whom I introduce briefly below, I argue, best capture something of dying experiences. The individuals you will meet in this book will, of course, be presented in more depth in the narratives. I introduce them here as I first met them.

The principal respondents

Ben aged 63. He and his wife Eilish lived in a small, immaculate detached bungalow. He had retired from his work as a printer and they had one child, a grown up son who did not keep in contact. Ben was a non-practising Jew, whose testicular cancer had originally been diagnosed three years before our first interview.

Bob aged 56. He shared his semi-detached home with Sheila, his wife. His cancer of the colon had meant he had to give up running the small, family painting and decorating business. An Irish immigrant to England, he was a lapsed Roman Catholic.

Clive aged 36. Single, he lived with his widowed mother in their rural family home. His testicular cancer had caused him to give up his position as lecturer at the university but he was still a practising member of the Presbyterian Church.

Gerry aged 35. Married to Claire who was pregnant with their second child. His non-Hodgkin's lymphoma had caused him to retire prematurely from his work as Marketing Manager for an international pharmaceutical firm. The family are Roman Catholic and live in an exclusive suburb close to both their parental homes.

Louise aged 36. Lived with her husband, Derek, and two young children in their family home, which was being renovated. Her breast cancer had forced her to leave her work as GP and she drew heavily on her Roman Catholic religion for comfort. Since being told that her cancer was no longer treatable, Derek suffered a stroke and brain haemorrhage, which left him severely disabled.

Rose aged 48. A single parent, she lived with her two teenaged children on a council housing estate. Her deteriorating health had caused her to give up her position as interior-designer. A second-generation Greek immigrant, she considered herself a 'lapsed Greek Orthodox'. Her breast cancer had initially been diagnosed sixteen years earlier.

Sue-Ellen aged 56. Lived with her husband James in a charming cottage. She was a Roman Catholic who had emigrated from Ireland to England thirty-five years ago and although not having a family, she had never worked for a living.

Susan aged 42. Divorced and with no children she lived alone in her bijou terraced home. Although originally a Roman Catholic she described herself as 'more spiritual than religious'. Still doing some minimal lecturing at a school for further education, Susan was struggling to come to terms with the recurrence of her breast cancer.

Vera aged 64. Married to Albert she lived in their semi-detached home. She was retired from her position as school-dinner lady, when initially diagnosed with her ovarian cancer. A practising High Anglican she was in regular contact with her son and daughter.

Bereaved respondents

Ash aged 43. Recently widowed, he lived with his two sons and mother-in-law in a smart, suburban detached home. He was a shopkeeper; his wife, Gita had worked as a fashion-designer. They were first generation Kenyan-Asians and the family were Hindu.

Mary aged 76. Lived alone in her semi-detached, rural cottage and was mourning the deaths of both her husband and her son which occurred within a six-month time period. She was a practising member of the Church of England.

Sophie aged 37. Divorced, she had recently returned to work as a nurse following the death of her three-year-old son, Steve. She shared her smart semi-detached bungalow with her other son, seven-year-old Dean.

These are their stories . . .

2   Stage One – Departure

Symptoms, consultations and diagnoses

When I began this series of interviews, I was at first surprised by how almost all of those who were telling me their stories anchored their narratives by recollecting the discovery of their original symptom. This was the pattern, irrespective of the time that had elapsed. Although from the moment of birth everyone is dying; for most, that knowledge is disregarded until they are confronted in a direct encounter with death. This section charts the initial movement on the journey that eventually led through the respondents' physical decline and on to their deaths. It begins at the time when they were, unknowingly, just moments away from detecting their first symptom. This was a point in their lives when they felt secure and safe, substantial and complete in their physical bodies. This feeling of ontological security was, however, about to be challenged.

Exploring how bodily changes were defined as problematic by them and others, this chapter investigates the objective and subjective reactions to those changes and examines how others, their supporters, contributed to these experiences. It continues, examining how they dealt with the medical professionals involved and concludes by examining how the interviewees responded to discovering their diagnoses.

As biological beings, our bodies are constantly changing. For the most part, these changes are acknowledged and accepted as part of our normal development as, other than at puberty, these changes occur so gradually that they receive scant notice or comment. Bodily change, though, can sometimes signal potential physical problems acting to stimulate and mobilise defence mechanisms. It is how changes are perceived that affects the speed at which defensive action may, or may not, be taken.

The stories that I heard indicate that it is the personal perception of, and emotional response to, symptoms that most frequently served to lead individuals to seek medical counsel. The research indicates that, in the same way as illness itself is a cultural concept, the knowledge and

16

understanding required to make this transition has to be acquired. The respondents had to learn how to negotiate the practical problems they met, such as deciding when their bodily change was sufficiently significant to warrant reporting to the medical authorities. This process of learning to live with illness is social and is directly affected by culture and the input and attitudes of others.

When a dramatic symptom, for example a lump, was detected, a direct connection was sometimes made to cancer. This discovery shattered the individual's equilibrium and a typical reaction was one of shock and fear. Radley discusses the 'horrors' integral to narrative accounts of severe illness, observing that '. . . it is in the chasm between the mundane and the terrifying that the "horrors" of illness experience are forged' (1999: 782). He argues that 'the key lies, in some way, in a portrayal in which dreaded but unspecified events are figured in the benign, and especially in the innocent' (1999: 783). This might contribute to understanding why the respondents had such heightened recall of the moment when they detected their symptoms. All of them described the moment when they first noticed their bodily change with unusual clarity and detail, conforming to Brown and Kulik's (1977) concept of 'flashbulb' memories, which, they argue, are the result of moments of trauma. Shaving, breastfeeding and bathing are considered innocuous activities, usually performed privately within a domestic environment, and it may be that it is the juxtaposition of detecting such potentially threatening symptoms, such as lumps or bumps, within such a mundane situation, which stimulated and exacerbated the respondents' fright.

Finding the symptoms

Gerry

When Gerry found his lump, he was shaving. At that time, he had everything to live for. Claire, his wife of six years, was eight months pregnant with their second child. So secure did he feel in his position as Marketing Manager for an international pharmaceutical company that the couple and their four-year-old daughter, Diana, had recently moved into a luxury villa in a select suburb. During my first interview with the couple, held just a few days after his diagnosis and her giving birth, we were interrupted many times by the crying of their new baby, Angela, and by Claire's sudden discovery of yet another of Diana's toys spotted hidden in the large, well-proportioned family room. Gerry described how he had found a lump in his neck and gradually realised that it might be problematic:

On 22nd September, it was a Sunday; I had noticed a swelling in my neck, while I was shaving. I had spots on the side of my neck, acne, and I touched it and thought, 'Hey that's not like acne, it's deep and big, not tender.' Totally painless but it was a hard lump and it was really deep to me. It was about the size of an egg, a golf ball. Claire thought that as well, it was deep in and as I touched the side of my neck, I could feel the vessels going into it . . . I knew it was serious straight away.

Gerry's heightened recall was obvious. He names the day and also the date. His first thought was that it was acne, but, scientifically trained, he made a closer examination that highlighted the difference. He gauged its size, using common, culturally specific, items to indicate the extent of its mass. He then immediately said 'Claire thought that as well . . .' which suggests that he had been sufficiently disturbed by the lump to instantly call his wife for her opinion. Gerry and Claire worked together in their assessment of the lump as a partnership, although his final decision to define it as serious rested on his own, scientifically informed education.

He continued:

Sometimes when you get something you are not sure about that worries you, maybe a lump in your arms, you panic and go to the doctor. You think of the worst and it turns out for the best but in this one . . . it was almost parallel with a road accident. When you know you are going to have it you don't have the fear, you go for it or avoid it. I just decided that I was going to go to the doctor . . .

His scientific knowledge, coupled with the fact that his wife was expecting a baby in a month concentrated his mind, leaving him in no doubt as to what he should do next. He used the concept of a road traffic accident as a metaphor to illustrate his confrontational approach to his symptom. He paralleled his decision to seek immediate medical advice with the determination of a driver who decides to make a calculated crash, rather than risk an impetuous swerve.

Although the lump suggested a potential link to cancer, Gerry and Claire both preferred to ignore this and instead behaved as though they did not feel threatened. They appear to have collaborated in the mutual pretence that the lump would prove innocent. Although instinct, and the popular opinion that unexplained lumps equate with cancer, alerted the couple to its possible significance, Gerry chose not to display concern. I asked him about how he was feeling at that time and he said:

I didn't care. I decided that I wouldn't make any decisions on what I had; I just knew that I had to go and do this, so I wasn't frightened of going to see the doctor. I knew that I had to take this step and I knew it wasn't one of these 'iffy' things.

I knew it was a definite something here, what definite it was I didn't know. I knew it could have been cancer but I decided not to put that in my mind, the worry about it, at that stage.

Gerry unwittingly revealed something of his internal fear, by his unconscious use of the word 'I', fourteen times during his six-line explanation. I was, however, puzzled that he had not noticed such an exceptionally distended lump previously. He explained:

These are painless; I might have noticed a swelling . . . This is not terribly scientific but I will tell you about the doubling of cells. Different types of cancers have different growth rates; some grow slowly, some quickly. Some double in about 30 days; others take 90, which gives more problems. Lymphomas grow very rapidly and double the number of cells every 30 days. The amount of cells in growth phase at any time is important too. In a lymphoma, 90 percent are in growth cells, whereas leukaemia may only have 30 percent and that will affect how chemo works. The slower growing, the more resistant to chemo. If you take one cell and 30 days later it is two then four then eight, it takes about three years before you notice a big mass, when it gets big it can be two billion multiplying. That is why it seems that there is a big burst. That is why you don't find it till it is too late. A tumour, which is the size of a golf ball, will have billions of cells. That is why you act very quickly as soon as something is discovered, get it cut out.

Although aware that Gerry's first degree was in biology, I had not anticipated such a detailed response. His inclination to situate his symptom in a scientific parameter objectified and rationalised the significance of the lump and so, in containing the threat, may have rendered it less frightening and therefore easier to manage. It also reflects the extent of the effort he had made to research and apply his new knowledge to his own situation.

Louise

My first interview with 36-year-old Louise, which took place in her semi-restored, rambling Georgian home, was frequently interrupted by two tiny, human whirlwinds, her children, five-year-old Richard and four-year-old Laura. She explained that they lived there, with her husband, Derek, a former professor. During the course of her illness, as the result of a sudden stroke and brain haemorrhage, Derek had himself become severely disabled. All except one of the interviews we shared together were held in the chaos of the large, semi-completed farmhouse style kitchen and were subject to the 'interruption on demand' of the two children.

Finding her initial breast lump came at a time that should have been an exciting one for the young family. Louise thrived in her respected position as GP in the local community and, although her father had just died, she was full of anticipation as she had recently given birth to her second child, a much wanted daughter.

She began her story:

I am 36 years old, from a large family, one of 8 children. Studied medicine and graduated in 1985. Fell in love and got married in very dramatic style when I was 30. I had a baby [Richard] 10 months after and then the next year I miscarried. My father was diagnosed that same year and died of cancer. Then I had my baby girl [Laura] just a few months later. Richard was born in 1991, my father's illness was 1992; his death and Laura's birth were in 1993.

As Louise lived, she became subject to numerous complex problems, both physical and social, outlined in Table 3.

She continued:

In 1994, I was diagnosed as having breast cancer. I had a breast lump, had surgery, partial mastectomy, chemotherapy, radiotherapy and was told I had pretty tough cancer. It was spread into my lymph nodes and that it was quite a worrying spread. I never asked too much because nobody was saying anything too good but they were worried about the nature of this tumour although there was nothing inevitable. I was just to go on and see what happened, which I went along with. Just after I finished my treatments I developed a lump under my arm, went back into hospital and had that biopsied, developed an infection, abscess and had daily nursing [from the district nurse] for 6 months.

At the end of l995, my husband had a brain haemorrhage and his surgery went wrong and he had an enormous stroke and we had a couple of months when he looked like he would die. Now he has recovered to an extent but he has no speech, he is blind, he has difficulty comprehending. That is a minor difficulty, he is in a wheelchair, he is paralysed on one side, he has developed epilepsy.

In May 1996, I was diagnosed as having bone secondaries. I had known for a couple of months that I was in pretty bad pain and that I was ill, so I spent the summer having radio and chemotherapy. I was a pretty sick lady altogether, really thinking about dying. 'Maybe we have reached a point where you are not on top of your illness, my dear?' I would think, although never quite being prepared to live with that possibility. And then just bit by bit I pulled out of that and began to get better and better. Now some of that may have been anticipated medically but I think everyone is quite surprised at how well I am. The end of the year was complicated. Derek had epilepsy and, during a seizure, he fractured his hip . . . Just at the end of the year, I got another secondary in my ribs, which has been treated, so it means my life has completely changed. I have gone from being a doctor who loved being a GP, with a very intelligent, imaginative, lovely husband, who was my support in life with two kids and the money rolling in, ideas rolling out. I have a life threatening illness, I do not know how that will resolve itself, neither of us can work, can run the home and we have two wee children.

Table 3 *Timeline for Louise's Life*

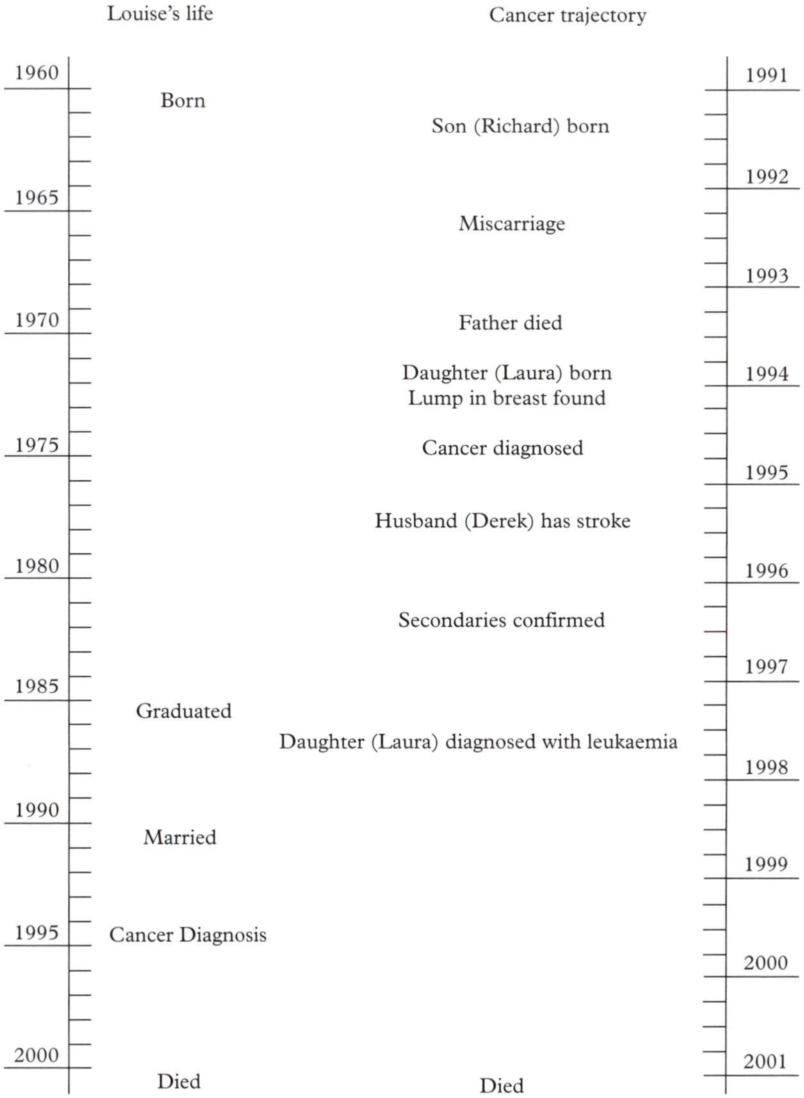
Louise's life
Cancer trajectory
1960
1965
1970
1975
1980
1985
1990
1995
2000
Born
Graduated
Married
Cancer Diagnosis
Died
1991
1992
1993
1994
1995
1996
1997
1998
1999
2000
2001
Son (Richard) born
Miscarriage
Father died
Daughter (Laura) born
Lump in breast found
Cancer diagnosed
Husband (Derek) has stroke
Secondaries confirmed
Daughter (Laura) diagnosed with leukaemia
Died

I have cancer. I have a primary and I have known spread, so I have metastatic carcinoma, which is an extremely serious situation to be in. According to conventional medical wisdom, I have an incurable illness, my prognosis is uncertain. Sometime ago I was told it was anywhere between six months and two years. I am not sure when I was told that, I have deliberately tried to forget, but maybe six or nine months ago, but another doctor has said, 'No, you may have six months, you may only have five minutes dear, I don't know. But with bone secondaries, you can live for a while. They don't all, but lots of them do . . .'

Louise actually survived for almost exactly three years after our first interview, during which time, her daughter, Laura, by then aged six years, was diagnosed with leukaemia. Much of this period of her life, not surprisingly, was spent fighting bouts of profound depression, as not only her health continued gradually to decline but also dramatic events occurred to others within her social group. She told me that following her own initial diagnosis, she:

. . . just sort of lost the joy in life, I couldn't be bothered. I was reading the death column in the Daily News and the thought came completely unbidden 'I don't care if I never get well.'

In the face of such adversity, it is surprising how many of the interviews brimmed over with laughter and good humour. This was especially true of the conversations with Louise. An intelligent and articulate woman, she appeared to use humour as a defence mechanism to counter the many tragedies that dogged her life. Having recited her litany of health and social problems, she confounded me by saying:

But you wouldn't believe how happy my life is. I can describe my life to sound awful or to sound very, very good. Through all this, I have had two lovely children, a family that you could not imagine and my husband who is my right arm; we are just spiritual buddies.

Louise settled into her story, telling me how her illness had begun. Happy and content in her role of GP, her scientific training encouraged her to rationalise a lump she had found and so she hesitated to seek specialist medical advice. She continued:

I had a baby in July, and was breast feeding in August and one night felt a definite lump, you know when you feel your heart fall and thought 'Oh my God! Don't worry about it dear, you are breast feeding.' Now this is another disadvantage of being a doctor, you can rationalise all these things away if you can go up another diagnostic track . . . Then I got the midwife to look at it; she said 'Blocked duct!'

Louise's narrative unwittingly serves as a classic example of her socialisation. Her first response was 'Oh my God!' which conforms to popular perception of lumps being dangerous. Her scientifically educated, and more objective, self then spontaneously interjected, immediately dominating. Consequently, she then read the lump through the lens of her profession as doctor, telling herself 'Don't worry about it, dear . . .' as it might signal any number of a host of lesser problems.

She made no mention of seeking her husband Derek's opinion on how she should react. Busy at university and in good health when she found her initial lump, he would later encounter his own tragic health problems. It must also be noted that, in spite of being a doctor herself, Louise did not turn to a peer for advice, rather she consulted her midwife, a person of lesser standing in the medical hierarchy.

She continued:

I love the sense of control my medical knowledge gives me, I worked in the hospital I am being treated in, I am on first name terms with the doctors. I think being a doctor made me very slow to present with my illness, because . . . I was almost embarrassed to turn up with anything other than cancer. I would have felt a bit of a Charlie turning up with a lump that was not and I think that that was a deciding factor in my not going to the doctor.

Louise's cancer caused her to endure two major losses. The first, common to all the respondents, was the loss of good health; the second, specific to Louise as a doctor, was the loss of medical control. Although on a cognitive level, her profession armed her with the objective ability to appraise her symptom professionally, her status also impacted negatively to neutralise the benefits of that power. She feared ridicule and the thought that her colleagues would label her a hypochondriac. This might be attributed to the conflict between two modes of normative behaviour that prevail in current Western society. The first informs the public to behave responsibly in health related concerns. The second counsels bravery in the face of adversity, likening self-awareness to vanity, a selfish form of weakness.

Louise explained that in the period between finding the lump and ultimately seeking professional help, she had at one stage:

. . . thought most of the lump had gone, it had changed. So in October I arranged to see a surgeon but did not keep the appointment because my mother was cracking up and I didn't think she could take it. She was to have minded the children and I knew I couldn't have come back in from the appointment and told her 'By the way mum, I have breast cancer.'

So, I took a chance. Christmas came and went; my husband was finishing writing a book so I said, when he finishes the book I will go. The book dragged on. By this stage, I knew I was in trouble but my powers of denial were so strong . . . I went to my friend who forced me to . . . In March I went off to hospital and once you are on the roundabout everything happens around you. Getting the foot on is the difficulty.

Louise had adopted a sophisticated series of delaying strategies, initially citing social causes as being responsible for her prevarication. She pleaded the fact that her mother was '. . . cracking up . . .' and said that she '. . . didn't think she [her mother] could take . . .' the probable cancer diagnosis. Although speculation might suggest that Louise was projecting her own psychological perspective and consequent fears onto her mother, this quotation is only the first of many which suggest something of the dutiful but also, at times, openly confrontational, relationship which existed between mother and daughter.

Despite admitting she was aware she might probably have cancer, Louise still postponed further assessment of her symptom, this time indicting the extended temporal duration of one of her husband's career commitments. It was not until March, a full eight months after detecting her lump, that Louise reluctantly relented to the badgering of a friend and sought medical advice.

Gita

Gita's death, before the beginning of my fieldwork, precludes learning directly of her experiences. However, I have chosen to include her husband, Ash's, recall of how she found her symptoms, because it affords a vital glimpse into how some individuals from non-Western countries react during the dying journey.

Ash and Gita, first generation Indians from Kenya, were settled in a small village. They lived there with their two sons, aged 8 and 14 years, and Gita's mother, in a smart, detached, mock-Tudor home. As I had been informed that I was to interview a recently bereaved widower, I was surprised when, on being taken into the living room, I was met by the entire family. They made me welcome, plying me with tea and biscuits. The younger son even presented me with a picture that he had drawn of his 'mum'.

Gita was 41 years old when she died, just six weeks before I interviewed her widower. Referring to how he believed her Hindu religion influenced her attitudes, Ash told me that Gita felt resigned to the course her life would take, telling me that: '. . . you accept what you have in life and you accept what you've got and you have to go along with it because this nature takes its own course'. In a later interview, he spoke of his own perspective on life, paradoxically condemning her behaviour and yet simultaneously supporting the philosophy that underlay his wife's views. Still in deep grief, he raged against her, saying: '. . . to me personally, she created her own death. Not by . . . but then who knows, if fate was written in that way, who knows . . .'

The rawness of his grief was evident in the angry and frustrated comments he made about Gita and how she delayed seeking medical advice. She had trusted her Hindu religion, whose philosophy taught her to let fate take its course. Ash told me what had happened when Gita had found the lump in her breast:

This thing happened in 1992, it was like a Smartie. Small, when we discussed, I said, 'Look you have to go see a doctor because this is happening, I don't think this is right.' I don't know if she is afraid of it, or just totally ignorant but she just left it and it started getting like a Kitkat. Four fingers and it was getting bigger and bigger, the breast was getting bigger. There was so much concern about it, I did tell her a few times, 'You go see doctor, I take you.' I booked appointments 4 or 5 times myself to take her there and she cancelled everything. And then in 1994 some of the time she was busy taking the children . . . [to school] but I take that as an excuse; obviously, she had a run around to do but that was not very important. I thought the way I was telling her to go and do this, and that, go and see the doctor, she just didn't accept that and it is something. It is very hard. If it was my son, you just give him a couple of slaps, put him in the car and drag him down to the doctor, but I cannot do that to her. She was a very intelligent person. For three years, she just neglected and she was totally brainwashed by her religion fanatic thing. She was devoted to this particular thing, I don't believe in it much but I believe in God. When you go too much in it . . . she totally neglected herself. So in the short term she has created her own death sentence where she could avoid that at the beginning.

Ash, a shopkeeper, referred to his wife's lump in terms of the familiar, applying the names of branded confectionery. Impatient with her fatalistic attitude to the lump and behaving much in the way a managing director might overrule a subordinate, he pro-actively tried to persuade her to seek qualified opinion. It is interesting to note that, however passively Gita may have behaved in her reaction to her lump, she was active in her determination not to seek medical help. Ash's words, it should be stressed, were spoken at the height of his grief and are imbued with his evident frustration and fury at the tragic outcome of her delay in seeking medical help. Although both were Hindu, their devotion to the religion differed enough to cause problems. His use of terms such as 'brainwashed' and 'fanatic' denote his frustration with how he felt she was influenced by her faith.

When I asked Ash if he believed she realised the potential significance of the lump she had found, he told me:

I think she knew, she knew in her mind. I think she was worried in a sense what would happen. She was not going to accept it that she had cancer, although it was there. She thinking that that wasn't a cancer, that it was just a cyst. When we were going out one night and she realised one breast was bigger than the other, that was when she realised there is something wrong with her. Then I had to cancel two appointments [with her doctor] after that . . .

Although by then Gita could no longer ignore the obvious physical mani-
festations of her, as yet, undiagnosed cancer, she still shirked from reporting for medical advice. However, it was Ash, not Gita, who cancelled the
appointments.

As an immigrant, Gita's late medical presentation might, in part, also
be attributed to her continued observance of many of her native culture's
strict behavioural codes, especially those concerning privacy. Although
the family were part of a large extended familial network, Ash told me
how Gita insisted on keeping her symptom private. Embittered by his
recent bereavement, he said:

> In the beginning, she did not want to disclose this business. Obviously, that is a
> private thing. She didn't want anybody to talk about it, she couldn't face it, she
> cannot face it, you cannot talk to her, you cannot criticise her. She was just . . . I
> know it is not nice to say this, because she was my wife, she was a totally selfish
> person; she was crazy.

Although Ash is not a native English speaker, his pattern of speech, specifically his inclination to switch between past and present tense, divulges
much of his state of mind. When he comments 'she couldn't face it',
he began by situating the event in the past when it happened but then,
presumably because his grief had revived the events that occurred, he
spoke as though the experience was continuing, telling me 'she cannot
face it, you cannot talk to her, you cannot criticise her'. Although on a
material level Ash undoubtedly accepted his wife's death, he was, not
surprisingly at this early stage in his mourning, still struggling to come to
terms with it.

Discussion

Bury (1982) describes illness as a 'biographical disruption' as it impacts
not only on a biological level but also affects how individuals perceive their
entire life trajectory. The time when they first located their symptoms was
then, not surprisingly, marked clearly in the minds of the respondents.
The clarity in their memories is evidence of how significant they perceived
the discovery. However, from the meagre references they made about
how they felt emotionally, it would seem that both Gerry and Louise
appeared to have experienced an instinctive sense of dread when they
were initially confronted with their lumps.

It should also be observed that it was the facts that were stressed rather
than the emotional reactions. Gerry and Ash both described the symptoms using culturally specific terms to indicate their size. Significantly,
all these terms, Smarties, Kitkats, eggs and golf balls have positive or

neutral nuances. None used negative terms such as louse or slug to des-
ignate dimension. This link to everyday items may be a subconscious
strategy to defuse the horror of acknowledging potential cancer.

Once the lump had been discovered, Gerry and Louise were alike in
that they drew on their education and both automatically attempted to
rationalise the symptom, seeking less threatening explanations for its presence, such as acne in Gerry's case or a side effect of breastfeeding for
Louise. Although Gerry instantly showed the lump to his wife, he chose
not to dwell on the probable implications. It would seem that Gita, too,
initially conferred with her husband and, much like Gerry at this stage,
did not allow anxiety over the potential symptom to disrupt family life.
Although Ash, bereft in his grief, describes his wife as being 'selfish' in her
repudiation of medical help, it might be that, as a mother, she quite simply did not welcome the idea of pro-actively recruiting the confirmation
of a cancer diagnosis into her home.

Lichter (1987) notes the part family response plays in the dying journey, observing that the patient cannot be at peace if other family members are tense and anxious. In response, patients often attempt to ease
the situation by masking their physical symptoms and true emotions, in
an attempt to protect those with whom they are intimate from the harsh
reality of their situation (Gyllenskold, 1982). This, though, entails performing emotional work for others at a time when they themselves are in
need. I argue that this heroic behaviour (see the Conclusion) could be
observed in how Gerry, Louise and Gita behaved even at this early stage
in dealing with their symptoms: heroes do not worry and most definitely
do not complain.

Gita was like Louise in her delay in presenting her symptoms for medical assessment and, also, in the fact that she chose to take 'a chance'. Both
instigated what proved to be fatal delays. Frankenberg (1992) alludes to
how individuals who present for medical opinion after an obvious delay
are viewed by doctors as bad patients, but this inclination to hesitate
before reporting may have its roots in societal attitudes. Despite rapid
advances in technology that facilitate early diagnosis and, therefore, early
treatment, impressions of the disease as an acute killer still linger with
the public. Many of the respondents delayed presenting their symptoms
for medical attention, often only going at the insistence of others. There
may be a number of reasons for this, including fear of what they will be
told.

Kubler-Ross (1995) cites the first stage of the move towards 'acceptance' of death as 'denial' and it may also be that it is, in part, denial
that sometimes allows symptoms to be dismissed. However, not all cancer experiences begin with the individual finding an obvious lump or

bump (Doka, 1993); many make their presence felt through symptoms such as changes in bowel movements, fatigue, general discomfort or pain. Some cancers, like that of the bladder, respond well to treatment if caught within a six-week period and so early diagnosis is vital. The problem is that, with these lesser known cancers, many patients tend not to recognise the symptoms and delay reporting for a host of reasons, such as not having a family history of cancer. That delay can prove fatal.

Once the initial bodily change has been personally defined as a symptom, the majority of respondents consulted with family or friends. With the exception of Louise, all of the respondents had informed supporters who proved their worth, being available for conferral when they were instrumental in motivating the respondents to seek medical advice. Reaction to their symptoms was contingent on their specific social situation (Zborowski, 1952); the respondents' decision to consult with the professionals was mediated by social factors (Zola, 1973). Relationships did sometimes impact negatively. In the face of opposition from her husband, Gita struggled to keep the knowledge of her lump from her family presumably fearing their criticism over her extended delay in presenting for medical treatment. Louise, too, shared with Gita, the desperate need to maintain dignity, the urgent need to retain self-respect, in a situation in which they gambled their lives rather than risk appearing foolish.

Consulting the professionals

Gerry

Holding Gerry's and Claire's attention for more than ten minutes, whilst I attempted to interview them, was never easy! Our time together was beset not just by the children's demands but also by the constant telephone calls from well-wishers and family, eager to support them through their difficulties. Even so, Gerry found time to explain how, as soon as he found his lump, he made an appointment with his GP, who instantly referred him to a consultant. Gerry went alone, as his wife was just days from giving birth to their second child. He told me that his specialist:

. . . touched my neck from a different angle, he went behind me, touched it. Apparently, you can feel it better that way than the front, and he said to me, 'not to worry it could be ten different reasons, including TB' which was on the increase. TB of the lymph nodes because I do a lot of travelling . . . He later told me that he knew it wasn't that but you couldn't be sure and that he wanted to rule it [TB] out. Also, I think it was the easiest way to keep my mind on other things.

It is interesting that, in reassuring Gerry, his consultant focused attention on the lump not as cancer but as a potential manifestation of TB, a disease that is easier to treat. He wanted to distract Gerry away from making the obvious connection of lump equals cancer equals death and onto another illness that, although serious, would not spark the same alarm.

When I asked Gerry if he had felt apprehensive about that meeting with the consultant, he told me he had drawn support from Claire, who encouraged him to do some basic research on what the lump might signify. I asked if he had worried and he said:

Not at that stage, I mean we talked about it, but we didn't . . . it was only after I came back from the consultant and told Claire some of the things that he said, that you [gestures to his wife and a medical encyclopaedia] got the medical book out and opened it up and by chance it opened at Hodgkin's disease, lymphomas. Because he [the doctor] mentioned lymphomas to me and I said to you [his wife] it could have been a lymphoma and I read it through. Every thing you looked up, swellings in the neck it said, '. . . of course not every swelling is down to cancer . . .' It just could have been an ordinary infection, but if you have any wit you know that an ordinary infection brings pain and swelling and redness, this was at another level. It was a lump.

Gerry, again, conformed to his pattern of analysing and began to ratio-nalise his illness. His medical consultation appeared to have moved him to realise that a cancer diagnosis was possible and he chose to deal with that prospect by arming himself with knowledge. Like many of my other respondents, Gerry and Claire worked as a team and initially turned to textbooks seeking further elucidation on what the lump might mean.

Anticipation of the tests, or biopsies, fuelled the respondents' angst, not just when the tests were being carried out but also before and after, when waiting for the results. Gerry, who required surgery for his biopsy, drew support from friends whose advice reflected the current upsurge in alternative medicine. He reported:

It was only just coming up to the actual day, the day before I was going to get the operation that I spoke to one of my colleagues in work who is into these homeopathic remedies and things. He had a lump on his neck a few years ago but he went to a homeopathic doctor who drained his lymph nodes and he was fine. Thankfully I did not take his advice.

Gerry's research into possible causes for his lump prompted him to ques-tion the proposed exploratory surgical procedure, even at this early stage:

Mr. S [the surgeon] then arranged for me to have the lump removed on Saturday 12th October, so from 22nd September [when he found the lump] till 12th October was not a lot of time. I did not worry too much about it . . . I wanted to ring to find out why I needed to have the whole lump taken out, why not just a biopsy, a sample. Mr. S wasn't there and I got his wife who is a GP. She explained to me that it was rather large and that, whether it was anything or not, it needed to be removed and there was no point in going in twice and sometimes the biopsy may not get the proper cells. So I thought it may be the surgeon wanting to make a few bob! So I thought about it and I said, "Well, ok. I will go ahead and have it out and I really did not worry about it . . ." Did I Claire?

Claire said: 'Well, you talked about your father a lot . . .' Gerry's father had died two years before and Claire made the connection between talking about his father's death and his anxiety. The twenty days between 22nd September and 12th October could, in such a situation, feel a long time, especially in Gerry's case when one of those days was his birthday. His tendency to rationalise is also evident when, attempting to explain the need for the lump to be removed, he suspiciously attributed the reason to pecuniary gain for the surgeon.

Gerry continued:

When I came around from the operation [the biopsy] later, Mr. S came in, and he has a habit of shaking your hand, and saying, 'Well, how are you, how are you doing?' as if he is a great buddy, but he . . . The way he shook my hand, and in fact clasped my other hand with great intensity, I saw something in his eyes, I just felt something, that it is more than just, 'You will be alright.' And also the state my neck was in, it was bad, it was really sore, and for just taking a lump out it was a hell of a lot of damage that was done and even now I still can't feel my ear and down the side of my face, my chin, under my neck, I have no feeling, nothing. Nerve damage. I found out later that they actually had to cut into my nerves to get this growth out because it was growing outside the lymph node but at this time I didn't know this. And the next morning the consultant anaesthetist came in and gave me the big friendly handshake I think it was their sort of support, I think they have seen enough of this, [they] knew straight away. So Doctor S was to get back to me on Wednesday with the results, I was waiting all day, feeling a bit anxious.

In his heightened state of concern Gerry interpreted the doctor's kindness and reassurance as preparation for the bad news, which he felt was forthcoming. He was also prompted by the 'state' in which the surgery had left his neck. The adjectives he used to describe it fit his psychological demeanour well: 'it was bad, it was really sore', there was 'a hell of a lot of damage'. Although when he says 'I have no feeling, nothing', he is clearly referring to the nerve damage, he might also have been describing how he was left in a degree of psychological numbness.

Ben

Sixty-three-year-old Ben and his red-haired wife, Eilish, had only recently moved to their pebble-dashed, semi-detached bungalow. They had enjoyed refurbishing their home, adding French windows to bring the well-tended back garden into their cosy living room. Their hospitality was overwhelming and extended even to inviting me to join them for evening meals.

Although I interviewed them as a couple, while Eilish prepared some refreshments, Ben told me how his illness began after he detected blood in his urine:

> . . . saw my GP and he gave me some antibiotics, which cleared it up and then it came back and it was up and down and up and down all the time. Eventually I had an interview with a consultant at the hospital; we went privately to see Mr. C. You would probably be better off talking to Eilish but there was lots of mistakes made by Mr. C. X-Rays were taken and then he didn't see them. Then I had a couple of biopsies and he said, 'You're fine, you're clear!' and Eilish wouldn't accept this. She knew I wasn't all right and I came out walking on air, and she said 'No', and she made me go back in. She said 'If you had abnormal cells last week they can't be normal this week, it can't happen like that.' So he gave me another biopsy.

Not surprisingly, Ben's symptoms did not respond well to the antibiotics, so the couple decided on a private consultation, presumably believing that this would guarantee a better medical standard. They were, however, let down on two counts: their faith in scientific medicine was to prove misplaced, as was their trust that their money would ensure preferred treatment.

Although not overtly describing how worried he was prior to learning the results of his biopsy, the fact that Ben describes himself as initially leaving 'walking on air' suggests that he probably had experienced some tension before the appointment. The quotation also indicates something of the power relationship between the couple. Ben describes how Eilish, 'made me go back in', which suggests that he was inclined to be the more submissive. It also indicates something of Eilish's commitment to their marriage. She was not going to permit Ben to accept anything that might jeopardise him or their future relationship.

When Eilish, who had made tea served in Prince Charles and Diana cups, rejoined us, she repeated Ben's story, echoing much of what he had said and expanding upon it. Telling the story from her perspective she stressed how difficult she had found it to persuade the relevant medics that Ben's problem warranted serious attention. This resulted in a series of what she deemed to be 'inexcusable delays', caused in the main by the human errors made by one 'incompetent' consultant. Ben attempted to tell me that at this stage he '. . . still didn't suspect it was . . .'

Eilish then interrupted, saying:

He had the blood test and within 24 hours a letter came to say abnormal blood tests and he had to see Mr. C straight away, which means cancer. It was in the blood stream . . .

Ben attempted to interject, stressing again that he '. . . still didn't know this was cancer . . .' Eilish told me how she empathised with Ben in his dilemma saying:

And he still didn't know because he said: 'What's abnormal?' I said, 'I'm sure it's nothing . . .' so I had to keep him calm . . .

Seizing control of the conversation, she went on to tell me of the continued confusion, which dogged his diagnosis, including how the consultant had based the diagnosis on notes belonging to another patient. This chaos had reigned from early February until Ben was ultimately correctly diagnosed at the end of July; six months of delay, well outside the optimum six-week window for beneficial treatment.

Sue-Ellen

Fifty-six-year-old Sue-Ellen and her recently bankrupt husband had only just moved to their charming, bijou cottage, adjacent to a railway station. During the first interview I shared with Sue-Ellen our conversation was interrupted frequently by the sound of the plumbers installing central heating and also by her husband. He paced the hallway, continually interjecting through the open door to correct her, in his attempts to ensure that what she said would be understood and interpreted correctly. Sue-Ellen told me what happened when she initially reported her troubling bowel symptoms to her doctor:

. . . first diagnosis was irritable bowel syndrome. I was not happy with that so I made three or four more visits to the doctor. His attitude was 'You're wasting my time.' I continued to visit him because I believed that it was serious. He sent me to the hospital for a test and I had to drink something [presumably a barium meal]. A week later, doctor telephoned me at home at 8.30 am and asked me to come around to his surgery immediately. Although I thought this was strange I saw him, thinking that he was only doing it to tell me there was nothing wrong and to get rid of me again. When I saw him he told me '. . . as far as I know you need a hysterectomy . . .' The doctor went on to tell me that I would have an appointment with a consultant in about a week's time. I was surprised to have the appointment made for the next day.

Problems with clinicians began early for Sue-Ellen, who soon learned that presenting promptly for medical opinion was not a guarantee of accurate diagnosis and appropriate treatment. Instinct warned her that her symptoms signalled something serious, which demanded more attention than her GP warranted, and so, because she felt uneasy, she continued to badger him hoping that he might eventually realise the gravity of her condition; her system worked. Having been referred for routine tests at her local hospital, she was surprised to be contacted at home outside normal social hours. Zerubavel (1981) argues that time has territorial dimensions and that as terrain can be breached by strangers, so can private time be intruded upon. This is effectively what the doctor did when he telephoned at 8.30 am. It is, though, interesting to observe that it was another temporal factor, that of the doctor's speed in arranging an appointment with a consultant, which alerted her to the probable gravity of her situation.

Discussion

Soldiers are rigorously disciplined to the realities of life on the battlefield and anthropologists are trained to anticipate and prepare for the period of acclimatisation encountered on entering new fields. However, for the most part, people about to embark on an illness journey have not been prepared for even the most basic pragmatic or emotional adaptations they will have to make.

This promotion from dealing with their GP into the realm of the expert effectively pushed up stress levels for the respondents and their supporters. The introduction of specialist assessment of their symptoms signalled the beginning of intense anxiety. They were now entering the new, and for the majority, previously unknown world of the medical; a situation where their worry would grow in proportion to the level of expert opinion that would now be involved.

As the respondents began to climb the relevant clinical hierarchies, they became enrolled into medical culture and had to learn to manage its attendant spheres. However, even with the help of increasingly sophisticated diagnostic tools, the diagnosis of cancer is seldom smooth or speedy. Costain Schou and Hewison observe how such an assessment '. . . often involves invasive procedures and repeated tests, as well as actual treatment processes (the line between reaching a diagnosis and beginning treatment is often difficult to draw)' (1999: 24). Anticipating such demands, the respondents turned for much needed help and reassurance to their supporters, who usually did not hesitate to meet the challenge. It is worth noting that all but two of the respondents chose to have a companion present when they made that first significant visit.

The value of being escorted worked on several levels. Besides being a prospective source of consolation, supporters could also offer practical help by, for example, taking charge of a severely shocked patient and providing transport home. The fact that the supporter was, to some extent, more removed emotionally from the trauma of the diagnosis, also facilitated a more objective account of what the consultant actually said. Supporters, by dint of this detachment, were also well placed to observe opportunities where they might elicit and retain further information.

Indeed, this tendency to have support was borne out during my periods of hospital based observation, carried out in a consultant's office, when people were being diagnosed at various stages of their cancer. All of the patients attending came escorted by a companion.

As part of these observations, I was able to study the interaction between a 78-year-old male patient, his daughter and the consultant. Although when he was being told that he had cancer, his daughter remained silent, she later assumed the role of guardian, questioning the consultant as to the specifics of his disease and how it would be managed. She was particularly interested in learning the practicalities of his treatment and the appointment concluded with her verifying the details of where and when this would begin. Although father and daughter entered and left the consultation room together, they did not, at any stage, make physical contact.

The choice of escort was not made lightly. In referring to how she elected who would accompany her, one of my respondents said: 'I recognise now that my friends all occupy a specific role and I needed someone who wasn't going to go to pieces on me because I was . . . I couldn't have my sister or my mother.'

Illness, even at this early stage, would, however, appear to bestow on patients the ability to transcend previously established hierarchies in power. As we will learn later, this switch in power relations was not always so well received.

Diagnosis

Louise

Louise came from a very traditional, rural family background. Her graphic and descriptive stories many times, during our conversations together, lapsed into deliciously inviting tales of, unfortunately, unrelated matters.

Having a medical background, though, would not appear to have cushioned her from the shock of her diagnosis. Louise, whose academic husband was busy at work, went alone to see her consultant for the results of her initial breast biopsy. Explaining what happened when he broke the news she said:

> . . . I grabbed the chart but maybe there were few cells . . . but the surgeon said '99 per cent definite you have cancer here.' I went on my own; all I could feel was just this . . . I felt it was a death sentence, two or three years max; unbelievable sadness for my children, what are they going to do?
>
> I remember he said, 'What are you crying for?' He is a difficult man and I said, 'My children are very young', the baby was 8 months and I have a 2-year-old boy. 'Yes', he said, 'They are very young and you are in a very serious situation' and I felt panic stricken, loss of control. I felt this is beyond my control. I will be swept away by this and my children are going to be left. Even pre-stroke they would not be left with a man who would iron uniforms . . .
>
> Panic and a chasm of sadness. Despair, absolute despair. I remember the sister told me to sit down. She said, 'Even in the bleakest of outlooks people do do well and you will have to look at every possible means of doing well', and then she gave me examples of people who survived. She wanted to phone someone but I just wanted to get in my car and go home. I had told people it was just a little problem, probably just self-delusion. I felt desperately sad, that is what the illness makes me feel most; it is that sense of worry for the children. Sadness that they would experience loss at that stage in life and a loss for which there is no true compensation . . . That is a huge burden to carry about.

Louise previously prided herself on her ability to be in control. This diagnosis specifically threatened that control and she was so astounded by the trauma it induced that she was spurred into physical action. Although physically weakened by learning her diagnosis, she summoned up her strength and mustered her medical training, feeling the need to observe and validate the empirical evidence of her tests with her own eyes.

Her interpretation of the test results as being a 'death sentence' contrasts strongly with her dynamic 'grabbing' of the chart at the beginning of this narrative. There is a stark distinction too between her own, powerful emotions evidenced in her words such as 'despair, panic and sadness' and the detached objectivity of her surgeon, who questioned the reason for her tears.

Interestingly, too, she observed the instruction from the nurse who told her to 'sit down'. In doing so, although a doctor, she was defining herself now as a patient. It was also the nurse rather than the consultant, who provided the key element of hope common at the time of the majority of critical diagnoses.

This quotation also provides detail about the degree to which Louise was socially embedded. On four separate occasions she referred to her children, at times seeming close to invoking divine involvement on their behalf. She feared for them, believing their future could only be safe with her and that without her, their security would be in jeopardy. She may also be projecting onto them her own sense of loss and anxiety about her future. Her other social relationships were also critical to her and this narrative reveals how she had attempted to protect others, as well as herself, from worrying about the appointment by minimising its potential gravity. This supports Seale's (1998) concept of the modern day hero. It is interesting to learn too that, although she had elected to attend the consultation alone, in suggesting that Louise contact her family, the nurse automatically assumed that she would benefit from social support.

Gerry

Although obviously comfortable, from a material perspective, Gerry and Claire were clearly suffering from the trauma brought about by his health problems. This was compounded by the additional pressure of living with a very new baby and suffering from the consequent sleep deprivation. Referring back to the time of his diagnosis, Gerry explained to me that when his doctor had:

... called me at ten past ten that night ... He said, 'Hello Gerry, I have a bit of news for you. The operation went well but you appear to have had some abnormal cells.' At that point, it felt as if my heart had stopped and Claire was trying to butt in to hear what he was saying and I was trying to spell the word 'Cancer' in the air to her. I said, to him, 'Abnormal cells, does that mean cancer?' and he said 'Yes, lymphoma', and I said, 'Hodgkin's or non-Hodgkin's?' but he said, 'Well, I don't really want to say as yet but the oncologist will call.' He said 'I will talk to you after you speak to him ... but don't worry I will be getting Christmas cards from you for many years to come.'

Gerry provided a good example of the difficulties many individuals experienced when being told that they had cancer. There are two major issues, which have to be handled simultaneously: dealing with the emotional aspects of the trauma that usually takes place within a social context and, more pragmatically, absorbing the technical facets of the diagnosis. In this quotation, Gerry illustrated how he attempted to deal with his own emotions, endeavouring to pass the information onto his wife, and also trying to absorb something about the specific mechanics of his diagnosis. Melbin (1987) considers how medical professionals use time, discussing how they have acquired the ability to break through the frontiers of the night, effectively colonising time. Whilst it might prove questionable should a nurse appear to be on duty after her allocated working time has passed, doctors retain the unquestioned right to be in contact with their patients at any time of day or night. When I asked Gerry why he had been informed of his diagnosis at such an anti-social hour, he vaguely dismissed the question saying '. . . the doctor is a busy man, he works all hours'.

The quotation is also important as it provides evidence of how, when breaking bad news, some element of hope is usually added. Lutfey and Maynard discuss how physicians communicate terminal diagnoses to their patients, quoting Sudnow (1967) and explaining that '"Dying" does not stand as a proper answer to a patient's question "What's wrong with me?"' (1998: 339). Instead, doctors frequently evade the direct question by categorising the illness, allocating its scientific name and describing the symptoms. They do not often candidly inform the patient that they are dying. Instead, they behave as Gerry's consultant did and highlight other aspects, such as the fact that there will probably be a prolonged trajectory by saying that he expected to '. . . be getting Christmas cards from you for many years to come'.

Gerry continued:

We were in the kitchen at the time. We went into a panic and Claire then phoned her sister overseas to tell her. I was feeling disbelief and yet belief because it confirmed what I knew, or what I thought would happen but it wasn't that I was thinking . . . I had put this thing I knew was going to happen almost in a box on a shelf and I thought I will reach for it when I need to but at the moment it is up there. I am not thinking about it, it didn't really worry me before but all of a sudden the box was open and the contents fell around me and I felt 'Oh shit! I have bought it' and later Claire told me when she heard it she thought, 'That was it.'

It should also be noted that, at this moment of heightened emotional crisis, the couple turned immediately to their social circle rather than waiting to hear from the oncologist. Gerry referred to 'this thing I knew was going to happen' suggesting that he was fully aware of the probable implications of the lump, although previously he told me that he had not been worried. He then said that he felt he would 'reach for it when I need to', which implied that, although knowing what the lump might signify, he still felt able to control his situation. It is, though, more interesting that he appeared to have distanced himself, splitting off his anxious feelings and envisioned them, contained securely, in a seemingly safe and innocent place; a box which, suddenly evocative of Pandora's, bursts open, discharging all Gerry's, until now, unacknowledged terrors.

Although shocked after learning his diagnosis, Gerry worked as a team with his wife. He put her need to seek opinion and solace from her family before his own desire for more information and waited patiently while she made the telephone call to her sister. The temporal order, in which the couple told others his diagnosis, reveals something of the hierarchy of intimacy in their social grouping. Zerubavel (1982) cites Lewin's

(1936) 'topological' analysis of the personality structure. He suggests that individuals can be understood as being situated at the centre of concentric circles that symbolise the various areas of their self. Those rings more closely aligned to the inner circle indicate that those within that group are more closely intimate with the subject.

In telling me what happened next, Gerry was sufficiently insightful to recognise the distancing techniques, which were apparently being employed by his new team of professionals as a defence by them against the reality of his illness. He said:

> The oncologist called. He said, 'Hello Mr. T, I'm Doctor Z, I'm going to be your oncologist. Mr. S has just been speaking to you.' Very matter of fact sort of guy, all, Mr. Mr. Mr. and it takes a long time for you to break down any type of wall that he has up and you can see why. These guys are the last bastions of what they can do for you on the health care services side, because if they are not going to help you, nobody is going to except, perhaps, the Alternative side. You can see why they do not really want to get emotionally or personally involved. Fifty percent of people or less survive my form of cancer.

> He [the oncologist] told me that I had Lymphoma and I said, 'What type?' and he said, 'Non-Hodgkin's' and I went 'Oh shit' because we had quickly realised that Hodgkin's was the easy one that was cured in 99 times out of 100. Everybody [they had telephoned] was trying to say, 'You will be ok' but they didn't believe it themselves and it was patronising. We are not so slow. Look we have the book in front of us. We thought, 'They don't believe it.' He [the oncologist] said that it was a very high grade, which is good news and bad news. They [the medical team] are right not to give you all the information they have because no matter how intelligent or how calm you think you are going to be . . . , I don't think anyone can cope with too much information at once. What he said, was, 'It may be curable but it will take six months chemotherapy.' My heart was in my mouth. I didn't believe it. Going from being a normal person to six months of chemotherapy is rough and eight sessions of CHOP . . . ? [the ironic acronym of the drugs currently given to some patients with non-Hodgkin's disease] It is imperative that it is dealt with urgently.

Claire interjected, telling me, 'I thought he was dying . . .'

Gerry had impelled his oncologist to reveal specific information, presumably feeling that increased knowledge of his illness might be useful. Rather than comforting him, however, what he heard compounded his trauma, as his own research, before the confirmation of what he suspected, had informed him of the harsh facts of this illness. Although he also felt disappointed in the reactions of those whom he telephoned, Gerry gave them the benefit of the doubt, and chose to believe that they also were in shock, rather than that they might be lying. When he commented 'I don't think anyone can cope with too much information at once' he might have been projecting his own feelings on to others and so referring to how he, himself, felt. His comment on how he felt he was 'going from being a normal person' might indicate how he feared he would become detached and separated from ordinary 'normal' mainstream life.

After being given his diagnosis over the telephone, neither Gerry nor Claire, who was due to give birth the following morning, slept. Gerry said:

> I don't know about Claire but I thought she was going to have the baby that night. Claire was due to go in the next day for an epidural to have the baby. . . . I did cry a lot that night in bed. I worried about . . . I honestly thought about me snuffing it. I thought . . . missing the family and not being there for her growing old and the children growing up. I could not stand the thought of me not seeing my daughter Diana at about 5 or 6 [years] and I could not stand the thought of that wee child crying for her daddy. Even now it makes me cry. I even cried for the baby but because she was not born yet it was Diana I was focusing on. I kept thinking, 'Why me, why me?'

Whilst the respondents were experiencing the development of their cancer journeys, events in the lives of others within their social network also continued to exercise an effect on them. Gerry's thoughts focused on the practical as well as the emotional and social impacts that he feared his diagnosis would bring about. He dwelt not just on his own predicament but also on how his shocking news might affect his pregnant wife, perhaps even accelerating the birth. His primary fear, however, was, understandably, for his four-year-old daughter Diana. His thoughts then became rationalised and he, again, compared his situation with that of a road crash:

> I very quickly stopped saying, 'Why me?' I will go back to the road accident. If there is something that you have done wrong you always think, 'If only I had looked at my mirror', because there was an event that you could have controlled. But no matter what I could have done, even though people say, 'It was stress, that job etc. . . .' Stress is in everybody's life and, if stress was such a big factor, why has everyone not got it? Maybe there are psychological reasons, psychosomatic reasons. Maybe chemical, environmental reasons, food things, toxins, smoke but at the end of the day you don't have control over it so you can't say, 'Why me, what if, what did I do wrong?' You have to stop that quickly. From the first few days after I heard, I stood on that notion and I have never had that notion back at me. It doesn't really bug me, it is there. If you have caused an accident that would eat away at you, seeing some one getting killed in a stupid accident but this is me, so it doesn't matter.

His tendency to rationalise demanded that he find an explanation of how his disease originated. Casting around for any possible causes, he reluctantly accepted that his disease was probably random. He commented:

Rather me than Diana or Claire. I used to pray a while back, 'If anything was
to happen, give it to me.' This was well before I got it. 'Don't let it happen
to my daughter, don't let anything happen to Claire because Diana would miss
Claire more than she would miss me, even though she would miss me. If you are
going to sprinkle some nasty pixy dust over this house, sprinkle it over me.' And
it is not being heroic; it is the only sensible thing. It would be easier for me. I
don't know how I could cope if it was Diana, it is a very selfish way of looking
at it.

Gerry's social role as father dominated his thoughts. Even before he
learned that he had cancer, he had pre-empted the tragedy and, being a
practising Roman Catholic, had attempted to bargain with divine powers
and have the disease himself. Moreover, in spite of saying 'it is not being
heroic', he knew that it was.

Bob

Although I initially met 56-year-old Bob and his wife Sheila whilst he was
in hospital having chemotherapy, my first interview was in their home,
a stylish 1970s, suburban, semi-detached house, fronted by an immacu-
lately kept garden. As I already knew Bob had been a house decorator, it
did not surprise me that their home was so elegantly finished. Bob began
by telling me he had had quite a radical reaction to the results of his tests.
He said:

We got a call from the hospital to see the doctor and lucky enough we met him
and had a chat and he just said, 'I have bad news for you.' When he said bad
news, I was really shocked. My wife and I were there just waiting for what bad
news there was and my wife said, 'What bad news?' He said, 'I'm afraid you have
cancer.' I was reeling, devastated because I thought . . . that was the last thing on
my mind. I was just devastated, I collapsed on the floor. I was devastated, really
devastated. The next thing he said was, 'You are in a bad way so we will take you
in to a side ward. I will get someone else in to see you.'

Bob's physical collapse, as well as his repeated use of the word 'devastated'
indicates the level of his trauma. Patients who are told they have cancer are
frightened. They do not understand how this awful thing has happened
and how it may shape their lives; all they know is that, suddenly and
terrifyingly, they have been plunged into a position where their life is at
risk and many, automatically, assume that they will die.

Like the majority of the respondents, Bob had attended for his consultation with a supporter, his wife Sheila. It was she who had prompted
further details of the 'bad news' and not Bob himself. He was immediately
removed to a side ward as a result of his extreme reaction to his diagnosis. Although this was probably to free the consultation room for other

patients, it allowed the couple privacy but, perhaps more significantly, defined him overtly in the role of patient rather than individual. He explained that:

Within 5 or 10 minutes there was Dr X, and he read all my files and said, 'I see that you got really bad news from the surgeon. I am the guy with the good news. I have looked through your files very quickly and from what I can see you have cancer but I think we can do something with it. I don't want you to ask any questions but I will see you one day next week.' He went away and said, 'I have an appointment next Thursday.' My wife and I went together and he told me I have the cancer in the coccyx. He told me 'There is a tumour, we have things . . . not to cure, but we can relieve you of a lot of pain and so, with time, there is possibilities with the stuff that we have now, with all the gear that we have now, that with time, we might get rid of it or repair it. It is as simple as that. There is a new research programme going on. Now you have a choice of three Cancer Research programmes.' He asked do I want to go on it. 'It is a trial but it is very successful in America and we hope it is successful here. You do not have to take it but I recommend that you take this.' So I said, 'Yes, by all means.' He said, 'Next week we will take you in. It will be in 48 hour periods which will mean that you come in on Thursday morning and leave sometime on Saturday.' I said that was ok.

The doctor began his consultation with Bob by contrasting the 'bad news' of his diagnosis, mentioned four times in the first quotation, with his being the 'good guy'. This marked the beginning of a much more positive series of meetings which were replete with upbeat terminology with the doctor referring to how '. . . we can do something . . .' and '. . . get rid of it or repair it'. Words such as 'simple', 'possibilities' and 'successful' also offered hope, thereby encouraging Bob to be more optimistic. The words 'you have a choice' may have been pivotal in realigning Bob's interpretation of his prognosis away from the more pessimistic aspects and onto a positive outlook. He suddenly began to believe that there might be hope of his survival. He felt he was in control. It is significant, though, that Bob only paid lip service to the fact that this new treatment would be part of a trial. As our conversation progressed I realised that this trial was randomly controlled and I wondered to what extent Bob's agreement to participate was based on his full and informed consent.

Close scrutiny reveals that the events detailed above actually occurred during two separate meetings. Bob, probably unconsciously, blurred the events, so that they appear to have taken place during the one meeting. What was striking was his precise recall of how the events occurred and the words spoken by both doctors. For example, his remembrance was of a vague diagnosis of 'cancer' during the first meeting, which contrasted, with the more precise description of 'cancer in the coccyx' during the second.

Such was the extent of his trauma that he told me he took some time to assimilate the shock of what he had learned. He continued with his story, explaining that he:

. . . was very low in the beginning and then when I had the two treatments and all the doctors told me about this and that and about what they could do for me, because it is a very serious thing I have got, and I just couldn't get over the effects of it. And it took me about two weeks from when I got the news in the beginning. I couldn't stop shaking, my nerves, I just took to my chair. In the end my wife said, she was going to get the kids, which I got four kids, very good, very loving, and they all came down and we had a good old fashioned chat, we were all having a little weep. Each one of us was crying, then I said . . . after a few minutes, I started to come alive again, because I got a good talking to from the family, they were all saying this and that, 'You could be knocked down by a bus, what you have is treatable.'

The trauma of learning his diagnosis caused Bob's physical and almost complete psychological collapse. Bereft of hope, all he could do was sit in his chair for two weeks, terrified of what he believed was inevitable: his impending death. His wife also feared for the worst but she, realising how he valued family life, gathered their grown up children around them and they comforted him; presenting a united front, they were able to inject hope into his bleak mood. Sheila summed up the family's view, saying, 'As we said, he is not dying with it; he is living with it.' Bob confirmed this change, telling me that, 'After about two weeks, I got up off my butt and I said, "Right, I am going to start living."'

Ben

Ben and Eilish's joint devotion was obvious, the two worked in alliance, at times even finishing each other's sentences. Ben's diagnosis threatened him, not just as an individual but also his part as active contributor to their partnership. As a result of a series of calamitous human errors, he, who had previously been told that he did not have cancerous cells, was given a final biopsy. He told me his consultant: '. . . came in and said, "You have got cancer of the bladder". Well that is like a sledgehammer hits you.'

I asked if Eilish had been present and Ben replied:

Yes, I looked at Eilish and I didn't know what to do because you are numb, absolutely numb, it's just like a sledge hammer hitting you on the forehead and we went and had a cup of tea in the hospital and it was a very quiet period. I didn't know what to say. We was lost for words, you know. It is like a death sentence; although it is only one word, it is like a sentence. So we had a cup of tea, then we spoke to him [the consultant] for about an hour and we said, 'What's the procedure?' and he said, 'Oh, you'll have radiotherapy twenty times in four weeks, five times for four weeks and that will clear it up, great.' But then I saw Doctor R. I went in to be marked up and she [the consultant radiologist] said, 'No! It has to be surgery.' And she showed me the book where it said where there is cancer in the diverticular . . . it has to be surgery. I agreed to surgery . . .

Ben used a metaphor of physical violence '. . . sledgehammer hitting you . . .' to convey how shocked he and his wife were when they learned his diagnosis. He emphasised the extent of the trauma by describing how they felt 'lost for words', a point which they continued to stress during the interview, telling me eight times, for example, 'we never spoke' and 'I was absolutely dumbfounded.' Herman cites loss of linguistic ability as a measure of trauma. In her description of how individuals react to trauma, she quotes the words of a rape survivor, 'I couldn't scream. I couldn't move. I was paralysed . . . like a rag doll' (42: 1992).

It is interesting to observe how Ben's first response to hearing his diagnosis was to look at his wife, presumably trying to read her reaction, also, perhaps seeking support. His next comment is vital to understanding how individuals respond when in situations of trauma. He says that he 'didn't know what to do'. This inability to react when in shock has been discussed by Herman (1992) who posits that traumatic stress falls into three categories: 'hyper-arousal', 'intrusion' and 'constriction'. Ben's narrative conformed almost exactly to her description of constriction. Herman observes:

Events continue to register in awareness but it is as though these events have been disconnected from their ordinary meanings. Perceptions may be numbed or distorted, with partial anaesthesia or the loss of particular sensations. (Herman, 1992: 42–3)

Eilish wanted to elucidate. Referring back to the beginning of that same appointment she described the events from her perspective, telling me:

We had a 2 o'clock appointment and we saw him [Ben's consultant] at 4. They could have said, 'You are going to be at the end of the clinic, go home for a while.' He sat there behind his desk with his [nursing] Sister. When she came in I knew there was bad news to hear. He said 'Mr. and Mrs. B, I don't know how to put this, you have the worst cancer you can have, in the bladder, it is invasive, and it is angry. What we are going to do is, I am on leave for the whole of August, in that time you will be having twenty treatments. I will see you when I come back.' I could have strangled him because we would not have been at that stage if only he had done his job properly at the beginning. If me as a layman knew, surely a qualified person should have known more. But I was so shocked, I was stuck for words, well, we both were. We never said a word; we came out of there like two mummies. We went up to the restaurant, they had not even offered us a cup of tea and I wanted to hug Ben, and I couldn't because I didn't want him to . . .

Ben interrupted Eilish explaining: 'Because we would both have broken down at that stage . . .'

Eilish's ability to pre-empt the diagnosis was based on two clues. First, the unexplained postponement of their appointment and second the appearance of a nurse in the consultant's office. Although I would speculate that the consultant rescheduled the appointment to afford more time for breaking the news, perhaps he did not enjoy the prospect of informing them and so simply put it off until later.

Just as both Louise and Bob's accounts specified the precise words spoken by the doctors, so too did Eilish's. Her version was more detailed and she also overlaid the facts by relating her feelings of rage and shock. She appeared furious, resentful that her untutored knowledge had proved more accurate than the consultant's specialist learning.

What dominated were her dual concerns of sheltering Ben from the reality of the recent trauma and her need to maintain the correct mode of social behaviour in a very public situation.

Eilish resumed, telling me how their predicament became exacerbated by the political relationship between the surgical and oncology teams, which resulted in a breakdown in communication. She said:

He [the consultant] had made this appointment the next week for us to see the oncologist, and be marked up . . . [the place for radiation] and she [the radiologist] said, 'Marked up, who does he think he is, I don't tell him how to do surgery, how dare he tell you to come to me? And for a month well.' Oh, this is awful, after hearing that; we don't want to hear this. She said to Ben, 'I don't know what to say really, you have eighteen months at the most, it's a very angry and aggressive tumour, the worst I have seen, it is invasive and it is everywhere by now. It has gone through the bladder by now . . .'

Ben interrupted, commenting: 'To her it's just matter of fact, like saying – "A cup of tea?"'

Although Ben drew upon basic cultural niceties, which include offering tea, comparing it to the thoughtless way in which the diagnosis was delivered, it is interesting to remember that the couple had earlier commented on how, after being delivered such dreadful news the medical team had '. . . not even offered us a cup of tea . . .'

Discussion

A diagnosis of cancer is rarely made on the strength of a single test. The individual concerned is often subject to a battery of examinations and tests that, when combined, present data that eventually result in an informed judgement. Costain Schou and Hewison suggest something of the hazardous course this process presents to individuals when they describe how the '... diagnostic course often resembles an obstacle course rather more than it does a neat, straight line' (1999: 50).

The attitudes prevailing within the medical culture are affected by wider social change. Thus, the decision of whether to give the patient a terminal diagnosis, or not, is contingent on temporal custom. Not so long ago, the clinical tendency was to withhold information of this sort; the argument being that it may have a detrimental effect on the patient's frame of mind (Christakis, 1999). Increasingly, however, the inclination is to foster a spirit of openness, with the patient being party to all facets of their prognosis (Seale, 1998).

The response to learning their cancer diagnosis was as varied as the individuals themselves, ranging from Bob's complete physical and psychological collapse to Louise's dramatic grabbing of the medical reports. They were similar, however, in that, in relating the events, all respondents were able to detail precisely the words used by their consultants.

It is also interesting to observe that, at this difficult time, the thoughts of the majority turned to how their illness would impact on their family and friends. Gerry feared especially for his daughter and his unborn child; Louise, not surprisingly, dwelt on how her infant daughter and son would cope with such a loss. Her narrative is redolent with loss and sadness to the extent that it might indicate some primitive form of anticipatory grieving. The nursing sister who proffered 'examples of people who survived' offered her hope. Gerry, too, drew solace from his consultant's casual remark that he would '... be getting Christmas cards from you for many years'. Most hopeful was Bob's oncologist who said, 'You have a choice.'

At this time of crisis, they were expected to cope with the shock of their diagnosis and be capable of retaining information about the nature of their cancer and the technical information on how they would be treated.

During my fieldwork, I frequently experienced more laughter than tears. This was certainly the case, when one, older, respondent laughingly told me how she and her husband had learned her diagnosis. Fearing the result of her medical tests, she told me how important it was that she knew the truth:

... right from the word go. Two and a half years ago ... [they]sent me into another room with the pretence that I was going to be examined. Because my husband is hard of hearing you have to shout at him so I could hear through the wall what they were saying to him, although I suspected what they were going to tell me ...

Although a cancer diagnosis is specific to a particular individual, entire clusters of people become affected by it.

We will meet Clive in more depth later in the book, however his experience of diagnosis is quite pertinent to this discussion. Clive, who was 36 years old, learned his initial cancer diagnosis when already hospitalised and alone; he did not need to fear how his supporters would react.

[I was] . . . told I had a tumour as part of the normal ward round and all I was offered was aspirin. Then they moved on to the next round. No counselling, no asking about my family, I was devastated. I was shattered because all along the hospital in town had told me there was no cancer . . . I was completely devastated and very emotional not ever having any experience of cancer in the family. People did not even say the word, it was always . . . 'The Big C . . .' I sat in bed and waited till my family came . . .

Having trusted medical science, he appeared to feel betrayed and rejected by the fashion in which his diagnosis was broken. Perhaps, just as he describes the disease as taboo, excluded from conversation, he feared that he, too, would suffer the same outcome. This quotation provides evidence of how mainstream perceptions of, and attitudes to, cancer extending to the employment of euphemisms can negatively impact and significantly influence how individuals deal with their diagnosis.

As we have already learned, Louise had her problems with her own diagnosis. I was, also, tragically, able to learn of how she responded to the diagnosis of her four-year-old daughter Laura's leukaemia. Louise explained:

When she went to school, I could just see that that child does not fit in here, there is something wrong and I thought she was unhappy but I could see a . . . hard to handle, I thought she was stressed . . . behaviour that I would have punished Richard [Laura's brother] for but, somehow, it was causing me deep, deep concern about the child, but I thought . . . I am amazed . . . I thought she could handle school ok, so I started, keeping her off a day a week, not making her stay for dinner at school . . . She might have been at the doctor if I had not been one; she just got very pale . . .

Although clearly aware that her daughter was not behaving normally, Louise sought psychological rather than physiological explanations. When she had found her own symptom, a lump in her breast, she had tried to rationalise it away, dismissing it as a side effect of her breastfeeding. In much the same way, she also delayed bringing Laura to see her doctor. When she did eventually take her to see her ex-associate, she told me that she '. . . knew before I went to see him what the most likely diagnosis was . . .' However, she continued to hope that the blood samples taken in his surgery would prove normal. She said:

He did not ring the next day, I was not too impressed . . . I thought, we have got away with this . . . so we got a bottle of iron, cooked lentils, no sweets till the plates were cleared and thought . . . it is only a matter of building her up . . . it was easier to believe . . . on Monday he rang with her blood results which 98 per cent confirmed that she had leukaemia. Then it was confirmed within an hour. I . . . in a way. . . . cannot afford to go back . . . I just went crazily hysterical when he rang. I was here with Derek . . . [her disabled husband] I thought it was appalling, the surgery is 3 minutes away, I thought he could have come . . . especially to a colleague . . . To phone me, he may have just said the words, I just lost my reason, I yelled, screamed, howled, knelt on the floor, hammered the floor . . . I thought I had every mother's nightmare which is your own life being in peril . . .

Again, it was a temporal factor, that of not making contact within the anticipated time, which caused Louise's fears. Nevertheless, because her worry was so real, she behaved as though she believed that all would turn out for the best. It is not surprising that she did not want to remember the events that were to follow. At this most excruciating of times, she not only had no social support but she was alone with her severely disabled husband. Learning that her youngest child also had a potentially fatal illness left Louise bereft of hope and plunged her into the depth of despair.

It is interesting to compare how Louise dealt with her own diagnosis and that of her daughter. The management of her daughter's diagnosis differs significantly from her own in three ways. First, she learned her own diagnosis during a face-to-face consultation with her specialist; she discovered Laura's over the telephone. Second, she responded to Laura's diagnosis with immediate anger, which she directed onto her doctor. When she learned her own diagnosis, she fell into complete despair. Finally, the shock of hearing her daughter had leukaemia propelled her to such a state of mental desperation that she became verbally incoherent. She told me that she 'yelled, screamed, howled'. Of the time when she herself was diagnosed she made no comment as to what she said immediately. When her doctor had asked why she was crying, she said 'My children are very young.' It seems, therefore, that at her own diagnosis she was able to express herself lucidly or, at least, on a level where she could maintain communication but her daughter's plight appeared to strike her at a more primitive level.

There is, though, one striking similarity between the two accounts. During both she describes how she gravitated into dramatic physical action. On hearing Laura's diagnosis she 'knelt on the floor, hammered the floor'; on hearing her own she 'grabbed the chart'. In spite of this moment of action in response to her own diagnosis, that account is redolent with a real sense of desolation, evoking something of the despondency into which she had been plunged. In her account of Laura's diagnosis, although conveying much of her depression, she intimates that this was not experienced merely as a passive period of melancholy. It was, instead, a time in which her excited emotions had become so frenzied that they had leaked through her psyche, creating and heightening her physical disquiet.

Chapter summary

Analysis of the interviews, in which the respondents described how they initially detected their presenting symptoms and then learned their diagnosis, suggests several significant issues. Those who located dramatic symptoms, such as lumps, had to first recognise them as atypical and then realise their significance. They were faced with the dilemma of how to respond. If they first became aware of disconcerting, rather than dramatic symptoms, the tendency was to take no immediate action and hope the problem would settle. The trend, though, common to both groups, was to report initially and confer with supporters as to whether or not the symptoms should be taken to a doctor. At this stage, the contribution made by supporters was crucial. They acted as witnesses in observing and confirming the symptoms and their validation of abnormality often served to endorse concern and motivate the respondents into seeking medical advice.

However, social pressures, for example those rising from the respondents' family situation, were sometimes responsible for persuading some not to report early indicators of a physical change. For example, Louise cited relationship problems with her mother as reason for not keeping medical appointments.

In the intervening time between detecting initial symptoms and reporting to their GP, respondents had a heightened awareness of their symptoms. When this was presented, the GPs did not always make an accurate initial diagnosis. There was, therefore, sometimes a delay in referring respondents for expert treatment.

Referral for specialist advice, when it occurred, acted as a catalyst to trigger several changes in the respondents and their supporters. Psychologically, the imminent appointment was viewed with considerable anxiety; on a practical level, it was met with a drive to locate information on potential causes of the symptoms and socially it initiated a process of vetting, canvassing and recruiting prospective supporters.

As respondents endured their exploratory tests and investigations, anxiety escalated. Their diagnoses were learned in diverse ways; for example, Clive was informed during the course of a routine ward round; Gerry was told by telephone. The majority were informed in the course of private appointments with their consultants. In the moments immediately before hearing their diagnosis, they would appear to have subconsciously engaged primitive monitoring strategies to anticipate its nature.

It is interesting to observe the stark contrast between the reports in which the respondents described reaction to hearing their diagnosis, accounts made rich with heightened emotions, and their accounts of how they detected their initial symptoms, when they simply presented the unembellished facts of the occasion.

The first response to the diagnosis was, typically, one of stunned shock, which left respondents traumatised and incoherent. The reports reveal emotions and sensations that might also be applied to people confronting a scene of carnage. This was a moment fraught with psychological pain and complete disbelief.

Individuals in the West are socialised to accept, anticipate and allow their lives to develop in a specific order, through to death in old age; an assumption a cancer diagnosis annuls. The shock is not just because the word is perceived by many to be a metaphor for death (Sontag, 1978; Gyllenskold, 1982) but also may spring from our socialisation, which fuels unconscious expectations of a life of at least the biblical 'three score years and ten'. On diagnosis, the respondents were confronted with the fact that they were mortal.

The disclosure of a terminal diagnosis, no matter how well prepared and anticipated, violently confronts individuals with the reality of their humanity and reveals the brutal certainty of mortality. Weisman (1980) succinctly describes this time of diagnosis as a time of 'existential plight', a period when the individual faces impending death. I argue that this shock stems, in part, from living in a society which, to whatever extent, denies death (Becker, 1973; Ariès, 1981). We spend our present not just editing and reliving our past but also preparing for the future and we project our hopes into that future (Platt, 1966; Bourdieu, 1990). We also take the existence of a future as an established fact (Laurer, 1981). Many innocently place their faith in what is, after all, an illusory zone and behave as though the future was guaranteed, considering it a safe haven in which to project, as yet unrealised, hopes and dreams (Platt, 1966; Bourdieu, 1990). This comfort zone was threatened by the respondents' cancer diagnosis (Del Vecchio et al., 1994; Nekolaichuk and Bruera, 1998; Nowotny, 1994; Radley, 1999). None said they had ever given serious thought to the idea that they might, one day, have cancer, never mind die. When they learned their diagnosis, all became traumatised, experiencing a sense of overwhelming and profound shock. The precise responses varied, ranging from Bob's complete physical collapse through to Louise's dramatic actions, which led almost immediately to her slipping into the classic heroic role.

Whilst the respondents were experiencing the development of their cancers, events to others in their social network also continued to exercise an effect on them. Their encounter with illness fitted into lives that were already established and their continued involvement with others kept them engaged and helped them cope. Such events, however, did not always have a positive effect. Managing one major life crisis is difficult but when the timing coincides with another landmark in life, such as the birth of a child, this forces events to be re-examined and, sometimes, priority is allocated quite simply on a temporal basis.

Coming to terms with their cancer meant that the respondents had to make major adjustments in their social and practical spheres. How these changes were experienced was, to a great extent, influenced by the extent and quality of support provided by others within their social groups. Whilst they were wrestling with the realities of the illness, normal life, which had to be dealt with, continued.

3   Stage Two – Exploration

Tests and treatment

This chapter examines the events that occurred in the respondents' lives between learning their cancer diagnosis and becoming established in their treatment. This was a time marked initially with disbelief, uncertainty and fear. Accepting the diagnosis of cancer was not the respondent's only problem. Coming to terms with it was exacerbated by having to accommodate to a new routine filled with visits to surgeons, oncologists and radiographers, etc.

Learning they had cancer triggered a host of changes in their lives. Until now, their perceptions of the illness were second-hand, based on the accounts of others with the disease or by learning about it from the media. Elsewhere, I have described how:

> . . . the initial weighing and prediction of how the disease will affect their lives is based on the myriad of information previously assimilated, however unconsciously, from a host of sources, not only from direct contact with others who have cancer but also from indirect sources which include the theatre (Duclow, 1981), literature (Guthke, 1999), art (Bertman, 1991; Guthke, 1999) and music (Neilson Chapman, 1997). (Armstrong-Coster, 2001)

Their diagnosis resulted in significant changes being made in how they continued their lives as autonomous individuals. Even at this early stage in the dying journey, social relationships, especially those that were intimate, were affected by the diagnosis and, as a result, their quality began to change (Young *et al.*, 1999). The aftershocks of their cataclysmic diagnosis extended to disrupt the balance of power that had previously underpinned their day-to-day life. Shifts occurred, necessitating re-evaluation and re-distribution of roles and tasks, which the respondents had previously believed to be fixed. Illness entailed, from a practical perspective, learning how to adapt and conform to the world of the medical, as well as preparing for the more tangible changes, such as hair loss, that might reasonably be expected as a side effect of their treatments.

For most, the majority of the dying journey occurs at home in the community. For others a significant part is experienced within a medicalised zone, such as hospital or hospice (Field, 1996). Wherever the bulk of the journey was experienced, their diagnosis served as a harbinger, which signalled the onset of prolonged periods of medical treatment as outpatients or inpatients in hospitals and in GPs' surgeries. The majority had previously encountered hospitals as places to visit others or as areas in which to receive treatment as day patients. Most modern hospitals are situated within buildings that have been professionally designed for handling the sick and injured efficiently and economically. Individuals are treated as units to be moved from zone to zone with the minimum of disruption and the maximum of speed. However, the bureaucratic observance of this professional efficiency sometimes resulted in respondents feeling as though they were being treated as interchangeable components rather than individuals and tended to depersonalise what was, for them, a critical life experience.

The space within the boundaries that demarcate the hospital buildings is anomalous (Lofland, 1978; Field, 1996), being perceived to be public, whilst simultaneously being the physical site of extremely intimate and private exchanges. Not only are the buildings usually alien in their architecture and population but also their culture operates on a regimented clock time, in the form of strict adherence to scheduling (Frankenberg, 1988). This institutional space enforces a rigidity of time that runs counter to the autonomy that the respondents had previously exercised.

Modern life has medicalised dying (Illich, 1976), drawing it into expert systems. Respondents made their initial visits to the hospital either to have consultations with specialists or for treatment. Some of the most critical exchanges they ever experienced, for example learning their cancer diagnosis, sometimes in a piecemeal fashion, took place with experts; people who were strangers to them and were often removed socially from them by dint of specialised knowledge. The modern hospital has the effect of alternately bombarding patients with public interaction while at the same time privatising the medical experience.

Being subsumed into the realm of the medical proved something of a mixed blessing. Whilst diverting attention from disturbing images of a lost future, integration into the new 'illness calendar' (Costain Schou and Hewison, 1999) of treatment seemed also to establish a new form of predictability within psyches, which had recently been confronted with their own mortality. Zerubavel (1981) cites temporal regularity of schedules, appointments and treatment as beneficial in that, by providing a definite structure to the patient's day, it minimises elements of uncertainty, which may prove comforting to those experiencing crisis. Once within the hospital system, as inpatients or outpatients, respondents were expected to meet a personal timetable of appointments with various medical personnel as well as conform, if they were inpatients, to the collective schedules that demarcated times for meals, medication, visiting times and resting hours. Del Vecchio *et al.*, quote a radiographer who commented:

There is a lot of housework, the boring part of getting people into radiation. All those little appointments and time schedules and things. All of that occupies the trivial time when you circle around each other perhaps. (1994: 857)

Medical treatment also became a time of social interaction (Costain Schou and Hewison, 1999). Asked how many people he might expect to meet during a day at the clinic, Ben told me:

On an appointment day . . . Mr. X the neurologist, then maybe the girls in Radiology and Dr. Y, he is the pain control expert. Then Ellen, who is the Macmillan Nurse, then all the other staff at the Hospital then usually Celia, who is the District Nurse, Dr. Z, the GP, and Jane the pharmacist who delivers the 600 methadone tablets to our home.

Ben referred to the more senior members of his inter-disciplinary team, (all male), by their formal title of Mister or Doctor. Those holding lesser status '. . . the girls in Radiology' and the nursing staff, he called by their Christian names. These individuals were all, presumably, strangers when he first encountered them; however, his repeated communication with them has engendered a social relationship that established a basic rhythm to the interactions. Such individuals appreciated consistency in treatment; it helped in transforming their image of a bureaucratic hospital into a centre populated by individuals they know. Another respondent, Rose, who we will meet later, and who was well established on her treatment, illustrated something of this when she told me:

I prefer to go into G ward rather than anywhere else, although I did go into a different ward to start with. I prefer G because that is the ward I have always gone into and I know all the nurses, I know most of the doctors and because you know the faces and you have been there a lot before, you kind of trust them more.

Some, however, found the sheer number of people they encountered, even when only on an outpatients visit, intimidating (Small and Rhodes, 2000). The sudden pitch into a veritable sea of strangers was most noticeable for those who spent blocks of time there. Young and Cullen observe that:

. . . hospital wards, . . . are sometimes like Clapham Junction in the rush hour, with doctors in white coats and solemn faces moving around continuously between their patients, nurses dashing from one bed to another, cleaners with mops, porters pushing unconscious people on trolleys and trying not to get the drips snarled up. This is the setting in which life-and-death communication has to insert itself into the bustle. (1996: 147)

Exley supports Young and Cullen and quotes from an outpatient whom she interviewed and who said:

You meet so many different people and you have so many different names to remember, it just sends your mind blank. We've got enough bleeding people involved with doctors and things; . . . once they start, they don't stop. They'll be camping out on the bleeding front lawn! (1998: 106)

The domain of the medical, into which the respondents had been involuntarily press-ganged, was for most very unlike their usual territories. They suddenly found themselves, like new recruits at sea, subjected to a foreign, intimidating world that demanded compliance to its exacting schedules. This shift sometimes proved disconcerting as it interrupted lives that were established on more autonomous and personal routines.

Spradley and Phillips (1972) questioned Peace Corps volunteers recently returned from developing regions about the adjustment necessary to live abroad. Although language was rated as requiring most adaptation, coping with the change in the general pace of life was cited second. Such a change, even when occurring in good health, can be experienced as both traumatic and psychologically exhausting (Laurer, 1981). Patients are expected to learn to accept, assimilate and, sometimes, live within a medical setting, the culture of which is not only physically but also, temporally disquieting. This drastic change occurred at a time when the respondents were still coping with the heightened psychological trauma of their diagnosis.

The experience of time during this period, when gradual, psychological filtering allows the reality of the diagnosis to permeate and, perhaps, become accepted, is reported as being quite different from the jarring, slowing down of time experienced during the diagnosis.

Advances in technology mean that consultants are frequently able to diagnose terminal illness in advance of the onset of many of the more obvious symptoms. The patient's defence mechanisms not only have to cope with the existential resistance to death but also bolster the denial that anything could be wrong in an a-symptomatic body. A cancer diagnosis comes primed and armed with the capability of disintegrating the practical, emotional and social worlds of the patient.

When the future threatens to be drastically foreclosed, then the present, too, is seriously disrupted. Time, which once, however unconsciously, served as the dominant framework of lives loses the meaning it held before and individuals become insecure. The respondents told me they felt they had nothing to look forward to, no planning for the future, no hope. They experienced this uncertain, limited time as emptiness and many lived in despair.

The tests

Louise

Having been diagnosed with breast cancer, Louise was forced to counter her protective tendencies and break the news to her family. This enabled her to draw on their support in dealing with the practical problems that arose from her consequent exploratory surgery. Explaining that this surgery was necessary, as it would determine the spread of her cancer, she told me how disturbing she found the evening before her operation:

I went in to hospital and I was hysterical the night before surgery, I had to get somebody, I could not breathe, I thought my head would lift off with anxiety and worry. The staff at the hospital could not have been better; the night sister was there the whole night. I could not regain my composure, I was disintegrating. I remember days after that, I had a mixture of being beside myself with anxiety, ready to scream. I didn't. Just a farcical sense of saying and doing things to make people laugh. Entertaining them. My family were devastated and I knew they were all crying. And then I came home very quickly without knowing if there was lymph node infection. The after effects took over and I went back in [to hospital] to be told six lymph nodes were involved. He [her surgeon] would see that as 'just chemo' [beyond surgical intervention] which left a drastically reduced survival rate. My sister went with me that day, it was my lowest point, the fuss had died down around me and I didn't want to start ringing around to say, 'It's not just bad, it's very bad.' My sister saw it in terms of 'Oh she needs chemo.' That was not the issue, chemo ends, but I am looking at a very poor chance of surviving this illness. I felt lonely; my doctor friend was the only person who appreciated the significance of that. That I had to carry for everyone.

Louise's narrative introduces a sense of the terrifying psychological ordeal that respondents experienced during their exploratory tests. Snatched from the safety of her family home, she found herself alone confronting her impending ordeal. Isolated in hospital, she took complete fright. However, although it was not where she wished to be, being in hospital arguably allowed her the freedom to vent the panic she would have had to repress at home. The nursing team, individuals unknown to Louise, 'outsiders', were safe repositories of the powerful emotions too dangerous to air within the family. Her pain was on two levels. She felt physically isolated from those who cared for her and a sense of responsibility for them, knowing that they would be affected by her illness and possible death. She knew she would have to minimise the extent of her predicament, effectively performing emotional work (Hochschild, 1983) whilst she, herself, was in desperate need of nurturing.

Her graphic mode of speech conveyed something of the desperate inner turmoil she experienced that difficult night. She described how she was 'hysterical' and 'had to get somebody', feeling as though she 'could not breathe'. This reference is hauntingly reminiscent of a person fighting for their last breath. Tellingly, she sums up, saying that she felt she was 'disintegrating'. Her psychic self was fragmenting and she felt, quite literally, in danger of falling apart. Having endured such a terrifying ordeal, it is not surprising it took days for her to recover; days in which she not only had constantly to repress the terror in which she now lived but also protect her family from the reality of her situation. It seemed she managed to obscure her true emotions from the 'insiders' in her group by mounting a series of manic defences, 'doing things to make people laugh; entertaining them'. In adopting the behaviour of the tragic clown, who hides his tears behind a painted mask, Louise was heroically performing emotional work, endeavouring to protect others when she was, herself, most in need.

As a doctor, Louise would have been fully aware of the significance of her test results, so it must have been difficult for her to endure the waiting. It is not surprising that she drew upon her social circle and went, this time escorted by her sister, to learn her prognosis. Her reaction, on hearing the findings, seemed somehow out of keeping with the turbulence and agitation with which she met her previous crisis, when she 'grabbed the charts'. Unlike her sister, who was not conversant with the facts of cancer, she had instantly understood the implications of what she was told. When she said 'I felt lonely', Louise was expressing the essence of the existential crisis. Deeply embedded within her extended family network, she could draw on social support almost at will but this loneliness she felt was a loneliness of the soul; no one could share it. It was as though she had been totally abandoned; the facts left her devoid of energy, vigour and drive. She had become ominously becalmed and she left the consultation in a state of complete stupefaction.

In true heroic spirit, Louise's immediate thoughts were of others and how she might protect them from the horror of her prognosis and impending death. She felt compelled to shield them by taking on their pain.

She told me how she managed the time that followed:

. . . life has to go on. Days at home with the children on my own, I had very dark thoughts then, it did occur to me to kill them all. If I could just kill the children and kill Derek [her husband] this problem is over, it doesn't matter and

I used to make myself laugh because . . . if Derek would come in and I would say, 'Would you like to go out for a drink?' and the shock of that would kill him cold for a start! [Derek did not drink] That would be him looked after and then I would inject up these other two . . . [I presume she means inject a poison into her children] and then I actually began to imagine the injecting up, that would have me in floods of tears. I just couldn't put a needle into their arms even, but it did strike me as a very attractive solution to the thing. I remember then, one day, I knew one of the nurses in hospital quite well, I was saying that to her, and how I ever got to the lengths of saying that to her I don't know, but she said, 'Oh you will feel like that but you will eventually realise that they have their own right to life.' And I thought . . . that is a good way of treating it; it was the first time their right to anything dawned on me . . . Derek has a right to life as well. Now I would go back to that when things are bleak. I just think well, 'I will just kill the wee things' and then I will think, 'No, I couldn't do that . . . .' but now that has got to the stage that they are much older and I could never do that, but when I feel sorry for myself . . . It will be sad, people will never understand it, these are the lengths a mother's love drives her to, but the blatant wrongness of that . . . I was thinking, 'Oh God it would be a great idea for all three of them . . .' and I would do it, plan it but that . . . but I just totally submerge into . . . what effect will this have on the wee ones, to the exclusion of anything else about illness. The other features of illness just don't cross my mind . . . too busy worrying about the children . . . very young children.

In spite of her almost impossible situation, Louise mustered all her defence mechanisms to help herself and her family to survive. She observed their need for routine and drew upon her sense of humour as a means of normalising the horror of her life. Her ability to rationalise pulled her back from the brink of total despair. As a Roman Catholic doctor, Louise had previously worked out her philosophy on euthanasia and abortion. She told me how she fervently believed in the right to life and now, at this difficult time, was challenging herself to live up to her beliefs. Fully aware of the futility of her situation, her deep love for her children and her belief that they needed her persuaded her to go on living and not to kill them. Part of her continued battle to survive might also be attributed to her highly competitive nature. She told me that she had:

. . . read somewhere where someone got a life-threatening illness and deep down relished the fact of taking it on. I would somehow admit that I, in some way, fall into that. I would hate if it went too far but there is a part of [me that thinks] 'Right, is that what you think? See you in a year!' It is a very exciting challenge; your life is on the line. It is not, 'Can you win a million pounds?', it is, 'Can I live and you think I can't? I am glad you told me that!' I loved doing exams, I loved going in there and putting it all down. I loved the challenges of being a doctor and, in a way, I feel the illness is just another of them.

She was, however, aware that she would not live for long. During one of our later interviews she said:

I know to imagine the future and you not being here is very strange. I thought the wee fire will be burning and the house will be here and I will not be in it. If plans occur you think . . . I will not ever do that.

Gerry

Gerry and his wife Claire, who was due to give birth on the day following the diagnosis, continued their story, relating the events immediately following the consultant's late night phone call. Gerry said:

After we rang Claire's sister, we rang one of my sisters, Lyn, who is a cardiac nurse and told her and she was shocked, again disbelief but being in the medical profession, she probably had a fair idea. She did think I was joking originally, everyone thought I was joking, because I do tend to joke a lot . . . but, in hindsight maybe, I should not have told her or others that night because they did not get much sleep and we didn't either. I also rang a colleague out of work and he was really devastated; in fact, most people are when they hear it. In fact, you like telling people because you like giving them this bit of scoop, you have a scoop here too. 'Wait till you hear this, I've got cancer, what about that?' It is almost like you have power to hit people with, you can throw it at them and you do. You don't mean it that way; you feel a real sense of . . . There are nerves in your body for another reason. You have this energy in you all of a sudden because you have been smacked in the face and this is you reverberating if you like. It is like an elastic band being stretched and you are twanging yourself forward or you have been hit off the ropes and you are bouncing back and that is the way it came across. Somebody told me and I had to go and put part of myself on them.

Learning you have cancer is not an everyday event; it is also potentially socially stigmatising to the individual involved. The diagnosis served to suggest that, at best, Gerry would experience a probable decline in his levels of physical performance; at worst it, effectively, acted as a herald of his death (Sontag, 1978). It served to disempower him.

In informing others, Gerry was, consciously or not, exercising some power in a situation where his control over his life was much reduced. Zerubavel observes that 'The degree of social distance is the most important factor in determining temporal boundaries' (1981: 144), which is borne out by the couple not hesitating to telephone their closest friends after eleven o'clock at night. Having consulted with his sister-in-law, Gerry chose to tell his sister, Lyn, presumably because, in her profession of nurse, she might have been able to contribute to his knowledge pool. Knowing that Gerry has a highly developed sense of humour and, not wanting to believe what she was being told, like Claire's sister, she initially tested the veracity of his information. Reflecting on that night, Gerry realised that, although they had benefited from those telephone calls, by unburdening themselves at such a late hour, they had potentially cost their supporters their sleep. He referred to his diagnosis as being a 'scoop' that, as an extraordinary 'What-a-Story!' event (Tuchman, 1973), has released the couple from observing normal social constrictions thereby empowering them to invade others' private time.

Knowledge of his situation appears to have been so overwhelming that it became impossible for Gerry to contain. He needed to 'throw it' at others. Describing how he broke the news, he drew on words that imply action, 'power', 'energy', 'reverberating', 'twanging' and 'bouncing'. Like a patellar reflex, Gerry seemed almost compelled to seek release from his shock. Although his diagnosis informed him that he would inevitably lose physical control, he used it to gain social power.

In our next interview, he expanded on how he had informed others, showing the dual role of finding an outlet for his emotions and exercising power. He said:

I decided to tell everyone I had cancer. I rang my boss because I wanted to shock him. He had called up to see me the day before to see my scar [resulting from the biopsy], to see how I was getting on. I thought I should tell him first. Later that day, I rang work, personnel department. I felt I had a lot of things to tidy up before I could start taking this forward. I felt it would be better for me, that when I met other people, if they knew beforehand then they wouldn't be embarrassed and therefore I would feel better about it. I wanted to tell people as early as possible. I wanted to go up and tell my mother and Lyn came with me. I went to see my own doctor to ask if she [thought my mother] could take the news, my mother has high blood pressure. I thought over what I would tell her and eventually told her that I had an infection. She stood there staring blank as if she could not make sense of it but when I think back on it, she knew it was not that but she was not sure what it was. I tried to tell her that it was possible it was something worse; eventually I just came out and told her. She was glad, she was shocked but she was glad. I don't think she was taking in the initial bit about the infection; she drew a blank on it. She has been great ever since, really strong, superb. Eventually we told everyone that day and then we went to hospital and booked Claire in to have the baby.

The knowledge of his diagnosis had acted like a pollutant and affected Gerry to the extent that he became frantic in his need to purge himself of it. He hesitated though, to tell his mother. Since his father's death two years before, he had assumed the dominant male role within his family. Fearing his elderly mother would react very badly to his news, he checked with her doctor and accepted the social support offered by his sister. He was acutely aware of the pain the information would cause. When Gerry described his mother as being 'glad', he did not mean that she was pleased, rather that she understood just how difficult telling her had been and felt proud that her son had chosen to entrust her with the truth.

Gerry found himself embroiled at the heart of two competing crises. He had to balance his priorities between the responsibilities that the birth of his child involved and to assimilate the psychological shock of his own trauma. He was further expected to comply with the daunting schedule of tests. He was being mechanically assimilated into the medical organism at a time when, as a new father, he most strongly felt a sense of his own destiny. The couple were also surprised and pleased to benefit from one of the unsought secondary gains which illness can grant: the ability to command the presence of others. Family members, who might have delayed visiting till the time of the christening, came to call and the maternity hospital gave them extra attention.

Practicalities caused by social niceties also entailed preparation. Gerry explained:

Before I was getting chemo I decided to get a wig. Not for my sake, but for Diana, my four-and-a-half-year-old daughter. I was worried about how she would react to me without hair. I didn't want to alarm her. All the articles advise you to get it before the chemo. As it turned out, for men, the wigs are awful. I have only worn it once when I still had hair underneath it. I think I was a lot better handling the hair loss than I thought I would have been.

Gerry had anticipated not only his daughter's reaction to this impending baldness but also his own and, not surprisingly, viewed it with some trepidation. Because of the birth, Claire had not gone with Gerry to the hospital for his tests but, now, a week later and because the imminent change in his appearance was important enough to warrant her advice, she resumed her usual role in his life by helping him choose a wig.

Established in his new sick role, Gerry became the subject of valued social support, which recognised and fed his desire for knowledge. He was assimilated into the cancer culture within his local community. He used this to his own advantage, learning from their experience and applying it to consolidate his own research. Being armed with more facts, he appreciated the importance of his early medical presentation but became curious about how he developed his cancer. When asked how he thought it originated, he cited environmental factors:

In my job, I travel a lot internationally, China, Mexico and other parts of the world that have a lot of chemical plants and produce various products. I went to one specific place in China where they produce an agro-chemical product. They are cited as one of the potential causes of lymphomas, funnily enough, but, since it has only been a few years since I have been there, it is highly unlikely that that was the reason that caused it. Because most of the western doctors would say that you need to be exposed to a causal agent like that seven years beforehand, because it has to affect the DNA structure of the cells. For example, there was stacks of lymphoma out of Hiroshima but the bomb was dropped there ten years before the lymphomas appeared. One of the plants I was in in China also produces one of these anti-cancer drugs I am taking. The top man of that facility was over here a few weeks ago and he heard I was not well and came to visit me. He could speak no English, but I had got on well with him when I was in China. Ironic that he produced drugs that might cure but could also have potentially caused this.

Gerry had been confounded by how his body managed to produce such a startling and ominously sly growth without his being aware of its development. Having a scientific bent he was curious for logical explanations, which would empirically validate how he contracted the illness.

The tests to establish the very specific nature of Gerry's lymphoma continued on what seemed to be an almost daily basis over a two-week period. Throughout the interviews I held, the very real physical presence of baby Angela served as a tangible reminder of how recently Gerry's cancer had been discovered. Those conversations were punctuated by Angela's demands for attention. When Gerry attended to her, he usually brought her downstairs, ostensibly for feeding or changing but really, I suspect, just so that he could enjoy her company.

I have noted previously how a cancer diagnosis is not usually the result of a single set of tests. Even following diagnosis, clinicians seek further information, refining their knowledge about, for example, the extent of the spread of the tumour, in the bid to identify the best treatment for a specific patient. Gerry found himself the subject of a gruelling battery of examinations:

The first one was a CT scan, which I was not concerned about. I knew that it was looking for evidence of other tumours or to see how the cancer had spread but for some reason I never got that worried about it. I went there, drank some horrible liquid, even I was nearly sick with it. I never really worried at the time . . . drank this stuff, had the scan, was reading magazines and was concerned about it but that was not that bad. Got the results on the spot and they were good, so the time did not allow me to ponder over it too much . . . the 'what ifs'. In to see the oncologist who told me everything was clear. Gave me a physical check up. Next was the bone marrow. That I was quite worried about because I had heard it was quite painful. It was very dreadful. I had bite marks on my fingers for a while after. You could see the needle mark – like a wasp sting on my hip, it had to be frozen. The guy stuck in the needle to suck up bone marrow and scrape out bits of bone. There was a harsh jolting pain in my femur. It was not nice; I would not like to have too many of them! What really worried me when I was reading the literature was that the bone marrow would be the last place they would find High

Grade. If it is there you are in stage 4 direct from stage 1, then it is much more difficult.

Those next few days were very difficult for me; I don't think Claire really understood what I was going through. They were the worst few days you can imagine because you don't know how good or bad it is going to be. The first part of the test they can tell you in 24 hours, the second part takes over a week to do. I was waiting to hear the results. I called him [his doctor] and he told me he had not got the results. I called the next day and thought he was fobbing me off. I found out on the Thursday. Went for the soft palate [test]. There was a possibility that I would need a severe operation on the back of my throat but when I got there I only needed the simple one. Mirrors and scraping. I did not feel a thing. It was all clear. Finally, got the information from the bone marrow test. It was an all or nothing for a 'yes' but not for a 'no'. So really, without knowing I had cancer on the 16th till the 30th, I got the best news I could ever have. I knew what the situation was at that stage. Two weeks. High-grade lymphoma, which had outgrown lymph nodes and into the nerves. They had to cut into my jaw. A bit more than a stage 1 but not as much as a stage 2. It was in its early stages though a heck of a size of a tumour, 4cm in diameter. Golf ball size.

Gerry innocently found himself in a regime of punishing tests, for which even his scientific background had not prepared him. Although he was familiar with the concept of a CT scan, like the majority of other respondents, he was not au fait with the rigours that it involved. Experiences which are entered into with no expectations are often easier to handle than those for which we are prepared (Kfir and Slevin, 1991) and this might go some way to explain Gerry's attitude to the bone marrow test which he endured. In spite of his attempts to hide his anxiety, his reactions are revealed in the vocabulary he used. Words such as 'horrible', 'painful' and 'very dreadful' seem apt in the context of tests which involved medical implements which 'scrape' and 'suck' and his having to imbibe 'horrible liquid'.

Why did he continue to subject himself to this cruel routine? Gerry trusted medical science. It had provided a diagnosis of the lump in his neck, which he thought appropriate, and it appeared able to refine its classification further and to propose remedies. Gerry, who as a result of his wife's recent delivery attended these tests unaccompanied, was aware of the possible consequences his cancer might exercise on his young family and felt obliged to pursue what he believed was his best option for survival: scientific medicine.

Gerry faced other challenges encountered because of his unexpected diagnosis:

Before I had the chemo, not long after the bone marrow test, my oncologist asked me to consider going to the sperm bank, because chemo will make you sterile. There is a possibility that it could be reversed but that is what normally happens.

I went to the fertility clinic that is located in maternity. As I went into the waiting room and it was packed and you stick out like a sore thumb because you are there alone. We decided we would do it because at the end of the day, it is an insurance policy. I had to have three visits. Apparently I am quite virile, which is a nice thing to hear. My chemo was stalled a bit till I got that sorted out because you have to do this before chemo. If you do not have the right [sperm] counts you need more visits.

Gerry used the various stages in the development of his continuing assessment to function as temporal benchmarks. He was given the news immediately after the birth of his second daughter and he and Claire had anticipated having, at least, two other children, one of whom, he hoped, would be a boy so he was alarmed when informed his treatment might render him sterile. The practicalities of attending the fertility clinic three times for treatment were also discomforting: Claire's confinement had meant his going alone. It seems particularly ironic to note that at this critical time in his life, when confronting his own mortality, he found himself in a maternity hospital, surrounded by encouraging signs of new life.

Discussion

As a consequence of my research, I became aware of a particular and distinctive way of life and living or culture of which I had no prior knowledge. Those whose cancer diagnosis was provided through their contact with the National Health Services most usually tended to remain the prerogative of that agency, conforming to the officially sanctioned forms of treatment and therapies. However, these individuals were also at least aware of, if not actively contributing to, another phenomenon, which appears to have formed around individuals with cancer, and is what I refer to as the 'cancer culture'. I would speculate that this indeterminate culture most probably has its roots in the spirit of self-help that, as we will learn, exists between individuals affected by cancer. A cancer diagnosis would seem to prompt the individuals most concerned into learning more about their condition whether via the media or personal interaction. As a result of these explorations, inevitably the individual becomes cognisant, not only of the relevant facts of their illness but also of others who also share their prognosis. Consequently, many participate, to varying degrees, within these groups or networks of others with cancer, whether that be at local, national or international levels. These associations, although most usually voluntarily organised, serve as vehicles to research and communicate information about the illness to others. Whilst most often including and encouraging the traditionally approved bio-medical ethos and attitude to disease, these groups also tend to embrace and promote a host of alternative philosophies, which become shared throughout the group.

Gerry and Louise, both aged 35, each had two very young children. They were both professionals who were financially responsible for their families whom they cherished. Their scientific background meant that they were also aware of the implications of their diagnoses and their probable prognoses. Consequently they were desperately concerned and felt the pressure of worry about their supporters and how they would cope in a situation that implied inevitable loss. However, rather than display their understandably disturbed emotions, they chose instead to repress them, using humour as a tool to alleviate tension. Louise appeared to have direct insight into the reasons for her manic behaviour, understanding that it was an attempt to divert attention away from the reality of her position. Her comments on how 'my doctor friend was the only person who appreciated the significance' and Gerry's remark 'I do not think that Claire really understood what I was going through' are crucial to understanding how individuals, who find themselves in this desperate position, feel and react as their journey with cancer progresses. The pressures inherent in the dying situation result in a reversal of normal behaviour, with the more private, vulnerable perspective of self being revealed to those, like medical staff, who are, in effect, strangers, whilst the staged face, which hides the true, subjective emotions, is the one which is ultimately presented to intimates.

At this stage, both Louise and Gerry put their faith in medical science. Louise's medical training informed her she had no realistic chance of survival; she was becalmed, trying to handle the depression and despair that she felt. Gerry, in contrast, was less knowledgeable and, therefore, more optimistic and was kept occupied, not only by his wife and young family but also by tending to the practicalities which had to be organised. Purchasing a wig and donating to a sperm bank were not events that he had ever foreseen. In being advised to bank his sperm, however, Gerry was being informed that his masculinity was under threat. The birth of his child, though, meant that he lacked the social support that might otherwise have been available, particularly his wife's support, when he attended the sperm bank alone. It should be noted it was Gerry's own personal decision to donate his sperm and not all individuals would perceive the prospect of infertility as so threatening. Although aware that his sick pay would allow financial stability for his short-term future, Gerry and Claire were aware that their long-term financial, as well as physical, future was not secure. This added yet another psychological pressure, that of deciding whether or not to remain in their recently purchased home.

For Louise, this was a time of bleak despair; for Gerry, thanks to the hope offered to him by his doctors, this was a time marked by fluctuations between trust and suspicion, terror and relief.

Treatment

Vera

Sixty-four-year-old Vera lived with her 'older man' – husband Albert who was 78 years old, in their modern terraced home. She told me how she experienced her radiotherapy treatment during our first interview when I saw her in hospital. She was:

> . . . absolutely scared out of my life about it. I had heard lots of funny things about it and people shouldn't say that because you get very frightened. Apparently they 'tattoo' you, mark you where they are going to zoom you [with radiotherapy]. I had to lie on this table and be marked up with a tattoo, they said it will not wash off, I had five days of radio [therapy] and I was absolutely terrified. They said 'There is nothing to it. It is just like an X-ray.' And I thought 'Oh yes?' You go in and you see these people sitting there with these terrible scars where it has all gone red. I went into this room, absolutely scared out of my life and I laid on the table. They were lovely, lovely people. I think they were all hand picked. They lay you on this trolley thing and I said, 'How long?' [will the treatment take] and they said 'A couple of minutes.' They line you up with like an X-ray machine and the machine comes down to you, so you have to lay how they place you and you must not move which is frightening. The only fault I found with this room is that they have nothing that you can focus on to, that would make it easier. They said, 'We will leave you but we can see you. Don't move; you will hear the door click as we go out and you will hear the machine start. Don't be frightened.' I said, 'All right, Two minutes.' I played the game that we play at Cubs trying to time a minute and I focused on what I could see and started to count. I got to 41 and heard the machine stop. I thought, 'That is not two minutes', and all of a sudden the door opened. They said 'Stay there, it is all over.' It was as easy as that. You go there, and you are out in 15 minutes.

Vera was terrified by what she had heard about her impending radiotherapy. She felt she had no choice but to take the treatment and was initially sceptical about what her medical team told her. Her fear of what she firmly believed was her imminent ordeal was compounded by her observation of 'people sitting there with these terrible scars where it has all gone red'. She was experiencing 'embodied paranoia' in that she felt 'threatened by institutions ostensibly designed to help' (Frank, 1995: 172). It may also be that Vera was displacing her fear of dying and death onto the machinery. It is not surprising, therefore, that her terror was at such a heightened pitch. It is interesting, too, that she focused upon the temporal duration of the therapy. Hassard (1990) considers the importance of anticipation, arguing that it is possible to bear almost anything, if we live in the certainty that it will ultimately pass and that better times will come. The staff seem to have gone out of their way in their efforts to reassure Vera but, in spite of this, the release she experienced when the door of the treatment unit opened was palpable. Like Gerry, Vera alternated between trust and suspicion, terror and relief.

Her chemotherapy was even harder. In spite of her radiotherapy, she still experienced pain:

Radiotherapy is not so frightening as chemo. Chemo there is nothing actually in what they do to you . . . I didn't have really any after effects with the radiotherapy, I was just very tired but they told me that I would be.

Dr T told me it was still the ovarian cancer, so that is why he is doing chemo. He gave me a choice. One that he put me on, which is a very strong chemo has a 50–50 chance of survival or a lighter form which is just a tablet and that has a 20 per cent survival rate or to have no chemo at all and you could be dead within three months. I said then 'I will take your advice because I owe it to my husband who I love very, very dearly and I have two kids and three grandchildren. I owe it to them to have a fight.' That is why we are on this terrible, terrible chemo. It is terrible, terrible. I was crawling around the house because I couldn't stand up.

Given such a bleak choice, Vera decided to trust her doctor. She chose to simply abrogate responsibility, optimistically leaving the ultimate therapeutic resolutions to the medics. Her love and regard for her family acted as a debt, which she could only settle by doing all she could to ensure her own survival.

The third time I met Vera, I had to hide my shock as she was totally bald. She laughingly told me that she was delighted to be 'still here' and that her continued survival was a result of:

[her] . . . faith in this man, this Dr T, the same as I have a lot of faith in my own GP. Although I don't see Dr T very often, he is a very clever man I think, he just has pinpointed my case, I don't know. Seems to have pulled the right strings for me. But I just feel that on the two occasions that I have had the chemo, he has got it right, but whether he will always be able to . . . I don't know. You get to the stage when you know you are going in for chemo and you think 'Oh God, I really don't want to go in', get a bit of a panic on but you go because you want to get well. It is getting well or going down. When you go in and see a lot of the other people you think . . . well you can't be anywhere near as bad as some of the others but then they all seem to come through it. But then they do marvellous things now with this chemo; they are learning the whole of the time. I don't know. I just have faith in Dr T and in the chemo girls [nurses] because I know they are only doing a job and it is his brain piece that is doing it but I think you have to have that. I'm sure there is times when you lose it and you think 'Oh no, this is not going to do any good' but we are getting there.

In desperate hope of a cure, Vera surrendered her body to the medical profession. Objectively, she realised her treatment might prove curative. However, it was a treatment in which her vulnerable body would be subjected to the indiscriminate effects of a harsh regime of toxic substances. In spite of the debilitating side effects, she opted to continue with this torturous treatment. Why? Those who have cancer are not the only ones who suffer. Their social group shares in the ravaging consequences. Vera was so deeply embedded within her supportive social network that she could see the damaging effect her cancer was exerting on that group. She could see how her illness impelled special effort from others and, as one who had previously been empowered to give to them, she felt reluctant to drain the group of its supportive resources. Consequently, she felt it her duty to maintain her position regardless of her personal physical and psychological suffering. Whether Vera would have persisted with her chemotherapy if she did not have such a supportive network is debatable. These relationships appear to have directly shaped her decision to cling on to her life.

When I remarked on the many get-well cards that ornamented her living room, she told me:

I have a thick pile like that from when I first was poorly. The neighbours are kind, people that I have known, if they don't phone me or send me a card or ask how I am or send me flowers, it is unbelievable. I have a lovely young girl next door with her first baby girl; she comes in to see me, which is absolutely wonderful.

Vera's cards reflected the degree of her value and standing in the community. A retired school-dinner lady, she actively contributed to the Church where her husband, Albert, was an elder. Her popularity might also have arisen from the bakery skills she loved to exercise at almost any opportunity and from her tendency to mother people. During our interviews together, she would frequently ask after my children and exclaim appropriately over stories of their most recent exploits.

Gerry

As baby Angela grew older, Gerry became established in his treatment. Discussing his feelings about it he said:

I was looking toward the chemo, not looking forward, it was starting 16th November. My attitude was, 'Let's go for it!' People asked if I was annoyed about it and I was but I was still of the attitude, 'Let's go for it!' I hate needles. I always look away. I had it [the chemotherapy] every Saturday. After the first, I thought, this is a piece of cake, felt great. Could not believe he [the oncologist] had given me 23 pills to take. It was the CHOP regime. The first session does boost you a little. I came back to the house and I was really hungry, so I had some Marks and Spencer Tuscan Bean soup, my mother was down [had come to visit] and I felt great! About 4 o'clock I began to feel mildly nauseous; Claire said I went bright green. Then I really began to feel bad, after that I was violently ill. This is a bit from my journal:

Saturday 16th November: 5.45 pm violent vomiting. Sick again at 6.15. Rang doctor to check if I should take more pills. He was unconcerned but told me to take more. Sick again 7.30 pm, 9.30 pm and 11.00 pm.

Sunday 17th November: Feeling really, really, sore; felt very strange.

Monday 18th November: Felt very beat about inside, very tired.

Although Gerry approached his chemotherapy with a very positive attitude, his opinion was influenced by the perceptions he had formed before he was even aware that he had cancer (Armstrong-Coster, 2001; Kfir and Slevin, 1991). Although still obviously suspicious of his treatment, in opting to comply with his doctor's recommendations, he was placing his trust in medical science. The physical effects were also compounded because Gerry's mother was visiting them and he felt obliged to maintain his attitude of bravado to protect her.

Some of the side effects of chemotherapy were less easy to deal with. Established on his treatment, Gerry explained to me what he experienced when he suffered his consequent hair loss:

I am going to lose it anyway, so let's get going here, even though I was not deliberately pulling it out. I would have told people for their benefit. Sometimes it irritates me when people tell me it will grow back, as if they were making me feel better. It never really bugged me that much. I went to scratch my hair one day and I had none. I never worried. I was joking about it to my mother. I was like the mummy in Raiders of the Lost Ark; became 140 years old in three seconds! Looking really old. Scary looking and I noticed Diana getting a bit scared about it. The next day, I got it cut off and there was an amazing difference. I went in looking like someone who was sick and came out looking as if it was on purpose. I instantly felt much better. When I caught sight of myself in a mirror . . . it hits you, you forget there is something wrong with you supposedly, but this reminds you, visibly until it becomes the norm again. 'Hey there is something wrong with you!' We had a visitor who didn't know about the cancer. Most people who knew I had cancer might have half expected it. He said, 'Did you get it cut or are you on medication?' He was the most openly shocked but most people knew before I met them. Sometimes you are conscious of people looking at you. There are not a lot of guys standing in a bar with no hair at my age, particularly now that my eyebrows are away. I look like a hood [criminal] with no hair, I have not lost any weight, so when I wear my jeans I look like a hard man . . . but when I walk into a shop . . . you do see that people would look at me differently. If it is really cold, I will feel it. It reminds you that now this is the norm.

Gerry did not want to appear to be ill or to be associated with a disease that is connected in the public imagination with death. Frank argues that the 'Restitution Plot' is the predominant position assumed by individuals who are ill, having the basic storyline: 'Yesterday I was healthy, today I'm sick, but tomorrow I'll be healthy again' (1995: 77). Impatient to leave the liminal sick role and resume his position in mainstream society, Gerry placed his faith in the chemotherapy. Knowing that it probably would cause his hair loss, he anticipated it and tried to maintain control by having his hair cut or pulled out. Although he was aware that his hair loss made him appear older than he was, he used humour as a defence against the psychological pain. It is, though, interesting that the parallel he drew refers to himself as looking like a 'mummy', someone who has lost their living identity and become recognised only as a corpse. Socially responsible, he had thoughtfully informed most people in his social group but was embarrassed when, on meeting people who did not know, he realised their shock. This contrasts interestingly with his earlier attitude during the initial stages of his diagnosis, when he perceived the news of his cancer to be like a potent tool '. . . you have power to hit people with . . .' He was also hurt at the reaction of strangers who stared at him, passing judgement and labelling him purely on the basis of his appearance. Practical problems occur as well, such as feeling colder than usual; Gerry, though, did not wear his wig, instead resorting to wearing an eclectic collection of hats.

Not surprisingly, he was perturbed that his illness affected not only him but also his family. Being on sick leave challenged him to fill his time in other ways but, by opting to take medical advice and treatment, he had effectively lost a significant part of his ability to control his own life.

Six-week-old baby Angela was, unwittingly, the cause of further stress to the young couple. Religious and social pressure prescribe that, as practising Catholics, they should have their newborn daughter baptised. Consequently, Gerry who was now self-conscious about his appearance, found himself being induced into organising this grand affair at a time when he felt decidedly under par. He told me he was simply exhausted after the christening, feeling as if he had had only two or three hours sleep every night. His dramatic illness was being back-staged and the social focus was directed away from him and onto baby Angela. Four-year-old Diana also found herself affected. She had to contend with the psychological adjustment necessary to 'only' children who suddenly find themselves with a new sibling; she also had to come to terms with her father's dramatic change of appearance. Claire told me that Diana: '. . . did not want him [Gerry] to collect her from the school gates because the other children poked fun at her because of his baldness'.

Gerry had, though, also drawn comfort from his social circle. He explained that:

People want to help you. Friends of Claire's from school [Claire was a teacher], teachers who have in-laws with cancer, telling me to call them. A lot of people come to give support. Some have been unbelievable to and for both Claire and me. Always asking after me, Mass cards, bouquets, oil, prayers, relics but it was the thought that was coming to me. Supportive help, emotional help was the biggest thing you needed at that time. I could not take physical help because there was nothing wrong with me. There was this particular lady, who comes always with fabulous wheaten bread; she comes and talks to me individually.

He felt something of a celebrity. Friends and well-wishers wanted to make direct contact with him. The community seemed united in their support of the family and their choice of gifts, Mass cards, prayers and relics, reflects their Catholic perspective on the family's situation. His social circle was offering him hope, in the form of prayers. Gerry remained stoic in denying his need for physical support. Later in our conversation, he came back to this theme of social support:

People come and call on you who you have not seen for a long time and that is nice. Glad to see me and sad at the same time but helpful. You get a lot of nice thoughts. Sometimes you are inundated . . .

Claire who had remained silent through most of the interview interjected, telling me that she felt that, 'Too many people call, all the time.' Gerry added:

But at the same time, it turns out . . . even though you don't want them here, you do enjoy them here. But it gets a bit wearing . . . There is a wider social scene. People do care for you, you see a genuine side of people's nature; something you might forget about. It is no skin off their noses that I have cancer but they want to go out of their way to help.

Again, Claire explained how she felt, 'But it is the constant phoning, calling . . . They ring for me too because people think I need support. The phone never stops ringing and it can be very wearing.' Gerry tried to sum up how they both felt, commenting that, 'On the one hand visitors coming are a morale boost but it can sometimes be too much.' Claire realised that there might be deeper issues underlying their experiences, saying, 'But maybe it is that I would like my life to be back to normal and this is not normal.' Again, Gerry interrupted telling me that:

There can be conflict between husband and wife because you are at home so much. There are times when the baby is asleep and a visitor comes but what can you do?

Discussion

The respondents' assessment of how their future lives would be affected by their cancer was, to varying degrees, influenced by both its type and severity and the information they had assimilated about that illness. Individuals become aware, however unwittingly, of the facts of cancer not simply by meeting or learning of others with the illness but also by interpreting media messages (Armstrong-Coster, 2001). What they have absorbed, however unconsciously, about that disease prior to developing it themselves shapes their reaction at the time of their diagnosis as well as their perception of their impending treatment.

All the individuals I saw during my research were subject to a host of treatments, which covered surgery, radiotherapy and chemotherapy. In line with this variety in treatment, all reacted differently in their approach to their prospective cures. Some like Gerry, focused psychologically on their beneficial attributes but suffered from physical after-effects; others, like Vera, who had dreaded the thought of her radiotherapy treatment, were delighted when they realised, with relief, their fears were largely unfounded. Unfortunately for Vera, the converse was true when she began her chemotherapy regime.

Although practicalities shaped how the respondents lived their daily lives, it was not these that caused the major upset, rather it was social issues. Until now, my interviewees had lived their adult lives with a fair degree of autonomy. Their illness, though, provoked responses from others which, however well meant, resulted in them feeling a loss of control.

Due to the unusual situation where she and her husband were both incapacitated by illness, Louise was reluctantly forced to consider accepting financial help from friends. She told me how she:

. . . just felt suffocated by the help but I was scared to antagonise anyone. We had no income and people were giving me literally thousands of pounds and I was having to bite my lip and say, 'Oh yes, give me the money.'

Having previously enjoyed a life of independence, feeling forced to rely on the goodwill of others did not come easily. In one interview, Louise returned to the theme of re-negotiating relationships:

. . . it is like an army coming through the door, I feel totally invaded. I would say during serious illness . . . Even my next-door neighbour, he did my garden when we were not well enough and I was not able to negotiate that in any way. Now I would have trouble stopping him doing things to the garden, which I may not want done. He has taken that over.

Her choice of military metaphors illustrates well her seemingly hopeless plight. She was battle-weary, having surrendered to a relentless, physically powerful, virtual militia, which struck at the very core of her dignity and privacy. Even her neighbours appeared to conspire in ensuring her continued ineffectiveness. She felt as though she had lost control.

More problematically, Ben and Eilish felt surprised at the lack of interest and support shown to them by their only child. They explained to me how bewildered and disappointed they both felt by his reaction to being told that Ben had cancer. Ben said:

We have one son; he lives some way away. He has three children and I phoned him on the Wednesday when Mr. C said I had cancer. He was very quiet and then he didn't phone again until two weeks after that. I was very hurt by that, I really was.

The couple who had been left 'dumbstruck' after hearing Ben's shocking diagnosis, suffered the pain of being let down by their son, to whom they had presumably turned, seeking support at this difficult time. Reflection suggests the hurt was made worse by their geographic distance from him and also from their grandchildren.

Similar problems were faced by 42-year-old Susan, who we will meet in more depth later. Because she was divorced and living alone, absence of rephrase support at such a critical time also left her feeling perplexed. She told me how hurt she felt when a trusted friend let her down:

When it came time to deal with the cancer, she was not there in person. Notes and messages on the [answering] machine, 'I am there in Spirit.' I was so angry and eventually got around to talking about it. I wrote her back firmly. It seemed like I was getting platitudes. The flowers are lovely and the cards are lovely, as are the messages, but the main value is someone standing looking directly at you holding on to your hand, telling you how difficult it is and at least they are standing there. I am not alone in this. Ok this is going to be rough, but . . . 'I am here with you' and that is what I find most valuable and this woman let me down when I needed her most; she let me down. Complete strangers didn't let me down but someone that I had invested a great deal of time with over a 5 year period . . . We shared a great deal of stuff and I thought I had made this really valuable connection with her and when I needed her most, she was not there. And instead I got these silly letters and cards, which I just found very annoying.

The horror of having to come to terms with cancer was compounded by her sense of abandonment. Susan felt rejected, baffled and angry at her friend's behaviour. It might, alternatively, be observed that her, understandable, sense of anger may have originated in her diagnosis and then been projected on to her friend. She believed that she had contributed a great deal to their friendship and, now that she was in need, was dismayed to find her only reward was a telephone message. This perceived betrayal occurred at the time when she was most in need of consolation; instead, she found herself alone, finding solace in the company of strangers. Zerubavel writes:

The fundamental difference between intimate social relationships and pseudo-intimate social situations is particularly evident in the case of situations that involve pronouncedly dead-end, short term, fleeting relations with total 'strangers' (Simmel, 1964: 404) such as taxicab drivers (Davis, 1959: 160) or passengers aboard trains, ships or aeroplanes. It is precisely *because* the partici-pants are quite confident that they would never meet those strangers again that they feel so comfortable to share with them some of the most intimate exclusive information about themselves [his italics]. (1982: 102)

Susan continued:

You know that adage of a friend in need. I have certainly discovered who my friends are. I have discovered the most amazing thing. First, that people I don't even know have made contact with me. I know that I am a very outspoken person and I have gone public with my disease and it is out there in the public arena and therefore . . . It is almost as if they have a right to get in touch with me and acknowledge some of the positive stuff I am doing and they also tell me their own cancer stories, which is very humbling at times. I feel very supported by complete strangers. I have had people, who I thought did not care, who knew me . . . Colleagues at work, etc. I have had them make contact. People who you are in conflict with over issues . . . For them to contact and set the conflicts to one side and deal with the life threatening stuff has been enlightening. I have had people come up to me in the street. People do what they would consider petty, minor things, like a hospital porter who, when I was looking for change, gave me seven 10ps and would not take it back. Just a lovely gesture, which meant a great deal. In terms of family and friends, they have been forced to deal with it.

Susan had made clear distinctions between individuals with whom she has come into contact. She divided them into three categories, first, strangers, 'people I don't even know' who make her 'feel very supported'; second, acquaintances, 'people who I thought did not care' whose behaviour is 'enlightening' and has 'meant a great deal'. It is only after dealing with these two categories that she suddenly singled out 'family and friends' and, referring to them in almost direct contrast to those others, almost bitterly commented on how 'they have been forced to deal with it'. It is worth noting that, even at this early stage, Susan looked outside her circle of intimates for the emotional attention that she felt she needed. The order in which emotional succour is derived has been completely reversed from what might have been anticipated.

Susan explained to me something of the problems she experienced, because her mother:

. . . cannot deal with death and dying and cancer issues and she spent twelve weeks here, which drove me crazy. She was here to support me and the biggest support she could have given me was to go away and to stop feeding me and to stop turning on the damned oven and putting food on the table. It was a nightmare. That's mum.

Another respondent, 48-year-old Rose, whose primary breast cancer had been diagnosed seventeen years before her eventual death, had to contend at that time not only with the prospect of her own imminent death and the symptoms of her illness but also with an extremely dramatic reaction from her mother:

When I was ill in hospital, they gave me ten days to live . . . I actually had to get my mother thrown out, she went hysterical. She couldn't cope. She started screaming. Every day; she did this to me for a fortnight. 'What am I going to do, how could you do this to me?' She was screaming at me and it was terrible, I couldn't take it. And in the end I was getting so upset, the nurses told her not to come and see me any more, to leave it for a few days. I think it was reaction . . . She just couldn't cope.

At the time of her original diagnosis, Rose had been given only a few days to live. This was a time when it might reasonably have been expected that she be allowed to spend any remaining time in peace but she found herself beset by her 'hysterical' and 'screaming' mother. In her unrestrained articulation of her pain, her mother might also have been confronting Rose with the very emotions Rose hoped to deny feeling herself.

Louise, too, felt challenged by her mother's behaviour. She told me how her mother:

Just walks in and doesn't stop to say 'Hello' or anything. Just starts tidying and cleaning – pokes through my cupboards for whatever it is she is looking for. I ask her 'Would you do that to anyone else?'
I remember hearing all the furniture being moved about. Derek has partial vision, a lot of perceptual problems and I organised the furniture to help him with his wheelchair, but she moved it all back. I would leave doors open at night so he could get to his breakfast easily, and every night she would lock the doors.

Susan, Rose and Louise would all appear to have become infantilised by their mothers who, well-meaningly enough, attempted to inject practical help. However, the mothering impulse to nurture, instead of helping, exacerbated the problems.

Others, at this stage, appeared to feel the benefits of their social relationships. Bob, who had been hospitalised for chemotherapy, was, unusually, very positive about his treatment, perhaps because of the pain relief it brought. He was quite delighted to explain that:

There were the nicest nurses and doctors there that I have seen in all my life; couldn't do any more for me than what they have done. They put me on this chemo. I was on it from Thursday till Saturday morning and it was like a miracle! The pain was gone, the lines in my face was gone – it was like the cream you see on television! After one treatment the pain was gone!

This was the only account from the respondents that did not castigate the treatments, which were intended to be beneficial. When treatment or its side effects were discussed, the reports from all the other respondents were redolent with nuances of dread. Living with cancer and its treatments is very, very difficult.

The side effects of chemotherapy seemed particularly to tax the interviewees. Rose was one of many who suffered as a result. She found especial difficulty:

. . . when getting out of bed. Takes me half an hour and every little movement is so painful that I am sick when I do get out of bed. And then it takes me five minutes to walk down the landing to the bathroom. I have to sit down six times before I get to the bottom of the stairs and I know I can't get back up those stairs again.

Having been told something of the harsh realities of the effect of chemotherapy on people, I accepted an offer to observe events in a chemotherapy clinic. An excerpt from my field-notes which describes events in the waiting room reads:

Blue carpet and beige walls. People of all ages and from all sorts of backgrounds, which is reflected in their clothing. Most are wearing hats or wigs. I could be in a dentist's waiting room, a completely full house. Wall of information up: 'Chemotherapy – How To Deal With It', '10 Different Symptoms of Bowel Cancer'. Fingers strumming. Nurses in plastic aprons – neat dresses. Woman takes appointment card.

Most people are there alone. Some with a partner. There is silence, not a lot of talk. The extracts, which I do hear, are interesting. 'We meet again!' 'When they told me it was back, I could not believe it, I thought they were joking.' People watching others – listening in to their conversations. 'Still working?' 'They are advertising my job, but I am not worried about that.' A lot seem to be immersed in reading the magazines.

Staff with clipboards 'Do you want anti-sickness tablets?' 'Oh, yes please.' Predominance of women staff, doctors, nurses and assistants. People clutching appointment cards. 'I am bringing you forward two days, because I am away on the Friday, is that all right?' 'Yes, alright'. Some treatments seem to go really fast. New appointments made.

The large airy room in which the therapy was administered was very comfortable. Somehow feminine – blue chairs, huge! Sage green carpet – tasteful. Televisions, videos, stereos, beds, separate armchair cubicles. The patients here are offered endless cups of tea and coffee. The technical equipment would seem to be state of the art.

The nurse manager told me that: 'When they come here first they are freaked; need everything reinforced. The interview room is the most important place here. Anything else can go, but not that.'

Then I was brought 'backstage' to the room where the pharmaceutical drugs were infused. Sterile cocktail laboratory – all white surfaces. Amazing side-wards, like nuclear bunkers built for nuclear medicine. Windows blocked off etc. 'We put their food through a special hatch.' The manager there tellingly remarked 'We wipe them out with chemo and then try to bring them back again.'

Many of those who are prescribed a course of chemotherapy have internalised a fear of the treatment that, initially, they appear to project onto everything connected with it. The waiting area was actually, a comfortable, if bland, environment designed to counter and pacify heightened anticipation of the treatment. The administrative area was integrated into the waiting facilities, reinforcing the openness in attitude by the staff, offsetting any possible nuance of secrecy. This appeared to reassure those patients unfamiliar with the routine; it seemed to be the lack of familiarity with the procedure and technology involved, which initially heightened fears.

Living with cancer in the present day United Kingdom means having to learn the minutiae of the practicalities involved in high technology medicine. However, journalist John Diamond, who would ultimately succumb to his own cancer, commented in his wry depiction of cancer on how eventually even: '. . . the exciting and the terrifying can become transformed equally by familiarity into the banal and the boring' (1999: 105).

This may account for why eventually attending chemotherapy sessions was something that most respondents did alone. Initially, they were so daunted by the prospect that they took a supporter but, after they realised that the drug infusion was not threatening, most were prepared to go alone.

Learning how to accept and cope with these very different life changes takes time, it is a period in which the non-verbal rules of terminal illness (Mamo, 1999) such as when, where and with whom to wear wigs, are assimilated. A Macmillan nurse described to me how the patients often attempt to 'pass', disguising or camouflaging their 'sick faces' by wearing heavy make-up, prostheses and wigs. One of the ploys used to assess more accurately the true state of their patient's condition is, therefore, to arrive 'early' for home visits, before the patient has time to get dressed or made up. Louise and Vera tended to wear wigs in public. Although Gerry had purchased one, he ultimately decided not to wear it, preferring instead to sport a series of unusual hats. This tactic seemed to work well, perhaps because it allowed him to feel in control of his situation and, in highlighting his more idiosyncratic characteristics, it served to distract others from the problem of dealing with his sudden baldness.

This tendency to play down the harsher realities of life with cancer are considered by Charmaz (1991), who argues that maintaining a good physical appearance is an indication that the disease is contained and controlled. Applying Goffman's (1963) concept of passing to the chronically ill, she argues that their desire to pass has two reasons. First, they believe their illness might count against them, and second, patients fear the embarrassment that would be caused should their illness be discovered.

Wigs, however, are cosmetic and basic physical performance can still be achieved without them. Louise and her disabled husband Derek found their son, Richard, assessed their physical competence on their use of mobility aids. Louise, laughingly told me how Richard was:

... not very engrossed in his sister's illness [his sister had been recently diagnosed with leukaemia]. He couldn't really work out that she is sick. It is very obvious that there is something seriously wrong with Derek; he can't walk and he can't talk, and he looks funny. I had a walking stick and that was always his [Richard's] measurement and he would say, 'Send that back to the hospital.' If I came downstairs, he reported to his gran ... 'She must be better, she is downstairs.' The wee one [Laura] is peculiar for him to figure out; she doesn't go to school but she was only at nursery for a week, nothing has really changed. She sits up, eats her tea, fights a bit, she plays a bit, lies on the sofa. There would be nothing there that he could identify as ... Her hair will fall out [from her impending chemotherapy], that might change the tune, but I don't really know ...

A strong public presentation of self not only bolsters what may be a flagging sense of self esteem but 'looking good' also distracts from private dwelling on the illness and the associated thoughts of death. There are, however, moments when the physical intrudes on the psychological, as when Gerry caught an unexpected glimpse of himself in the mirror. It may be this threat of a physical confrontation with the bodily markers of death that is responsible for individuals who are dying being excluded from large areas of public life (Blauner, 1996; Field, 1996).

The reaction of close family to a potentially fatal disease can vary. Lichter (1987) observes that feelings of guilt are common in the relatives and can spur excessive demonstrations of love and care but also denial of the illness that can result in physical and psychological hardship to the patient.

Rose told me how she believed her mother was, quite simply, in denial of her illness, explaining to me how once she had said:

'You know mum, please stop planning the future with me in it. You are looking ten, fifteen, twenty years down the line. I am not going to be here!' She said 'Oh don't be stupid, of course you will: grow up.' So she is totally denying that I can die. I told her that the disease was spreading . . . She walked out of the room.

Rose felt frustrated and alone. Gerry, Louise and Susan, too, experienced the existential pain of their aloneness at this time of heightened crisis. Susan explained how:

When the hospital closes down for the night and you are there in the room alone, it is a very scary experience. [She began to cry]. It is a very scary experience . . .

I waited for some minutes and then asked her what scared her. She told me:

Being alone. I think it is a very natural thing to be afraid of . . . It is a child-like thing. When children are scared you just want to give them a cuddle and hold on to them until they stop shaking and stop crying and to be on your own is a horrible experience . . . I am a single woman who enjoys being single, but that is through choice. But when you are alone, and you think . . . when you are alone and you have no choice and you are facing this really horribly scary thing and there is no one there to say that it's going to be alright . . .

Susan, who lived alone and felt abandoned by her friend, felt herself to be in need of someone who would 'cuddle and hold on to' her until she was able to stop 'shaking and stop crying'. She directly summed up the central motifs of existentialism when she said '. . . you are alone and you have no choice and you are facing this really horribly scary thing . . .' When I asked Louise directly if her prognosis frightened her she said 'No!' then 'I . . . Yes, every now and then my heart just chills and I say, "Right I could die", and then I say, "We all could die", I am doing everything I can not to die. Yes, my heart just chills . . .'

Others were not so direct, hinting more obliquely at something of their terror. Vera said:

. . . there is days that are bad, when you can't . . . and they say that you have to think positive, but you can't always think positive. It is one of these things where you think 'Oh God, I could die.' I really don't want to die. I have so much living I want to do . . . but you feel like . . . I want to give up. The lady in the bed across, at the hospital . . . I have lost a bit of weight but this lady really was ill and I said to myself, 'What do you do?' I know we have all got to die because that is the human race but it must be like a condemned person because that is how I feel . . .

Chapter summary

The reports the respondents made about the events in the period between learning of their diagnosis and embarking on their treatment highlight several pertinent concerns. During this time of tests and subsequent treatment, they felt impotent and, in that ineffectual condition, believed their best hope of cure lay in opting to receive traditional, scientific treatment. To varying extents, they were all aware that their lives were now under threat and, although they responded in different ways at this stage, they all complied in this choice. They felt that by doing this they were maximising their chances of survival. I do not know whether any of them even considered any other form of treatment. However, their adherence to conventional treatment meant that they had to suffer the loss of autonomy, which compliance to the scientific medical world demands.

This liminal time between diagnosis and treatment was a period when the support of their social groups proved critical; however, these relationships also unfortunately, came under intense pressure. The respondents' reports reveal early indicators of the sweeping changes that would come about in their social relationships. At this critical juncture and, as a direct result of their illness, the established social groupings were subject to shifts of power. These changes were not easily made but required sensitive and prolonged periods of verbal, and sometimes non-verbal, negotiation. Nettleton sums up something of the complexity of the contributing factors to how illness is experienced when she writes:

... responses to illness are not simply determined by either the nature of biophysical symptoms or individual motivations, but rather are shaped and imbued by the social, cultural and ideological context of a person's biography. Thus illness is at once both a very personal and a very public phenomenon. (1995: 69)

Whilst social input was valued, it was, sometimes, experienced as intrusive; family, especially, tending at times to interpret vulnerability as weakness. Instead of helping, this inclination to intervene, no matter how well meant, often had the effect of exacerbating the very real crisis.

The psychological pressure they had to endure and the side effects of their tests and treatment were beginning to tell. It is the cultural norm for people in new or unfamiliar situations to cope by putting on their 'best face' (Laslett and Rapoport, 1975). Conforming to the norms of conventional behaviour in order to maintain relational systems (Coser, 1961) does not explain adequately how such behaviour is actually learned when living within a society that prohibits an open articulation of any matter concerning death (Gorer, 1965). The pressure respondents experienced as a result of having to meet the criteria for a 'best face' was sometimes, unhappily, discharged at supporters.

The underlying cause of some of this tension may also have originated in the existential crisis that was experienced to varying degrees by respondents. As they became increasingly enmeshed in their medical regime, they became conversant with the implications of what their future might hold and, consequently, became more sensitive to existential concerns. Some conceptualised and articulated sound questions as to the nature of the human condition which, when scrutinised, revealed the depth of their inner despair.

Feeling overwhelmed by tumultuous events threatens to neutralise our sense of psychological autonomy but this potential vulnerability might, in part, be countered by seizing control over personal appearance. Coming to terms with the practical aspects of their treatment was difficult, as it meant consciously acknowledging that they had cancer and preparing for the physical changes, such as hair loss, which might result from their treatment.

Following the detection and diagnosis of their cancer, the respondents came to be the physical targets of whatever medical treatments were judged most appropriate. These treatments were all intended to have beneficial effects. The problem was that both chemotherapy and radiotherapy tend to have a ravaging effect on the whole body, often causing intense discomfort.

Their supporters too pro-actively prescribed and provided assistance which was exercised sometimes arbitrarily, whether it was wanted or not. Many of my respondents found themselves in the difficult position where they were often the involuntary subjects of overwhelming and oppressive intrusion.

Having been diagnosed with cancer, the interviewees became the focus of their social groupings, who, perceiving them to be in need of emotional support and practical help, took immediate steps to address potential problems. Many of the respondents found themselves in the difficult position of being the involuntary subjects of well-meant but overwhelming, oppressive intrusion. Much in the same way as the chemotherapy invaded the whole body, good cells and bad, to the respondents, supporters pro-actively prescribed and provided assistance, sometimes exercised arbitrarily, whether or not it was wanted.

Being informed of the results of medical tests is described as 'learning' a diagnosis. Having endured the trauma of hearing that diagnosis, the respondents were now, quite literally, beginning to 'learn' how to live with their cancer. Almost no aspect of their lives would remain unaffected by the changes their diagnosis had brought about. Their practical, emotional and social worlds would be subject to, at times, almost revolutionary change.

4 Stage Three – Anticipation

Remission and recurrence

So far, we have considered how the respondents came to be drawn inexorably into the realm of the medical expert and how they were subjected to a range of high technology curative treatments. Eventually, this treatment drew to an end but as Costain Schou and Hewison observe: 'The *illness calendar* [which] begins with the diagnostic period . . . In a sense [it] never really comes to an end – the patient will always be subject to reviews and semi-annual checks after treatment is completed' (1999: 49) [their italics]. Being seen by others to be physically recovering well from a life threatening illness is important but, during these periods of recovery, how the respondents perceived their own progress was often in marked contrast to their external appearance. Periods of remission seemed to be marked sometimes by as much psychological turbulence as the other, more obviously dramatic, moments in their trajectory.

It may be that some primitive element of self-blame is experienced by those who have cancer (Armstrong-Coster, 2001) but, whatever the cause, the interviewees all, to varying extents, tended to play down the pain of their illness, focusing, instead, on protecting those for whom they cared. Before Kubler-Ross's (1995) critique of 'modernist medical care' written in 1969, individuals who were dying were tangible proof of the failure of science to cure. They were an embarrassment to the 'experts' of the medical profession, which at that time was virtually unchallenged in its dominance of health related matters.

The recognition of dying as affording opportunity to earn heroic status was also made possible as a result of Kubler-Ross's (1995) good death thesis, which so revolutionised perceptions of dying, that something which was previously perceived to be negative (Saunders and Baines, 1983) was transformed into a positive, a condition which could actively enhance one's persona. Although, indisputably, Kubler-Ross's work has gone some way to redress the issue of death and dying being taboo, death still challenges the moral social order. How then are we to deal with people who are dying?

In the Introduction, I noted how Seale argues that, as a result of Glaser and Strauss's (1964, 1965) work on awareness contexts, in late modern society, heroism has not disappeared but has modified its form, opening up the role to embrace the idea of 'ordinary heroes' and so making it potentially achievable to all through their dying. Seale cites the dying self as being:

> . . . engaged in a heroic drama, involving the facing of inner danger, engagement in an arduous search, defiant displays of courage, and the demonstration of the (once 'manly') virtues of compassion. (1998: 92)

The repression of strong emotion results in home life becoming effectively a crucible, testing the strength of relationships. A referral for a hospital stay might then be viewed, by patient and carers alike, as a diversion from a situation of extreme stress.

If cast in the heroic mould, when and with whom can individuals who are dying express their true, private feelings or emotions openly? My research has shown that, contrary to that which I had anticipated, the safe recipients of 'risky' emotion are often not those with whom we are close or most intimate.

For the patient who is diagnosed as dying, to whom is it safe to turn? Gergen describes how, in modern life it is safe to unload emotional baggage onto those with whom we are unfamiliar, wryly commenting: 'One can let the internal fires rage in Paris, because the folk in Peoria will never see the glow' (1991: 67). Perhaps a hospital nurse may find a few moments to listen, or should the hospice be in a position to afford it, perhaps a social worker or therapist? Maybe even an interested sociologist? As my relationships with the respondents deepened over the course of the research, I often found them confiding in me about how devastating the effects of their illness had been. Louise told me:

> . . . I have been ill where I have been incapable of getting out of bed, of swallowing a drop of water, where I had no interest in the children or anyone, where I could not care how they were at home. I have been admitted to hospital, dehydrated, knowing my breathing was going, nurses urging me to hold on and thinking I am slipping away . . . I have cried with pain . . . I have been sick.

Although patients who are approaching this period of their illness enjoy the opportunity to re-enter normal life symbolically by sharing in the details of mundane, domestic life in the ordinary world, they are heroically constrained by the need to protect their family and carers from the harsh realities of their own position.

Who will listen to their pain? The people available to talk with them are others like themselves, people who, a short while previously, had been strangers. Wolff quotes Simmel who writes:

> . . . distance means that he, who is close by, is far, and strangeness means that he, who also is far, is actually near . . . the fact that he often receives the most surprising openness – confidences which sometimes have the character of a confessional and which would be carefully withheld from a more closely related person. (1964: 402–404)

Sharing the same geographic proximity and the same urgency of their predicament accelerates and sets the bonds of friendship. Rose told me that when she was in hospital:

> I think the fact that there are other people around who have your illness helps . . . You see, when there is six of you in a room and you are all suffering from the same thing, it makes you feel a lot more normal. When everybody around you is healthy and well and don't really understand the problems you have, you feel very different . . .

Prior to being diagnosed with cancer, the respondents had considered themselves to be normal. They had their own perceptions of how people with cancer would look and behave. However, Costain Schou and Hewison describe the diversity of individuals who have cancer, commenting how in clinical waiting rooms:

> . . . advanced illness, the ravages of treatment, survivorship and the many faces of 'cancer' as a collection of different chronic illnesses are visible on a daily basis. Contact with other patients seemed to have had a dimensionalizing effect on individuals' expressed views of their illness: a spectrum of cancer diagnoses/prognoses and cancer patients had replaced what for most people was limited or no experience with either. (1999: 39)

When patients enter the cancer culture, the boundaries that delimit and separate them off from mainstream society, ironically, also function to solidify the structure of their new group. This empowers them to share with others the knowledge and experiences of their illness without fear of losing face (Costain Schou and Hewison, 1999).

It is these other patients, as well as the informed and interested medical staff, who now form the dying patients' main social network, enabling the disclosure of private emotion to be freely discharged in the security of an understanding audience. The psychological adjustment and stark physical realities involved in a chronic dying trajectory entail a shift away from the concerns of mainstream everyday life, towards a coming to terms with the new. Family, once intimate, are now partly outsiders, strangers to the everyday life within the hospice or hospital. In their place, the staff and other patients become insiders, sharing the common bond of experience.

Louise

Louise, in spite of the many, very real, calamities that had befallen her, did not bemoan her lot, she quite simply got on with life and endeavoured to distract and protect others from her own, dismal prognosis. She told me:

. . . my mother feels that the rest of life should be called off, holidays are to be cancelled, we should [Louise parodies] 'Not watch that television programme, are you sitting there reading the newspaper? That child has leukaemia!' But there is nothing else to do, the leukaemic child is over there playing with her bricks, it is very hard. My reaction is always to keep family life going, you can't just sit down and wallow in yet another illness . . . How else do you survive?

When I met Louise she was in remission from her own breast cancer and, although much of our interviews were taken up with her relating the various pivotal and competing events in her life, she did tell me something of the trivia too. During our second interview she described how:

Since February I have been doing small but creative things, doing embroidery, patchwork, garden, recycling etc. I love all that. Most of my time has been taken up taking care of my husband and two children. I have changed the system of people coming in to do housework. I have got quite a lot involved with the kids, I put them to bed every night, take them to the shop but it can be a bind, because they now expect it. But I enjoy it and they deserve it because they were deprived of me for quite a long time. Now their expectation is that I do the thing. Spend a lot of time trying to motivate my husband, which is probably the best diversional therapy going, fling yourself into someone else's problem.

Although life seemed relatively calm for her then, the presence of her disabled husband and the input he required from Health Service providers probably functioned as a jarring reminder to her that her remission would one day end. Nonetheless she revelled in the fact that she was now, for the moment, able to resume her role as mother and wife.

All of the conversations we shared were marked by her need to regain autonomy; she frequently referred to how she had 'a plan, there is a plan of action' and the fact that she had a 'master plan'. In fact, so desperate was she for her problems to be resolved that she tried to persuade herself that her physical condition was not as grim as she, in reality, knew it was. She told me:

I mean, I don't think I live under a death threat any more, and it would be great to have that confirmed and I often think I would love a sign from heaven, to say,

'Yes, you will rear those kids. Confirmed!' My absolute priority is . . . I don't want the children exposed to the sadness of losing their mother at that age and I would love that confirmed to me. I would love a little vision, 'I guarantee that . . .' I would be very happy with that . . .

Louise's obligation to her family was the dominant and driving force in her life. She sometimes drew upon memories of just how bad her condition had been to stress what she hoped was evidence of her continuing improvement. She said:

I have had three months, where to get out the door required help, using a walking stick. I could not have made a cup of tea, I would have cried with pain. I have been much, much sicker than I am now, where my life has been just symptoms with no other life. Symptoms can take away your life. Now I have no pain, good energy, if I am just slightly careful. A great interest in life. I am back to being the mother in this house. I have my children; they are an interest again. I did not know that you could get sick enough to where you just didn't care. I didn't even care if I got washed; it was just too much of an effort. I get help now, I am dictating the pace, I can go out with friends, go to church, do all those things so, in that way, I would rate my health quite high. My mental attitude is back again. I am recovered to the extent where I think, 'Oh yes, I love it living here, I want to be alive' and that gives you a great sense of health. I am on no medication and I have been on morphine, begging for it to be given to me early, '. . . but don't tell the doctor'. Yes, there will always be this thing on a chart, primary breast cancer, bone secondaries. Not a very good outlook and I have been trained as a doctor, so to me, it was always, 'What it says on that chart . . .' But over the years, I have moved away from that to . . . Health is something quite, quite different . . . That will always be my chart but my plan in life is that I continue to improve. I loved being a doctor, the order of medicine, diagnosing things . . . this is all a departure.

Louise experienced her illness as sufficiently terrifying to describe it in terms that suggest that she had felt in real danger of losing her life. When others, presumably, became sufficiently alarmed by the change in both her physical condition and social behaviour, she found herself the object of their judgement and was, in being 'admitted to hospital' virtually declared incompetent. Lawton's hospice-based ethnography describes the transition of self to object observing '. . . that selfhood is fundamentally tied to bodily capacity, with a loss of self occurring as patients lost the bodily ability to perform tasks for themselves' (2000: 101). So great was the extent of Louise's loss of physical control that she described herself as being 'incapable', 'dehydrated' and requiring 'help' even to the extent that she had to be prompted to 'hold on' by caring others. Bearing in mind that she believed herself to be 'slipping away' and was enduring pain, which appeared at times to have reached agonising peaks, it is not surprising that she found herself 'begging' for morphine. It should, however, be observed that, even in extremis, her social instinct intervened and, perceiving that her request might be construed as weakness, she conditioned her plea to her carers with the request not to 'tell the doctor'.

What had alerted others to the fact that her condition was abnormal was their connecting those physical symptoms with her behavioural changes. On four separate occasions she commented that she 'had no interest' or 'could not care'. Indeed, so great was her growing detachment from the basic tenets of Western life in general and her medical training in particular, that she told me that she 'didn't even care if' she 'got washed'. She was not able to get out of bed, her mobility was affected and the fact that she had lost her social role as nurturer of her family was summed up in the telling words 'I could not have made a cup of tea.' The extent of this complete departure from normal social interaction was all the more marked when it is remembered that this is the attitude of a woman who 'loved being a doctor'. Analysis of what she has said suggests that her illness not only caused her physical suffering but also rendered her socially inept and emotionally deadened; she seemed to be unable to feel interest or to exercise choice. Her physical pain framed and shaped how she interpreted and behaved in society.

More can be gleaned about how she perceived her cancer from a practical and social perspective by briefly considering some comments she made during the next interview:

I have been in hospitals twice . . . with the side effects of chemo and I, basically, didn't give a damn about the children. Someone put a drip up on me . . . And I just really left them all to it, you know my sisters all fill in immediately . . . I have been in bed unable to do anything, that is fifteen months ago, that is the pits. Somebody else has to come in and do it all for you, you just lie there and it all happens around you. I hated that, couldn't do anything, couldn't walk across the room, couldn't sit up in the bed, could maybe sit and sip some water until I fell asleep again. It is terrible, because you might as well be dead.

Louise's plight at that time was such that she had surrendered control of her physical body to others who were now responsible for its maintenance. Just as the broader society in which she lived had recognised and made professional provision for those who would require such assistance, so too, her own immediate social grouping took steps to ensure that the practical affairs within her domestic environment continued to be regulated efficiently. The input provided by both public and domestic spheres effectively sanctioned her full participation to the sick role (Parsons, 1951).

Perhaps, though, it was the shift in her emotional attitudes that reveals most about her state of mind then. Direct evidence of the dramatic switch that had occurred was presented when Louise made reference to how 'I basically didn't give a damn about the children' and 'where I could not care how they were at home'. These words had been spoken by the same woman, who at the time of her diagnosis, said that she '. . . felt panic stricken . . . my children are going to be left'.

What has happened to effect this revolutionary change? I would suggest that it transpired because of the extreme pain and weakness she had to endure and also because, at that time, she believed she had no hope for survival.

The depth of the despair she must have experienced is happily presented in direct contrast to her quality of life at the time of the interviews. She was almost euphoric when she told me 'I have a great interest in life, I am back to being the mother in this house, I have my children, they are an interest again.' Louise was joyous in surviving that harrowing ordeal and blissful at being back in control of her home and family, where she belonged. The effect of her physical suffering, which had caused her almost complete physical and social collapse, was over and she was no longer introspective and withdrawn but able to resume her role as a social being. However, the degree to which those who cared for her allowed her to resume her autonomy did not meet her expectations or approval. Louise explained to me that:

> . . . as you get more ill, as your physical symptoms override . . . I don't think a loss of control is totally dependent on you; it is dependent on the people you are dependent on . . . And there are some people interested in letting you have control but most people are not. They will remove control and my game plan, in a sense, is to have people who will let me have control into positions of strength round me, you know that they will be the lieutenants in crisis and they can send the others packing on my behalf. My mother took my life out of my hands just as quickly as she could. I thought 'Oh they are cutting the keys to my door and giving them out to each other, they are all going to walk in here as they see fit . . . I love it . . .' [spoken with tones of extreme irony] Even though I had a phone by my bed it would be answered downstairs. When I was in bed with my husband, my mother would think nothing of walking into the room. I have seen my mother opening drawers in my bedroom, which I don't think you should do in your married daughter's bedroom. That is how I experienced it, a complete invasion of every aspect of my life . . . Like 'Don't mind us, we just live here!'

Now more physically able, Louise felt in control of her affairs. She was, though, only able to exercise that control with the support of others, 'people who will let me have control' and who permitted her to be their commander. Indeed, the family help had proven to be so intrusive that it actually would seem as though Louise's voice and ears, her telephone that was her access to her social grouping, had been removed. She returned to her plan to take up more fully the offers of help from friends rather than family but felt hesitant to ask because she was aware that:

I am asking a lot, I am asking 'Please all be at my beck and call, and the minute I need someone, I want someone.' I find that I am gravitating towards friends a lot and using friends a lot . . . The friends come prompt on the nail and leave when you ask.

Being ill and having to accept help has cost Louise and Derek their position as leaders of their family, as well as their dignity and privacy. Louise seemed to feel endangered, both as a side effect of being subsumed by this well intentioned help and by the awful fear that her cancer may return.

My field-notes, recorded after my fourth interview with Louise, read:

Saw Louise in her home in the evening time, as usual. She seemed to be very tired and in pain. She was not herself. Up until this visit all of our interviews were in her large, homely and incredibly untidy kitchen but this evening I was brought instead, into a beautifully proportioned drawing room. Even the children's mess did not distract from its elegance. The pictures were all originals and the predominant colour was green. The room was full of books and photographs. Pictures of Louise and Derek on their wedding day and lots, too, of the children. As the interview was beginning, some care workers came to the door to assist Derek going to bed and, as I went out to open the door to them, I met for the first time, a wheel-chaired Derek. He was much older and more gaunt than I had imagined. Richard, who is now six, ran in and out of the room several times before selecting a book, which he announced he was going to read to his father. Throughout the interview I felt troubled, I think it was caused by observing Louise's body language. Although she never once complained, she constantly shifted position and would not settle. As I was leaving I said something like 'You are tired aren't you?' and she answered by quizzing me on why had I said that. The many changes since Laura's [her daughter's leukaemia] diagnosis seem really to have exerted their effect on her.

During this, which transpired to be our final interview, she spoke to me about how she worried about her cancer recurring:

I would say if I sneezed I would think, 'Oh God, it is back!' If I do not feel like my breakfast, I would feel quite frozen with fear. It is like being pregnant, you are aware of it all day. You can go on but the one thing is that you are aware of it. It does not particularly influence what you do, but you know it. I would say it is never out of your head. If I yawn, then I think, I am getting tired . . . It is back but it is reasonable enough to be tired. I would still feel a sense of dread until that goes away, the other day I got the tiniest little pain in my hand and deduced . . . even a pain in my instep . . . If I even scratch . . . I have had asthma all my life but now when I get it, I see it as an unusual presentation of lung cancer. When I went in [to hospital] last March, I refused to have X-rays. The doctors laughed but they do not understand the fear. Today, I did not buy sweets and worried the whole way down the [hospital] corridor that my appetite was going. There was a time I thought I was losing that dreadful fear . . . I would say that is one of the worst things about cancer, everything that happens you wonder about. I would not get under a scanner for anything. It takes very little to highlight it.

Her experience of illness had been so traumatising that the fear of it returning dominated her life. The very idea threatened her to such an extent that she felt 'frozen with fear', and had 'a sense of dread'. She was in a position where she monitored even her body's most natural and spontaneous functions such as sneezing and yawning, in a desperate bid to pre-empt and deal with the most primitive signs of the sly return of her cancer. Most tellingly, though, Louise drew an analogy between cancer and pregnancy. Stacey considers this well established link and comments:

With pregnancy and cancer, where is the certainty of separation? When is the cord really cut? The tumour promises separation after surgical delivery into the world; yet the bond continues with the threat that some malignant cells remain in the warmth of the body to shelter from outside attack. (1997: 91)

It seemed ironic, too, that Louise detected her lump whilst breastfeeding her infant. The act of nurturing new life had become contaminated with nuances of death. Her tendency toward self-scrutiny might have been more alarming for her because, as a doctor, she had knowledge of the seriousness of any potential symptoms. Louise believed that her medical training had made appointments with health professionals more difficult than for a lay person. She told me:

It is good in some ways having medical knowledge. I suspect that makes it worse but I would hate to be without it. There are some things that I can rationalise but I am no different from Joe Bloggs when I get the things. When I see the other patients, I envy them; one thing does not inevitably lead to another in their heads, the implications of things may not dawn on them. I see them with test results and still smiling. I think it makes it easier for the doctors in one way, because they can talk in medical terms; doctors love that. I have worked there and know them very well. But if things go anyway other than perfectly, they hate it, because if you start asking . . . I can see that they do not know that much at all. It is fine if everything is going well, if not then I think they get a bit shadier. Start avoiding me. I think they find it merely interesting. If I ask about the side effects of a drug, they hate that, wish you could turn into a non-doctor for the duration. To get around it, they treat you as a doctor, as if 'We are all discussing another case here.' This patient, who just happens to be me, but they forget that and get technical. 'An interesting case now let's go on our way.' It is almost easy for me to fall into this, I sometimes acquiesce and then, in the car, wish I had not been such a doctor but more like a patient. Sometimes I feel as if we are not discussing me or my child, [Laura who has leukaemia] but a case of something else and I let them do that. They do not like my knowledge. The conversation comes to a halt if you show you are upset, it is 'Get her out!' They don't want you really involved. If you say, 'Right, abnormal liver function, what is the most likely cause of that?' they are much happier with that factual exchange. [Louise then parodied herself as being ignorant of her medical knowledge] 'No, I'm not concerned with her wee liver, it is not that important is it?'

Like Douglas's (1984) anomalous categories, Louise found herself being treated as 'matter out of place'. She had received a medical training like her doctors, she even knew 'them very well' but, in the role of patient, she had stepped outside of the category in which she was previously recognised. They did not know how to deal with her, as a former colleague with whom they probably even socialised. This caused the boundaries in their relationship to be redefined. As a result, they, not surprisingly, felt uncomfortable; she had become an embarrassment, someone to be tolerated with politeness. Louise believed that the doctors who treated her perceived her to be in some way threatening. As she said 'the implications of things may not dawn on' other patients but they are frighteningly clear to her. When she attempted to consolidate her knowledge of her own illness by asking questions, the doctors became 'shadier. Start avoiding'. She believed that she may actually have been thrown out of a consultation because she 'can see that they do not know that much at all'. Her training enabled her to see the bare facts, like the child in the fairy story of *The Emperor's New Clothes*, and that reality threatened her doctors. This does not seem surprising when she told me that she believed:

The death rate from breast cancer has not changed. Say all the people who got breast cancer the year I got it . . . they [the doctors] knew quite well that most of us would have had a recurrence within two or three years and probably be dead. I don't feel that they [the doctors] are honest enough to say that and that this treatment will make no difference. There are a lot of lies told about cancer. Say the lymphomas . . . The survival rate has risen, early detections changed things, skin cancers account for a lot of what they call the high survival rate. Bowel cancer detected early . . . But the biggies, lung cancer, non-Hodgkin's, there is no change using conventional means of looking after yourself. There is a bleak road ahead of those people. Should they tell people that and say, 'We don't have the answer, look elsewhere?' I think it is a sham, bringing in people with cancer and filling them up with chemo. If I had cancer again, tomorrow, I would have the surgery, but I wouldn't go through the chemo.[1] They damn well nearly killed me. They wanted me to have treatment earlier this year, 'Just a chemo thing, a couple of shots.' I kept pushing and pushing, 'Why, why?' and the doctor said, 'Well, at least it would make us feel better.' I am not having that. It is a lottery, you can do whatever you want with statistics, you can prove that people who default from follow-up have longer survival. They are, in fact, likely to do better! Last year,

[1] You will remember how, in the section of this book called 'Departure', Louise's four-year-old daughter was diagnosed with leukaemia. That diagnosis occurred some weeks after this interview, that November. Louise did, in fact, choose for her daughter to be treated with chemotherapy and she herself went on to receive two further lines of it before she died.

summer/autumn, I was to have six to eight rounds of chemo, all building up to this big megadose of stem cell transplant. Take you in and blast you with very high dose, I was dreading having to go in for it, the first dose literally . . . I nearly died, ambulance to hospital. Physically, I feel I am dying, I couldn't describe how ill I was and that was treatment making me ill like that. I read quite a lot of research articles and chemo's effectiveness in breast cancer has never been proven.

At this stage, Louise had become so firmly established in her role as patient that, when referring to her experiences, she labelled the doctors as 'them' and aligned herself with 'us', the patients. This significant switch was evident when she said 'I don't know how many would have got breast cancer the year I got it, but they [the doctors] knew quite well that most of us [the patients] would have had a recurrence'. Her medical training also seemed to count against her as it equipped her with a realistic map that defined the boundaries of what scientific treatment can and cannot do. Her knowledge of these limitations caused her to question the integrity of those doctors who, she thought, cannot even be 'honest with themselves about what they are doing'.

In view of this belief it is not surprising that she informed me later that she had:

. . . removed control from the doctors. Now, I love the doctors who look after me but they do it too much. I didn't go to them with my symptoms, I thought, once that is mentioned, there will be a chain of events over which I have no control. And that is the big thing, I can never get them to say, 'This is the story, this is what you need to do now.' It is very hard to retain control in the hospital. I told them I don't want to come back unless I need to. I told them, 'I consult lots of people about my health and I do consider you a cog in the wheel . . .' I spent half an hour making up for the insult. I pulled out of the hospital. They ask me if I have appointments and I say, 'I don't know!' I see them [her appointment cards] and tear them up. I know them both [her principal doctors] very well, and they are lovely. They are both in a very medical model and they feel they own the cancer. Sorry, that is not the way I see it at all, and I feel they will have me cared to death if I allow it. Not what I need at the minute!

Louise was hurt and angry. Instead of having the power to help others, as she did when she herself was a doctor, she was now reluctantly, subject to that power. She was fighting to maintain some level of power in the unwelcome position in which she found herself but, even when she did manage to articulate something of this anger and lashed out at her helpers as being just a 'cog in the wheel', she felt so bad that she spent 'half an hour making up for the insult'. Could it be that she felt herself to be the cog rather than her doctor? She appeared to need what it was impossible for her to have; certainty of survival. Hurt and angry, she needed to prove that she could still exercise some element of control, even if the only channel left open to her to vent her frustration was by symbolically ripping up her appointment cards! In doing so she was committing symbolic violence toward the very system which made her feel so constrained, and which, as she told me during the opening moments of our very first interview, she realised was:

... not going to cure you, save your life. Perhaps no one is going to save your life but you are going to have to make a fight for it yourself.

Losing control over her life was something that she wrestled with. She told me that:

I accept . . . I know tomorrow . . . Anything could happen to me . . . I don't think it will anymore. There was a time I just sat waiting for whatever would crop up that day. That feeling is gone, because I feel I have now started to do things, which I know can cure cancer. I can't say that they will cure my cancer but I feel I am tackling my illness again on every front, mainly dietary. I am doing this for the long term, other things to help me cope. That is where I am at. My major preoccupations are, to get well, to aid my husband to get him as well as he can and to bring up my children, run my house and everything else . . . I have a big spiritual aspect to my life as well, which I would be trying to develop. But things like social life, career ambitions, even the ordinary getting of life has all gone by the wayside, I feel I am on a definite project of getting myself well, perhaps even claiming my future. It is hard to be disciplined; it demands a bloody mindedness . . .

Although aware that her future was out of her hands, Louise was incapable of sitting back and passively accepting what might come. Her terrible experience with her chemotherapy left her glad to be alive and anxious to do all she could to ensure that she would stay that way. She had prioritised her life and was determined to make it a success; she explained how she is:

... no longer feeding my body anything toxic, I am feeding it very, very healthy nutrients, I would practically bless the food before I eat it, I wish it luck, 'Go in there and work for me!'

At this stage, Louise felt really positive about her ability to change her future; she even discussed some of the benefits her illness had brought. She felt that her cancer had removed:

. . . responsibilities from you. Folk think I am a hero if I get up out of bed in the morning. I worked bloody hard to be a doctor but no need to bother with that any more. If I smile, I am just beatified and you are awarded the position, 'Isn't she bloody marvellous!' and I now know that position and it is great to be in . . . I am removed from competition. I don't feel that sense of embarrassment I got when people asked if I was a partner [in the surgery where she worked]. I am not in that competition any more. Those are the things that I am consciously away from. I am in another wee world that none of them know anything about. I can be a little hero without having to do all that much.

In line with Parsons' (1951) criterion for the sick role, her illness had sanctioned her withdrawal from employment, absolving her from not only her duties but also the psychological strain of striving for promotion. Further, Louise herself had become aware that the community in which she lived applauded how she managed her life, to the extent that she realised they interpreted her behaviour as heroic. She continued with that theme later, explaining how when she worked she:

. . . had to make massive adaptations. As a doctor I was always aware that I could do that. Move to a new town where I know no one every six months. But in all this illness, I was awarded a hero status by people. I wonder if I would find it so easy to adapt if that wasn't the case. There has been no personal hurt in my things, like if Derek was having an affair; that would be different. Could I adapt to that? I have no doubts that I can pull us through this; I don't know that Derek could. I have no doubt that I will bring those children up.

As a doctor Louise had a very demanding schedule, compounded by the necessity to uproot herself socially at regular intervals. She thought it ironic that, when an intense pro-active response was required just to maintain her job, this went almost unobserved by her friends, but when in remission from a critical illness and she was experiencing her life to be calm and passive, she was lauded by her social group and 'awarded a hero status'. Louise appeared to feel that her cancer had acted like a membrane, which had distorted how others perceived her. She had adapted from living in a situation where she was responsible for making life and death decisions about others, to one in which she was, at times, 'not even able to have made a cup of tea'. Now that she was more able and could exercise some power, she remembered how terrible was the loss of that power. Pensively, she told me that she believed:

. . . we are completely in God's hands and that there is no point in my trying to worry or control the situation. All I can do is be this child's mother [her daughter Laura], that is all I can do. Look after her for as long as I am allowed to do that. What is the point in me railing on . . . and getting upset? Now having said that, I am not sleeping right, I have enormous cares about the child but I also have the sense that . . . suddenly I am being carried on an eagle's back, something is carrying me, I don't know where. I am living in a way that I never lived before. I thought I had lived it before but today at the hospital they started to tell me [Laura's] future treatment schedule and I could feel the lip beginning to go. They are doing a test in three weeks and she [Laura] is to be in remission then and I thought, 'Well, what if she is not?' And then I thought, 'Well, we will have to deal with it when it comes' but I have heard that so many times before, that means shit. I had a friend who said 'Get today over with first!'

Susan

I first met 42-year-old Susan sixteen months before her death. I was aware, even before then, that she had recently been the subject of a BBC documentary film on living with cancer. As we sipped coffee in her living room, replete with souvenirs from her travels and work in the US, she explained that she was a PE teacher, who came from a family of eight children and that she was divorced and lived alone. She was in the shower when she found her original tumour, one year before we met. She saw her GP within 24 hours and had a partial mastectomy and radiotherapy. Having been pronounced cured, she almost immediately found another lump in her other breast and again endured a battery of gruelling tests and this time had a radical mastectomy. These events sparked a crisis. She told me that she said:

'You Bastard, God!' God and I have had real choice conversations, not 'Why me, why am I in this place again?' but 'I don't know what You are playing at, I got the point last time, I changed my life, I know it has to be somebody.' But I just couldn't believe that he was putting me through this again. I said, 'You better sort this out, I will deal with this, provided there is a reason, I will put up with this, but I can't see why. I don't have time, so sort this out!' When you are in the first three or four days of a cancer diagnosis you don't sleep, you are not conscious of sleeping to any great state, it was 7[am] and the answer was at the end of my nose. I should have done something with my previous cancer experience, I benefited, but I didn't do anything beyond me, and suddenly I knew I needed to tell my story. I have lots of connections with the media, I rang a producer friend and told him I wanted to tell my story. He agreed. An hour later the BBC rang and I knew the [documentary] programme was going to be done. People have said to me, 'How could you do it, expose yourself to that extent?' I have no idea but I know that from that moment on, I never stopped to think. I just kept moving until the thing was finished and it was six months worth of that project. I was inspired, it was not me that was doing it.

Scrutiny of Susan's quotation might reveal elements of what some may consider to be Kubler-Ross's (1995) bargaining and also of the altruism referred to by Young and Cullen (1996) who discuss how people who are dying often cultivate their sense of altruism, tending to turn away from self-love and developing their benevolence toward others.

Susan told me that:

I know in my heart that I am not dying of cancer, at least, not now. I have no idea what is around the next corner. I know that I have been set free for a reason, the programme . . .

Becker (1973) argues that much of human culture is constructed in an attempt to evade the fear of death that he believes to be inherent. He suggests that, haunted at a subconscious level by this knowledge, individuals throw themselves into a host of projects much as Susan did. Arthur Frank's book, *The Wounded Story Teller*, specifically addresses the stories told by people who are ill and questions why these stories are told. He writes:

Seriously ill people are wounded not just in body but in voice. They need to become storytellers in order to recover the voices that illness and its treatment often take away. (1995: xii)

As a consequence of her surgery Susan felt secure, certain that she was cancer free, to the extent that during that first interview she told me:

I am not sick at all. In other words, I do not feel sick. I have had a problem with this. In the course of the first and second cancer, a friend heard me say that I have had cancer. I have had it and I don't have it any more and she was very concerned for me because what she heard was someone in denial, denying the seriousness of the situation. She challenged me and, over a period of weeks, we had huge rows. She wanted me to be realistic about what was going on. Cancer is life threatening, people die from cancer. I am aware of that and also aware that many, many people survive cancer, so there was no reason for me not to be one of the ones who survived it. So when I say, I have had cancer, I mean, I have had cancer. I have had surgery to remove the diseased cells and they are gone, the malignant cells are gone. I have had treatment, radiotherapy and chemotherapy to chase the rogue cells and to deflect the possibility of it recurring. I still feel comfortable saying, 'I have had cancer but I no longer have it.' But I am aware that I live with the threat and the possibility of it coming back. When I say, 'I am living with cancer', what I mean is, 'I am living with the threat of cancer.' I have been the one woman in twelve twice [she was referring to statistics on women with breast cancer]. To have it once is unfortunate, to have it twice is downright careless. I just get on with it. I have had worse period pains, worse headaches, regular illness, but I have never felt sick with cancer. You expect to be at death's door, to be constantly ill . . . cancer does not make you ill, the treatment does.

Susan was angry. Her experiences had left her feeling so vulnerable that she had resorted to reciting a virtual mantra 'I have had . . .' fixed, it should be observed, firmly in the past tense, and which, in the above quotation alone, she used nine times. Her need to believe that she was 'cancer free' was so great that she placed it firmly in the past, a situation that, she persuaded herself, held no relevance to her current life. Unfortunately for Susan, this is not how the disease is perceived by mainstream society and she found herself challenged by a friend, confronted by the reality of her situation. As the only way she could cope with her position was by situating the threat in the past, her relationship with her friend suffered, they had 'huge rows' in which both parties remained so entrenched in their own convictions that they extended 'over a period of weeks'. Her family, too, found her position difficult to understand. Sometimes, she needed to:

. . . sit down and talk about stuff that is going on and a lot of this stuff is very hard for some members of my family to take on board. I think I am fairly unique to my reaction to my cancer, I am seeing it solely as something of value and I know from talking to people that that is a very different approach. I don't see myself as a victim, as 'Poor me', somebody who has to be taken care of. When people come to me with that voice 'Susan! How are you?' and the head goes on one side, and the face scrunches up, I don't need any of that! A lot of my family are of that ilk, where it would be a huge drama, toeing the medical line, not arguing with doctor and so on. I believe that they find my approach hard to take and, therefore, they don't discuss stuff with me; a lot of it is done on a superficial level, 'How are you? Here is a bunch of flowers. Do you need anything?' kind of stuff, but very few . . . but that is the level of support that they can offer.

Susan felt frustrated. Although she most definitely did not want pity, there were times when she would have valued a simple conversation with her family about her position. She needed their reassurance. She was disappointed that they did not offer her that or even understand her need to question medical judgement. She did not complain to them but accepted instead the flowers they offered, realising that that was their way. However, she felt extremely upset when:

My partner at the time was particularly not there when I needed it most. He actually saw my baldness on the television. He works in the media, heard my voice on the programme, and was completely shocked. He was not happy with my baldness . . . Was not happy with the way I conducted myself through my illness. Thought I was exposing myself. I was being too revealing, so all of that was very difficult . . . He couldn't support me when I needed him most. He was there for the first surgery but not for the second, which was the more traumatic. The six-year relationship ended.

As a consequence of using her experiences to help others, she suffered. Susan, who believed her motives in contributing to the film were completely altruistic, felt bewildered and hurt. At the time she 'needed it most' she again felt abandoned and bereft of support. She was also shortly to be faced with an objective assessment of her position. She told me:

. . . the doctor who told me I had cancer took me to one side and . . . It is like a reality check. [her doctor said] 'Even though we have said you are cancer free after your treatment, there is still the risk of recurrence', and that hit me like a real blow because I was concentrating on the future . . . On moving forward and to be brought back to the reality that it could come back was a negative road that I did not want to go down. There was always the risk of recurrence. After the chemo, it is more fair of them to say, 'We assume that you are cancer free' rather than 'You are back to normal.' Normal being that you stand as much chance of getting cancer as anyone else but when you have been there twice, that is not very reassuring because you must be of a higher risk. She reminded me that there was always the possibility of recurrence and then I was annoyed.

In spite of the heightened vigilance that Susan exercised over her body, she still felt sufficiently safe from the threat of her cancer's recurrence to experience 'like a real blow' the threatening information which her doctor imparted. She had constructed and maintained a psychological haven in which 'there was no reason for me not to be one of the ones who survived it'. Although her doctor's words had confronted her with her own denial, she still felt determined that she would conquer her awful disease. She continued telling me her story, explaining how she felt she:

. . . was really well and looking fabulous. Three months ago I got a pain in my shoulder . . . was excruciating, worst I had ever experienced, they diagnosed a frozen shoulder . . . but it persisted . . . I decided to have them X-ray to confirm that it was a frozen shoulder. I was having to fight . . . They realised that they were dealing with somebody who is not going to give up, so they gave in. The timing is unbelievable. Whilst waiting for the results, I went back to the [cancer] support club where I work, as it was a year to the day since I had my mastectomy! They congratulated me for getting to the first year, which is like a milestone . . . The results confirmed the frozen shoulder but threw up hot spots on the rib cage . . . [The consultant] . . . came down, called me in, showed me the frozen shoulder and I said 'I am reassured.' Then he said, 'There is more.' He showed me shadows on the ribs. He said, 'I think we are dealing with secondary spread.' I heard those words and did not register and I asked what it meant. He said, 'Metastasis' and I knew . . . I stopped talking and went into shock. I could see [it] very clearly on three ribs. Later we saw a few more on other ribs. I sat down and he told me he wanted to do further tests. He said, 'If it has metastasised to the bone, it may turn up in other organs.' I said, 'When do you want me to come back?' and he said, 'Today!' That was the second blow. I thought, 'Oh this guy means business.' I asked if I needed to have somebody with me and he said, 'Yes I think you do.' So I knew I was in trouble. I had to think very clearly, 'Who do I call on for this one?' The sister that I needed, who has been with me for the past two diagnoses has gone to Nigeria. My other sister and my mother would go to pieces, which they did later but I have a friend . . . a master of controlling her emotions, she came. They called me in and said that the cancer had metastasised to the bone and the liver was highly suspicious. I went to pieces, because [cancer of the] liver is not good. One of the drawbacks of being knowledgeable about cancer, because of all my reading, you get to recognise the good, easy to deal with cancers, and the not so easy to deal with. Liver is not so easy to deal with.

Despite her physical pain, which suggested the symptom's gravity and the need for it to be taken seriously, she had to fight to have the X-ray taken. Frightened and alone, she returned to the cancer support centre, presumably to derive encouragement from her colleagues. There, she celebrated the first of, what I presume she hoped would be, many anniversaries of her mastectomy.

This was the state of mind in which she returned to learn her third cancer diagnosis. She was so traumatised by her doctor's words that they 'did not register' and she 'stopped talking and went into shock'. Although traumatised, she appreciated the need to 'think clearly' and seek immediate social support. She had, until then, been alone and now was in desperate need of comfort and assurance.

As that awful consultation continued and the information she learned grew worse, such was her emotional state that she eventually believed that she felt she 'went to pieces'. She went on:

. . . was just terrible. I went into my usual pain. I recognise my pattern; my body's ability to absorb shock is three days. I went into a three day complete blackness. All the support came out of the woodwork, the prayers started . . . This was the second day; you cry for twenty-four hours and then the tears stop. I started trying to work out my chances here. I had some practical support in that a friend, Amy, is a nurse from the cancer support group where I volunteer. Another girl in my group, Siobhan, had died of cancer, so we were very close. Amy came over and I said, 'You know I like straight talking and I also need you to be gentle, but I know the liver is not good' and Amy said, 'Yes, you are right, it is not good.' I also knew Siobhan had dealt with the liver before she died. 'It is not good but it is not impossible', she said, 'Yes, it is not impossible, but it is difficult.' I said, 'I am looking for something to hang on with' but she said, 'The difference between you and Siobhan is that, by the time she was diagnosed with the liver, she was in a very weakened state, whereas you are coming from a position of strength and power and good health and youth so your chances would be better than Siobhan's.' I still don't think I look or act or think like the stereotypical cancer victim. So that gave me a bit of hope and everyone was praying . . . One of the things we needed was the miracle that it would not be in the liver and you don't sleep through this whole period. At one point, I wanted to be on my own. You don't sleep but you don't want people around either because people are here during the day and you talk yourself silly and they are making all these reassuring noises and there comes a point when you just want people to go and be on your own.

This was the third time Susan had been confronted with the fact that her life was at risk. She had been in this awful position before and could recognise her own response and coping mechanisms. She could see and confidently discuss her 'usual pain, I recognise my pattern'. Her experience of living with cancer was not positive. She described how she endured 'three day[s] complete blackness', during which time her social group rallied together to offer her their support. She was sufficiently buoyed up to seek out one special source of potential reassurance and turned to her nurse friend. Her problem was that, as a result of having had cancer for such a long period, she had had friendships with others, who like her, have cancer. It is inevitable that she would have been affected by their deaths and learned something of the course she feared her own journey might take. Nonetheless, Susan clung to her belief that she was in some way different from others with cancer. She appeared almost desperate in her declaration that she didn't 'look or act or think like the stereotypical cancer victim'. She was splitting herself off from others with cancer in the hope that she might survive it, that she would be the special one. All she had was 'a bit of hope' and she hung on to the chance of a miracle. She drew comfort from her friends and family though she found too much social input intrusive: 'you just want people to go and be on your own.'

However, it was not, apparently, human contact she wished to escape but the social group as an integral unit:

I had been in and out of sleep and at 4.55 [am], rang a friend who just happened to have popped up a few days earlier and had not known about my cancer and was pretty devastated. John came over. [She began to cry] I just needed to be held. He held on to me for three hours and allowed me to cry. It was not an awful morbid situation, it was a very funny three-hour experience. We were down here, drinking orange at 5 [am], and I said, 'I am exhausted. I'll go to bed just to rest.' I laid on the line what I needed from him and he was there and we were laughing and crying and serious talking . . . At 8 [am] I turned on the news to find that the Orange men were not going to march and I said to God, 'I want another miracle', because I was going at 10.30 for a CT scan. 'As long as you are in miracle mode, don't forget me!' John was fascinated because he is not spiritual or religious and he allowed me to waffle on like an idiot. Two hours later I got the miracle I needed! The scan did not confirm cancer in the liver, I have bone cancer, so it is just a matter of making the most of a shitty situation. I was breaking that news to people who thought I was crazy 'She has bone cancer and it is good news?' But if God takes the difficult one and leaves you with the controllable one, that is good news.

Although turning away from her supportive network, Susan still craved social comfort, a friend who she believed could help. Her heightened recall of that terrible night reveals something of the strength of the friendship she shared with John. Contacting him outside accepted social hours was an indicator of the depth of that relationship. Although Susan telephoned her friend at 4.55 am and was probably aware that she was not only infringing on his privacy but also probably wakening him, her need of succour was such that she overcame this social barrier and shared what was left of the night, 'laughing and crying and serious talking'. Significantly, this friendship spanned their differences. John, was 'not spiritual or religious' yet Susan and the majority of her social grouping were. Susan, although terribly distressed, was obviously aware enough to realise that he 'allowed me to waffle on like an idiot'. She realised that her behaviour was not what might be normally accepted. It would appear that she felt that the crisis entitled her to disregard normal socially sanctioned behaviour to the extent of intruding on another's sleep, requesting their presence and then expecting their complete attention. Although we did not ever discuss politics, the fact that she was a Roman Catholic may have led her to perceive a political march from a Protestant group as threatening and it may be that she interpreted the group's decision not to march that day as a metaphor for the miracle she prayed for. Just as the Orange men's march was a threat to the political stability of the city, the body social where she lived, so too was her cancer spreading to her liver a threat to her body corporeal. When she learned that the cancer had not yet spread there but instead to her bones, she interpreted this as a sign from God and became elated to the extent that she feared that people might have thought her 'crazy'! She felt now that she had some hope of controlling her disease. She continued:

I began to plan my strategy. It is all about choices, decisions and accepting responsibility for your own recovery . . . The doctor wanted to begin the chemo right away. I am not convinced by the chemo because it has not worked. He is coming at me with a harsher regime of drugs over a longer period of time. That is all he knows. 'If one round of chemo does not work, we will try another.' I am not looking at it scientifically but from a logical, practical way. I said, 'This is what we are doing!' He knows not to patronise me and he folded his arms. I could see the nurses look but it is my game. I am the captain of the team. I am the All Star and I devise the game plan and when it is there I will share it. So long as everyone recognises that they are just team players but that I am the captain. We will break down consultant, oncologist, mister, doctor barriers that get in the way of healing. When I talk about my consultant I call him Paul and I have people tell me, 'Oh! "Paul?" You are on first name terms . . . ?' It is just that he is on my team. Get rid of the awesome stuff. [She then parodied herself speaking to her consultant, saying:] 'Please do not take offence, I am not criticising you, I am criticising the treatment which is on offer! Fact, the treatment has not worked. With utmost respect, all you [the medical team] know is to come at me with more treatment, so I would be a fool if I left myself solely in your hands!' I wonder, if and when he loses patients, does he think 'Was there anything else I could have done?' But he is tunnel vision medical. I said 'Paul, much as I don't want the chemo . . .' I could see the nurse shudder, because no one says, 'No', I am sure they have not come across too many refusals. 'I will go for your chemo but let's put a question mark on the eight [treatments], let's go for three and review the situation!'

Susan had examined her dilemma and, in the face of what seemed like a hopeless situation, had decided to assume 'responsibility' for her own recovery. She believed that medical science was continuing to let her down and so was challenging it. She used American slang and sporting terminology referring to herself as 'the captain, the All Star', of her team of professionals. Her final hope rested in her decision to make drastic changes to her diet:

Strand two of my plan is about my supporting the chemo with herbal remedies to bolster my immune system. Allowing the chemo to do what it needs to but also support the healthy cells. I also came across a Macrobiotic diet. Very strict vegetarian Japanese influence. Includes things we are not used to. I saw it five years ago, in pre-cancerous days. I thought, 'Interesting . . . but it does not apply.' It has popped up a lot but more recently in the past year, to the extent that I cannot believe I did not jump at it a year ago. But then there was no sense of urgency, because I was doing so well after the first cancer. After the second cancer, there was nothing [no hope]. Your third cancer diagnosis, it is like the biggest wake up call you have ever had in your life. This is my third chance. It is like God said, 'I told you there was a problem once and twice. Now wake up!' Now a sense of urgency that I need to go into some kind of action is here and I have switched. It is the most challenging process I have ever encountered beyond cancer.

If Susan had felt threatened by her two previous diagnoses, this third one galvanised her into immediate action. So compelled was she to do all within her power to continue living, that she was prepared to entirely remodel not only her diet but also her way of life. In telling me about her plans she, a non-smoker, drew an analogy with smoking, telling me:

To quit smoking overnight requires discipline and I recognise that, except that I feel that I have a motivation. For me it is essential. I equate it with someone holding a gun at my head and about to fire the trigger. This recent diagnosis feels to me like that. Like God has taken me by the scruff of the neck and given me such a shake. He fired two warning shots and I thought I had reacted appropriately to my cancer but I really didn't. Think about it, what person with a cancer diagnosis goes out and makes a television programme about it. I was well intentioned, for other people, but what about Susan? It was such a misuse of energy in terms of Susan, the person who is of value . . . if someone I know had done that I would have said, 'You are crazy!' My counsellor calls me John Wayne, kicking open the bar room door, storming in with guns blazing and cleaning up the town. I needed to do it to recognise that it was the wrong thing to do. I'm not blaming myself but God said, 'Yo! This is your third go!' The analogy of a gun pointed at your head is pretty scary; that is a frightening thought. It is like Russian roulette. The gun at my head . . . I know that sounds like a scary idea but I am not doing that to frighten myself but to remind myself that it is this crucial. Getting it right means taking care of me, which is my strategy. Six months, totally dedicated to Susan. Nobody else.

Susan was frantic to do all within her power, anything that might con-tribute to her survival. So desperate was she that she used the metaphor of violence, 'someone holding a gun over my head and about to let go of the trigger', telling me it was as though 'God has fired two warning shots'. Not surprisingly, she felt terrified. Attempting to alleviate her plight, she decided to turn away from the social, even to the extent of avoiding what she might once have seen as special treats, like birthdays. She did not care what conclusions others might draw, she felt that she had nothing more to lose.

She believed her plan was working as, during our third interview, she optimistically explained to me how she felt she was:

. . . well on my way! But then the hospital have a different outlook, very different markers, for example, the activity of the white cells. If the immune system is damaged, which lowers the white cells, they cannot give you chemo. They monitor that carefully. Sometimes it drops, which annoys me because I am doing everything not to allow that to happen, in terms of diet, rest and relaxation, so that unnerves me a wee bit but the hospital assures me that that is normal. Still I agitate that my body does not do what I tell it to do but Paul who refers to me as his 'big strong woman', said, 'No, no, I am confident enough to give it [chemotherapy] to you.' At the next treatment, it [her white cell count] went down again and he talked about a series of injections to artificially bring the count up. Unfortunately, I have spoken to one woman who told me that they are worse than anything you have ever had. Even worse than the cancer and stupidly I bought into that. What I know is that that was her experience, it does not have to be mine. But it unnerved me when I heard him talking about them. They [the medical team] brought me in to start the injections. I was thinking, 'I don't want to have these, I hate these injections.' I had felt really good and I asked them to test my blood and it was up again! So I am back in control again. I am fine. This time last weekend I was in bits but I have reconciled myself that I have to take painkillers. With this diagnosis, I am feeling pain that I have not felt before and that is because the cancer is in the bone, so it is natural that it is sore.

Susan was, of course, aware that her condition was anything but normal for those in mainstream society. She felt frightened and frustrated because, in spite of her desperate efforts to maintain her health, she was still experiencing worrying dips in her body's performance. She was aware that her body would just not comply with her wishes. She was psychologically shaken by what she heard about her proposed treatment from others, although she acknowledged that, as an individual, she might respond differently. Her relief at being told that her blood count met the criteria for her chemotherapy to be administered was palpable. What is important about this quotation, though, is that it provides evidence of the extremes of emotion, which are experienced as part of a cancer journey. She began by using upbeat terminology; she had felt 'Well on my [her] way!' but went on to confide that she 'agitate[d]' to the extent that she became 'unnerved'. There is a dramatic switch then to her feeling 'really, good' to the level of saying confidently 'I am fine'; all of this though is set against 'This time last weekend I was in bits' and the fact that she is 'feeling pain that I have not felt before'.

Through all of this angst, she attempted to keep her spirits up. She said:

At the time of the diagnosis, I was so frightened I could taste the fear and it was awful. The worst taste I have ever had. That has disappeared and I am wildly excited about where I am now.

Although by our last interview her cancer had in fact spread to her liver, she closed it on a positive note:

In my heart, I know that I have the solutions to my problems . . . to my cancer problem, my soul knows how to deal with this cancer problem. You have to ask the question, ask yourself. Only someone with cancer knows . . .

Rose

Estranged from her husband, 48-year-old Rose lived with her two teenage children, Marie and Tony, in a terraced council house that was part of a scheme originally built for travelling people. Some months after I began interviewing her, she confided that 19-year-old Marie was pregnant and would give birth in January. She was concerned, too, for 18-year-old Tony who, with financial help from her mother, was in the US attending a specialist course in flying, which she hoped would serve as the basis of a worthwhile career. Once a successful interior design consultant, living with her cancer, originally detected seventeen years earlier, had caused Rose severe financial hardship resulting in bankruptcy and devastating what was once a very comfortable way of life.

Her knowledge of design and colour was evident in how she had decorated the small sitting room that faced onto the hardstanding at the front of the house. Elegant, antique French sofas and swagged curtains, contraband from her earlier life, jarred with the tyreless cars, up on blocks, that loomed through the window. The cream on cream heavily embossed carpet was, in places, badly soiled and came to stand for me as a metaphor for her cancer.

During our first interview she began her story:

I had problems breast-feeding both my children and, after my son was born, I developed lumps in my breasts, particularly my left. By the time he was nine months old, they told me that I had a lump in the breast, which could be cancer. I had a lumpectomy, about two-thirds of the breast taken away and I did have breast cancer. I also had it in my lymph glands under my arm. At that time the medical team decided that 'it wasn't worth treating me' and they gave me radiotherapy for the pain. However, it returned six years ago. So I had about ten years of remission. Obviously, I was ill first time around but not as ill as I am now. Five or six years ago, I had terrible pains in my head, I couldn't move. I was feeling really tired and all sorts of symptoms and over the last five years the cancer has spread. I now have a tumour in my spine and five or six hot spots. I have four hot spots in my ribs and one in my right shoulder. I have since then lost my right breast in a total mastectomy and had my lymph glands removed from the right side as well. I have lost the total use of one lung, which has filled with fluid and can't have anything done to it because it is not solid. I have some, 25 to 30, small satellite tumours around my right side, I also have had a hysterectomy and, during this time, I have also had kidney problems. I have had umpteen operations, so basically that is where I am now.

She remembered clearly the events of six years before, when her cancer returned and how she had to fight the medics to learn her prognosis:

They didn't tell me, I asked them. I said to my Macmillan nurse, 'I know I am very ill and I don't know if I am going to make it or not.' She said, 'Well I don't really know, you must speak to the doctor.' I said, 'I want him to be perfectly honest because I have a young family and there are things I need to sort out.' My consultant came to see me and he said, 'Yes, you are very ill' and I asked him, 'How long?' [left to live] and he looked at me. I don't think he really wanted to say but I pushed. I said, 'I need to know, it's not that I want to know, I have to sort my affairs out. I must know.' So he said 'Very well, in that case, we can tell you. Ten days. That is the best scenario that I can give you, I can't give you better.' I actually expected it to be shorter, so it was a bit of a boost. I didn't expect that much, not the way I was at the time, I mean I had gone up to 16 and a half stone [twice her normal body weight], I had three double chins, I couldn't walk, I just had to move myself slightly and I was sick. I just couldn't do anything. So when he said, 'Ten days', it might have surprised some people but not me. Bearing in mind that I have had this disease for a very long time, so it is an old enemy, it is not a new one. I had some idea.

Rose, who had recovered well from her first cancer, was sufficiently astute to realise that her second cancer was more serious. The level of pain and her impeded physical performance were sufficient to inform her that she might die. Her primary concern was to provide for her children, so she directly confronted the medics, hoping to gain further information. She needed a realistic appraisal of her condition in order to prepare herself and others for her death. As she told me 'the only thing I worried about was that if I went . . . the children were so young and I knew that their father really wasn't interested in looking after them. So I did worry.' The information she sought, even when it came, was not given freely. Her consultant said:

. . . there was absolutely nothing they could do. I was sleeping one hour in twenty-four. The medication wasn't working . . . I had gone past desperation. At one point, I got so desperate, I was so frightened, I was so petrified . . . And then I thought, 'Well, I can't be petrified because my children will sense it, it is not right. If it is time to go, it is time to go, there is nothing that I can actually do to actually control that.'

Although she had been in remission from her cancer for ten years, before the second diagnosis, much of that time had been spent living in daily fear of its return. Now it had reappeared in such a vitriolic and accelerated form, she was aware that medical science was not as curative as she had hoped and this second diagnosis left her feeling 'desperate', 'frightened' and 'petrified'. However, she valiantly attempted to override her emotions and to mask her true feelings from her children. Rose continued:

I was so ill at the time that I couldn't cope with anything . . . It devastated me, totally devastated me, I cried for the whole time. The children were wonderful, they came in and almost treated me as if I wasn't ill, which was like a tonic. I needed that, I needed someone to say, 'God, you look terrible today' or 'You look really good today, Mum! Have you just washed your hair?' The most important thing was to feel normal . . .

Rose drew consolation from her children who, she believed, were in urgent need of her protection. Rather than becoming introspective and withdrawing from her social obligations, as the sick role entitled her to, she made every effort instead to ensure a stable future for her children. She told me:

I don't know if it is faith or if it is just bloody mindedness but for me to be told ten days . . . my initial reaction was . . . inside, 'Don't be so bloody stupid, like hell, I'm not going anywhere in ten days!' but my outward reaction was 'Ah! I have to do something practical.'

Although her immediate reaction to being given ten days to live was denial, the knowledge of the probable impact of her death on her children excited her sufficiently to allow her to seize psychological control. She told me:

. . . this was my fourth or fifth day and I had to sort out my will and pay for the funeral . . . Well, I felt I'm quite a practical person and I had two little ones, 12 and 13 and I thought, 'How on earth can I leave the children to face sorting out the funeral and possibly a legal battle with their father?' So it had to be done and it was like a great weight lifted off me when I had done it. The thing is the funeral is a bit financially past it now and will probably need a top up because of inflation. If I had a partner, it probably would have been different but I was alone with two children and my first thought was for the children . . . Basically, I arranged all that.

We have already been told that Rose felt desperate, frightened and pet-rified, emotions that might create psychological need to seek physical escape. Rose, though, was so weakened by the physical symptoms of her illness that she was unable to move. She was distraught. As a mother she could foresee something of the crisis that her impending death would cause. She knew that dying intestate would probably result in legal battles between her elderly mother and her ex-husband. Consequently, she urgently needed to make a will. She also wanted to protect her mother and children from the pain of having to arrange her funeral. Her emotional turmoil was so great that it motivated her and, in spite of being bed bound, allowed her to maintain a sufficient level of psychological control to ensure that her wishes were obeyed by others. She might not have been able to go out to meet her solicitor and funeral director but she arranged for them to come to her. The knowledge that these practical tasks had been resolved gave her intense relief.[2]

Amazingly, Rose recovered from that crisis and was given a further six months to live. Six months later she was still alive and was then told by her consultant that she could live for another year and a half. Later, she was told she had, at best, perhaps six to eight more months to live. She told me, laughingly, during our first interview just six months before she eventually died, she had outlived so many estimates of her predicted time span that, once when she made her visit to her consultant, she had:

. . . ordered another ten years! I feel no fear now. If I am going to die, I am going to die, although I will say that at this particular moment in time I am not in as critical a situation as I was then, as I have been many times. Maybe it is because I have been through it so many times and maybe it is because I know I should be a lot more ill than I am. I am ill but I have lost friends who are less ill than I am, which doesn't seem very fair. It seems rather sad that they have gone and I am still here but then, even though I have my problems, I think half the reason why I am still here is because I am totally happy with my lot.

During all the interviews over the six-month period that remained to her, Rose stayed rooted in her need to present me only with the positive elements in her life. Close scrutiny of the interview tapes, however, suggests that the reality of her life was somewhat different. Rose, who always presented such an upbeat view of her experiences, probably felt something akin to survivor guilt when friends from her cancer culture died whilst she continued to live.

This current, and third, recurrence of her disease saw her cancer spreading to new areas of her body and this heightened her anxiety. Rose told me four months before she died:

[2] Some days after Rose died, her daughter, Marie, telephoned to ask me if I was aware of where her mother had kept the official documents relating to her Funeral Plan. Sadly, I was unable to help, however, Rose's mother took out a loan which paid for her daughter's funeral. To the best of my knowledge, the monies paid into the Funeral Plan by Rose have never been recouped.

I'm all right; I'm a bit better than I felt yesterday. I've had a few ups and downs because it has spread to my jaw and up to my ear. I'm all right but I get these sharp pains through my ear, which are rather disturbing and the jaw hurts rather a lot . . . It's funny, because every time I get something new come up, I sit and I think, 'Is this it?' But at the end of the day, I've had so many new places come up it is a silly way to think but I can't . . . It's just you can't help what goes through your mind and I find it sort of frustrating that I still have these notions every time. When the old places come up, it doesn't seem to bother me so much, it is when I have something new, it worries me, so I find that a bit frustrating. I think, 'Is this it?' And then you have to sort of try and think about it logically and think well . . . I have been very much worse than this with pain and, 'No this isn't it.' There is no way I'm going to let it be it. It takes a day or two to react and sort it out in your head. I don't let the fear take over.

In spite of realising that the spread of her cancer was not good, Rose attempted to gloss over her more recent symptoms. Although she had lived with her cancer for such a protracted period, she could not repress or escape, in spite of her best efforts, the horror of her inevitable death. Twice she questioned 'Is this it?' Rose was in no doubt of the reality of her situation; however, she could only deal with this by attempting to rationalise her fears.

Two months before her death, she told me:

The first couple of years I was in and out of hospital, so close to dying that every time I went in I went in to die as far as I was concerned. And it didn't matter. Is there any point in panicking any more? The disease no longer stresses me, I don't think like that any more. I think when my number is up, I will go and that is the end of it. For me, Dr T just shrugs and says, 'Well, you know, what can I say? You should have been gone already, so let's say three months, six months, whatever!' and he says that every six months. So there is no point in worrying. I just keep going the best I can. He has in fact said to me, 'All I can do is give you palliative treatment to stop the pain, I can't do anything to halt the disease, whatsoever.' He has made that clear, because I have asked; not just once, I kept pestering him, so he said, 'Well, that is all we can do now, because we can't stop the disease, it has gone too far.' Radiotherapy is not a curative treatment, it only shrinks the tumour; it doesn't stop the disease. It will still come back and, because I have it here at the back of the brain, I don't suppose I have got a year left. But I want to enjoy that year. It took me a long time to be this way. At the hospital they said that I am living proof that if someone wants to live they will go on. I don't actually know what it is that I do; all I know is that I love life.

Seventeen years of Rose's life had been driven by her cancer. Although she had spent ten years in remission, that period, too, had been difficult, as it was a time spent monitoring potential symptoms. She had lived through physical and psychological experiences, which threatened her so severely, that she might have been living through a war. She attempted to counter these threats by mounting a psychological shield to protect herself from the continued onslaught of her illness. She tried desperately to normalise what was occurring in an attempt to persuade herself that she could maintain control. During almost every interview we had, she offered evidence of her continued resistance: 'I think to myself, I have too much to do. There is no way I'm going anywhere . . . I'm involved so much with my children. There is just no way but it does take a while to adjust.' She insisted that she and not the cancer would control how she lived her life as she had 'too much to do'. There were practical issues to be resolved and she believed they required her personal attention; 'There is no way' she was going to die. Rose's priority in life was her children, whose attitude to her cancer, she felt, enabled her to withstand the worsening effects.

She told me:

I think that they have helped me an awful lot, the children, because I have never really treated them . . . made them treat me, as if I am ill. And to that end, they take advantage of me. [Laughing] My son will come in at 10.30 at night and sometimes I can hardly move and he'll say to me, 'Do me a bit of bread and cheese mum, you know I can't cut the bread and the cheese goes all crumbly on me.' So they make me feel quite normal. I will say, 'Oh go away!' but I don't really think, 'Oh go away!' because it is what keeps me going. And all the children's friends come in and at times it is like Piccadilly Circus. And sometimes I sit here and I close my eyes, put my hands over my ears because the noise is too much but it is not really too much, it is what keeps me going, I know this. So in a way it is wonderful, because I haven't got anyone actually fussing over me. I have to get on and do it myself, which I think helps an awful lot, because by nature I am a fighter anyway.

Rose desperately needed to feel that she was still able to contribute meaningfully to her family. In spite of her debilitating illness, she persisted in her principal role, that of mother, not invalid. Her son, daughter and their social group ensured, by normalising her illness, that she could play that role. She struggled to maintain this pretence through the continuing deterioration of her illness.

Rose's success in maintaining her position within her immediate social group rested in her ability to control her independence and lay, in part, in her capability to manipulate how others read her behaviour. It seemed that she had, at times, an almost professional capacity to stage manage how others perceived her. She told me that:

Every time something happens [with her cancer] I tell them [her children] but I don't go on about it. What is the point? I don't want them to think about me as an ill mother. When I go, I want them to think of me as Mum. I don't want the thing that they remember about me to be that I was ill. People say to me, write a book about how you feel, about what is wrong with you, your pain and everything, and leave it for the children, but whatever for? – Whatever for? I wouldn't want that for the children, I don't want to leave them poems and stories . . . I don't want any of that . . . I just want to be as normal as possible. I don't want the children ten years down the line saying to their children 'Poor old Gran, she died of cancer' and that is what they will remember. I want them to say, 'Oh she was great fun!' or 'She was a lovely mum!' In fact, this is what has kept me going right the way through. I need to be me! I don't want to be the lady that is suffering from cancer.

Rose was well aware that her spontaneous reaction to her pain, along with the apparatus she had to use to enable her to continue to live in the community, tended to swamp her primary identity of mother. She knew that her illness was in danger of becoming her master status and so, heroically, she attempted to counter this by minimising the extent to which she revealed her pain and her dependency on her children for physical help.

She was not, though, so adept in managing the impressions of her wider social group who were not as sensitive as her children. She told me how:

. . . things happen, which make you feel even worse. Somebody who's always been what you considered a reasonably close friend, more than an acquaintance, will actually cross the road rather than walk past you and say, 'Hello'. Purely really because they don't know how to react. They are frightened, number one, of catching it, which you can't, but this is a fear. Number two, they are frightened of . . . they don't know what to say and they don't know what you will say but they don't want to know about it, they don't want to be upset about it, nothing to do with them, but something awful and take it away. I had that happen an awful lot.

Rose suffered from the spoiled identity arising from her cancer (Goffman, 1963; Sontag, 1978). She understood how it felt to be frightened, alone and in desperate need of knowledge. In a later interview, however, she told me how she was able to apply information gleaned about her own cancer to help:

. . . a lady in the waiting room last week . . . She said, 'Yes, I've got bone cancer, I'm going to die!', and I asked her where she first got it and she said 'In the breast'. And I said, 'You haven't got bone cancer then' and she said, 'Yes I have, I have it in my hip' and I said, 'No. Bone cancer is different altogether, you just have breast cancer which has spread to your hip.' She was quite . . . she perked up a bit. She was convinced because it had spread to her bones that she had bone cancer. It is a different disease, that works a different way. It is very, very difficult because people do go into shock . . . and that shock feeds the cancer and I have seen people, well people die through fear.

This inclination to support weaker neighbours appeared to be beneficial to both parties involved. Rose went on to illustrate this again. She told me something of the time she spent recuperating from a near death crisis in hospital, when she believed that:

... what helped me a lot was that even as bad as things got, I could see there were a lot of people around who were also ill. I would go and sit next to somebody's bed and hold their hand and talk to them or if somebody was being sick, I would hold the basin for them and it would make me feel as if I was contributing something. You feel useful, because when you have this disease, you feel as if you are totally useless. You feel as if you can't do anything. Everyone has to do it for you and I think it is very important to do for other people, to make you feel useful.

However, the behaviour of some individuals who did not understand the disease resulted in her feeling as though she was a contaminant, someone unclean and a risk to society. I was, consequently, interested when, three months before she died, she told me how, 'When I got this first, when Tony [her son] was a baby, I felt very polluted. I could not bathe. It was the whole of this area [indicating her breast]. Every time I moved, I had to change the bandages just to try to take up the pus.' Because of her cancer, she found herself becoming marginalized from mainstream interaction to the extent that she told me how sometimes she yearned for:

... someone to ... put their arms around me and I know we all feel like that sometimes. I'm not feeling sorry for myself, I just felt that I want another human, to feel that other people feel that I am not untouchable, dirty, I haven't got a terrible disease that I can give them. And now and again, maybe it is reassurance ... Now and again, I do need a hug.

Rose sometimes felt herself to be alone. Her feelings of responsibility to others compounded her problems. I had learned that she would always 'go alone [for treatment]. I would never take the children or my mother. My mother would always have this pitiful look on her face and the children would worry.'

During our fifth interview, when I asked Rose how she had been since I last saw her, she said:

... they took me in, to mark me up [for radiography]. They lay you out on a plank of wood. I can't lie, I have to have a lift to get me down, so getting on was painful enough but lying on there was abject agony. They put a hard plastic thing under my head, to mark you up in the right place, and a thing between my chin and here [indicates her shoulder]. I was taped here and here, so I was lying on this lump I have in my back, which was very painful. The girls [the radiographers] know me well and we chat about what's wrong. They very rarely ever say anything but it is so funny, isn't it ... ? I never thought I could get upset by something somebody has said but, because I suspect that this in the back of my head is a brain tumour, not that I have been told, but I know ... I have had it for over a year now and it is getting progressively more painful and it is also getting progressively larger. My head is swelling up and I am getting a sort of a lump. She [a radiographer] said 'Do you know which part we are marking up today?' I said, 'Well, the pain is across here.' 'Right!', she said, 'Now is that nerve or brain?' [Rose placed stress on the word brain] She assumed I knew because usually I know everything. She wouldn't have said a word . . . It is not her fault; not her fault at all . . . It is my fault because I always have this need to know. I feel that I can't fight or keep going . . . You don't fight and keep going to spite the disease . . . If I don't know what's going on, I can't stand it. So, of course to her . . . it was a remark that was unimportant. I was fine, I said nothing. I signed the paper and I left. They helped me up off the table; I have gone through so much pain on that table. As I was walking to the car, I just couldn't hold back, I started to cry. I haven't done that before and I don't know why I reacted like that; I still don't. When I came back I couldn't come in here, I went to my friend across the road, because . . . the last thing I want to do is upset the children. I just went into Pattie's [her neighbour], burst into tears and said, 'Please hug me.' If I'm still here . . . Pattie will have had a lot to do with it, they have been dear, dear friends and they treat me normally.

Rose's pain had been professionally assessed and she was prescribed treatment, not intended to be curative, merely to relieve her pain. Her friendship with the radiologists was not, unfortunately, of sufficient depth for them to realise the extent of the pain she was in during her treatment or the degree to which she masked her emotions. Rose's chief concern, at that time, was whether her cancer had spread to her brain. Three and a half months before her death, she told me: 'With a brain tumour, you can lose control over all sorts of parts of the body that are essential and once you lose those . . . then it is a different situation. With a brain tumour you can't really control your thoughts, so usually that is the way it ends . . .' Not surprisingly, she was torn between her anxiety for further information about the extent of her cancer spread and fear lest what she learned confirm her suspicions.

Earlier I discussed how the space within hospitals is anomalous, being perceived to be both public and private. At the time of her critical exchange with the radiographers, Rose was in a physically public place and was with individuals who, although known to her, were not intimates. Consequently, she struggled to adhere to the rules of conventional society and, at a time when she was desperate, presented 'best face' behaviour (Laslett and Rapoport, 1975) telling the radiographers that she 'was fine'. She was, however, only able to maintain that façade until she was alone on her return to her car, when she 'couldn't hold back' and 'started to cry'. In this desperate situation it is surprising that she chose not to seek solace in the comfort of her own home but, constrained by the responsibilities of her social role as mother, she instead 'just went into Pattie's, burst into tears and said, "Please hug me"'. Although Rose had had her suspicions, she had been so psychologically shaken by the apparent confirmation that her cancer had spread to her brain that she needed to be held, physically, secured by another. She wanted to protect her children, so she sought comfort from her wider social group, not her family; of her family, she said:

... they don't need to feel my pain. There is not any point to my telling anybody I'm in pain, I don't. When you talk to people you communicate. If you communicate laughter, people will laugh with you; if you communicate pain, people will feel pain for you. [She parodied a make believer listener who said:] 'This one is going to go on about not being well and I don't like this . . .' Or whether they sit there and they sympathise with you. They sit there with this pained look on their face, you don't want any of that and there is no point to your telling people about pain.

Sometimes the need to protect can become a problem. Rose experienced difficulties with her mother:

I keep reminding her that I am dying slowly and she says, 'Oh, don't be stupid!' and I say, 'Mum, I am dying' and she said to me, 'Oh you probably have toothache and ear-ache.' The first thing I did after this last diagnosis was to say [to her mother] 'There is absolutely nothing that can be done.'

Her mother's reluctance to acknowledge her prognosis caused Rose very real physical pain as well as psychological distress at a time when she might have benefited from a more empathetic approach. As a mother herself, Rose wanted the reassurance of knowing that her children could, after her death, be self-sufficient. She borrowed some money from her mother to pay for flying lessons for her son. This, though, proved problematic as the course he favoured was in the United States and so provision had also to be made for his accommodation there. Rose explained:

My mother absolutely forced me to spend three hours on the phone to all over the States and I was in agony with the pain. And then she said, 'You haven't finished phoning for Tony' and I said, 'For pity's sake, Mum, I am in agony, I can't do it.' 'Oh well, I was only saying . . .' And five minutes after that [her mother said], 'When do you think you will be well enough to phone?' So in the end, I said, 'Look mum, I'm in a lot of pain, I'm not well.' I explained to her that I think I have a tumour at the back of my head. Then I got the pained look, so I said, 'I have to go!' But I would sooner be treated like that, than have somebody walk in and stroke my hand and say, 'Don't move, don't move, I'll make the tea' for, at the end of the day, you can't feel sorry for yourself.

I suspect that although Rose did not want her children to think of her as an invalid, she would have liked to unburden herself to her mother had her mother been a stronger character. At this time, when she had such a short time left to live, she felt that she could not confide in those closest to her. She said:

. . . I can't get out of the chair and in wintertime I'm worse, because in the summer time, when it is warm, it takes some of the pain away. Because the pain is in my bones, the heat actually helps. But the worst of all is when my head is fuzzed, I can't describe it in any other way; when my faculties aren't there and I know they aren't and I know I am saying something I don't mean but something else is coming out of my mouth. I think that is why I stopped taking the morphine, I couldn't take the 'not being with it'. I'm not as with it as I used to be when I wasn't in pain, because the pain takes the edge off.

Rose felt she had to handle her severely limited mobility and extreme pain. She had long since come to terms with the gradual deterioration in her physical ability and she now struggled to maintain control over her mental faculties, which her drugs and brain tumour threatened to remove. Relinquishing these would be, for her, the final indignity.

However, she gained not just physical help but also much needed psychological support from others. It was not only other patients who could appreciate the full extent of what it is like to live with cancer. In talking of her consultant, she said:

The wonderful thing is that he actually hugs me and I know he does this with all his patients. He is the most wonderful person, he gives you so much. I have gone in there feeling . . . I don't know what . . . as though next week I am going to be rubbed out and he has put his arms around me and gives me a hug. He just hands you back your life. There are very few like him and, when you are that ill, it is amazing what that contact does, because he is actually saying to you . . . That he is looking at you, as being on a par with him. You are a human being and you feel so bad anyway, when you have this wretched disease. Dr T just makes me feel as if . . . Wow! I can go on forever.

Despite the front that she so courageously struggled to maintain, Rose sometimes unwittingly let slip something of her true feelings. Living a life in which she felt 'as though next week I am going to be rubbed out' cannot have been easy and the degree to which even a little social support was appreciated came across in the adjectives she used. The support of her doctor was much appreciated. Twice she used the word 'wonderful', she referred to his warmth as being 'amazing' and finished up, almost ecstatic with 'Wow! I can go on forever.' Whilst a response of this proportion to a hug might appear a little effusive, the magnitude of this reaction rested in the fact that she believed she was being treated with dignity, as 'a human being'. Rose trusted and appreciated her doctor.

When she had just eleven weeks to live, Rose trusted me sufficiently to show me some of the awful physical scars from her treatment. She began by lifting her long, lank brown hair to reveal that she was quite bald underneath what I now realised was just a top layer of hair. Her scalp was reddened and scaly. Lifting her top, she showed me the burn marks left on her body by the radiography treatment in addition to the scars caused by her many operations. Much of her pain was physical and even Rose, at times, felt provoked to anger. She explained how when she had the second recurrence of her cancer:

. . . it was a different cancer, a new cancer in the other breast . . . The surgeon didn't do what he should have done. He didn't remove my lymph glands, he just left the skin on here so it was all wrinkled up, filled with pus, it was awful and the smell, even if I washed every two hours it was still dreadful. So I went back into the hospital . . . They removed the skin, and took out the lymph glands, which should have come out in the first instance. They didn't, which is why my cancer spread. So, they weren't removed, when they should have been. I could quite gladly go and see the chap who did the original operation and give him the cancer. [laughter] I feel very, very . . . Well, I'm not so angry now, being angry is a waste of energy and when you get this ill you can't waste energy. The only thing you want to do is to love, communicate and do as much as you possibly can; you don't want to be angry, there is no point. But I was quite angry for a while.

Rose felt guilty when admitting her anger to me even though 'the chap' who she believed to be responsible for the spread of her cancer and her consequent death had virtually stripped her of her femininity, leaving her with foul smelling breasts, which could only leak pus instead of nutritive milk. Many might sympathise with her mildly expressed wish that he experience something of the hell which she continued to live through, as a result of what she felt was his ineptness.

During our last interview, just five days before she died, Rose described how her physical symptoms intruded on her life. She explained how much she wanted to be well when her 18-year-old son returned from the United States to be with her for Christmas. She said:

I don't think I'm going to be that well, this [recovering from radiotherapy] is going to be a slow process. I think this will take me into the New Year. Still the main thing is I get back on my feet at some time but I'm not going to be . . . I know I'm not, because I know how ill I am and I know that I won't be that well, even if I want to be, but it will come but it won't come when I want it to. I am fairly determined but the trouble is that I get weakened every time I have radiotherapy and I have had so much and am so weak that I just keep getting infection after infection and it pulls you down. There is still an awful lot going on and a lot I do not want to give up and I'm certainly not ready to die yet, there is just no way, I am not ready yet. Not until I see my son.

Rose felt impatient to recover from what she hoped was a temporary reaction to her treatment and to resume her role as mother. However, she had, at some level, an intuition that this time she was not going to recover. Rose's commitment to her family drove her need to continue the desperate battle for life. A life that was almost devoid of pleasure. In our fourth interview, she had told me something of how she imagined she would die, saying:

I don't know . . . I think . . . I know how I would like to die. When the time comes I would like to do it quick, like that, but that is not going to be, because it is a lingering disease. Just by virtue of my personality, I will probably linger. I would like to be without pain, I have had so much pain; it makes you so weak, it takes everything from you. It takes your dignity, it takes your self-respect, it takes everything and I . . . if I have to die, obviously I would like to do it without pain, which I know is not possible. So that won't happen for me but however I die . . . I had a friend who was really well, perfectly well one day and two days later she was dead, she had an internal bleed. You just don't know, I have seen so many people die. But I definitely would like to die in hospital, because when I was very ill before, they thought I was dying . . . My bowels, I was incontinent, I blew out like a balloon, I was sick; I don't want that for the children [to witness]. And I don't want to go to a hospice, I'm not an old lady . . . I really don't, if I have got to die, then I would like to die in hospital, don't want to go to the hospice, don't want to die at home. I don't want the children to see me dying. I know the amount of heartache that would give them. The one thing above all else is that my mother will not cope very well when I die and I know that she will not give the children any help. She will expect to be helped . . . But I have tried with Mum as much as I can . . .

Rose was frightened that her need to maintain control over her physical body would not enable her to benefit from the pain relieving drugs she knew were available. She also wanted to prevent her children from being confronted with the harsh realities of her own bodily breakdown, something she had observed happening to others. She told me how she believed:

. . . if you have that ability to love that little bit stronger . . . you ride over the pain . . . I know that I won't be pain-free [she was referring to her death] because of me [not wishing to take pain relieving drugs which 'fuzzed' her mind], not because I can't be pain free, that is how I am. I'm prepared to listen to the doctors and I am prepared to do 80 per cent of what they tell me but the other 20 per cent I must control. It is important for me . . . I don't think it is important because I think I am controlling the disease, I don't think I am. I think I am controlling my life, that part of my life that is still left . . . I don't think that I will die easily . . .

Her need to retain her mental control was in proportion to the despair she felt as she experienced her own body's surrender to her cancer.

I have to be very careful because I drop things and fall over because my legs do funny things when I least expect it. I used to enjoy a drink once in the blue moon, which I don't even think about now. I can't eat so many things. People buy me a lot of flowers and I give them away because I can't breathe [her lungs had deteriorated]. I say, 'Don't give me flowers and beside which, I am not dead yet.

Buy me flowers when I have gone!' [laughter]. The only thing I would like sung at my funeral is 'Amazing Grace' and I wouldn't like the hymn version[3] . . . it's a bit dirgey, very heavy. I don't want everyone to cry at my funeral, I have had a good innings. I can't complain about the time I have had, 17 years is a long time to be with cancer. I am very lucky, because not many people live this long. Five to ten years is the expected life span [following cancer]. With breast cancer, with secondaries, you don't expect to live 17 years, so I can't grumble. The saddest thing about the thought of dying is not that I am going to die, it is that I am going to make my family suffer and I really don't want to do that. I think to myself, how unfair. Maybe if my children were in their thirties and settled but Tony is 18, I can't bear the thought of dying and giving them that sorrow. That is not what I brought them into the world for, I don't know . . . Yes, send me flowers at my funeral but I don't like the idea of, you know, 'Dearly beloved we are gathered here today . . .' And I have not yet seen one funeral that I thought was nice, they are all so heavy and I don't want to do that to my kids. I'd rather say 'Bye darlings, love you all' and that is it, do you know?

Clive

Thirty-six-year-old Clive worked as a lecturer. He was a single man who lived with his widowed mother and was a regular member of the congregation at the local Presbyterian church. His testicular cancer had been first diagnosed four years earlier when he had been 'told I had a tumour as part of the normal ward round'.

He explained that having recovered from his initial cancer, when he then 'went for a routine check-up, they kept me in. Things happened quickly. I thought I was again sinking . . . I know Dr J was doubting the possibility that I would pull through.' Clive experienced the ensuing, sudden and dramatic, crisis in his health as terrifying. He had been alarmed to the extent that he 'thought I was dying'. Despite his fear, he told me 'I trusted Dr J and his understudies, although I didn't know where they were leading me but I put my faith in them.' In spite of his uncertainty, Clive continued to trust his medical team:

I struck up quite a friendship with one of the nurses, Sheila. She was one of these nurses who is very efficient but has such a way with her. . . . I could not have opened up as well with the other nurses or my family but I could talk to Sheila. She would just talk to me as a person and that is what was so important; she had a sympathetic understanding. The others were very efficient, very cheerful but not the same relationship with Sheila. I think that to have someone like her, could possibly mean the difference between life and death. Touch too is very important, a reassuring touch, that spoke volumes. I was not just Clive

---

[3] When I attended Rose's funeral, which was held in a Greek Orthodox Church, that hymn was not sung, but instead some traditional hymns were.

Black lying there . . . This was someone with deep, deep, worries and anxieties. That meant more than just the tranquillisers and sedatives. Also I was able to be very intimate with Sheila about another matter, which was troubling me, a relationship . . . Trouble I was having and she listened and understood, I could take her right into the very heart of the matter. She would just sit and talk to me; she was a gem . . . From that point of view I felt that all was being done that could be and the social worker came every day and chatted to me. That was my family, working staff.

Clive really appreciated Sheila, his 'gem' who 'listened and understood' him when he was in need. At the time this was happening, he was confronting a personal crisis. He was ill and in hospital; a culture with which he was unfamiliar. He was also removed from his family, of whom he says he 'could not have opened up as well with' because 'their line of defence was to hold up in front of me'. Who did he turn to at this difficult time? His new 'family, working staff'.

Clive told me how shocked he was, when it was initially suggested to him by a senior nurse, that his cancer might have recurred:

My mind was geared to absolute faith in medicine, the medical team and absolute faith in God. I did not recognise the symptoms as a reoccurrence, the tumour coming back. I put it down to an infection. Maybe I had to be shocked into the realisation of what was happening; maybe I was in denial. The Sister said, 'You know, Clive, the fluid . . . that is the tumour back.' I clung to the possibility that they may be wrong. I spoke to the other nurses and they told me that she had not had the confirmation back from the laboratory. They said, 'She is saying that from experience not from a scientific point of view . . .' but the next day the oncologist told me that 'Yes, it was confirmed that the tumour was back.' He told me there were '. . . two courses of action, one is that we will keep you comfortable and send you home as soon as we can', but not for any length of time is what they were saying. 'If this tumour keeps to its level, things will deteriorate very quickly. The choice is yours but there is an alternative, high dose chemotherapy.' To tell you the truth, I thought I had had high dose chemotherapy. He told me that I had to be aware that it [the proposed chemotherapy] was very severe. 'Quite severe side effects for you to cope with.' He told me that I had a thirty percent chance of surviving it. That was the choice that faced me in his office; really, there was no choice; I knew I had to go for it. He was used to talking to people in these terms and was just being the professional but a nice big hug would have said more. They were so remote with me. I walked back from his office into the ward and, I remember, I was in tears. The nurse was accompanying me and I was just crying out to be held in some way. She was a young girl but whether they are trained . . . but she was being the professional and keeping her distance. She gave me a few sedatives and that was it.

Like all of the respondents, Clive had been traumatised by this, his latest diagnosis of cancer. Having been seventeen months in remission, he had, though, believed that 'the medicine, the medical team' had cured him and that he was finally cancer free. So confident was he that he actually 'believed the tumour could not come back'. His conviction may have been rooted in his strong religious faith, a faith which went some way to supporting him in his bleakest hours. Alerted to the possibility of the cancer's return by the nursing Sister, he had steeled himself sufficiently to withstand what he feared he may learn from his doctor. It would seem that some protective mechanism cut in, detaching and disconnecting him, bolstering him up, in an effort to shield him from the shock of the news he was hearing. He was, during that consultation, shored up, braced to withstand the traumatic diagnosis. To be told that not only had it returned but was also back in such an aggressive form overwhelmed him. His effort to maintain self control appears to have almost reached breaking point and he cast around desperately seeking a safe haven in which to unburden himself. At this time, when he was most in need, he felt alone, bereft of human comfort. Clive continued:

That was the 27th November, the worst day of my life. How did I cope? I cried non-stop. Clung to people, held on to them, panicked. Did silly things, phoning everyone, telling them, just to talk to someone. I remember standing in the pay phone, weeping down the phone to everyone I thought would be sympathetic and asking them to pray for me and awaiting the beginning of the next day when the treatment would begin. I woke at 3.00 am and all I could think about was what would happen the next day. I went out and sat with the night nurses. I said, 'I am really afraid of this treatment that the doctor has in store for me.' I could almost feel it at that stage coming into my body, going down, this was coming into me and I was not welcoming it. I was fearing it, pushing it back. The day went on and that was the lowest plateau, the lowest part . . .

Unlike a drowning man who is confronted with the physical evidence of his dilemma, the threat to Clive was more abstract. The technological society of which he was a member facilitated a prognosis for which there was, to Clive, no visible physical evidence. Clive, whose life was not in immediate danger, had become so traumatised by this sudden confrontation with his own mortality that he was driven into a frenzy. He was scared. He knew he was mortal but this diagnosis provoked a crisis of awareness. He felt and acted on his need for physical action and sought release from what he had been told by attempting to share his burden with others. He was distraught. He clung on to complete strangers in a desperate bid to find safety in the comfort of others. Alone and left 'standing in the pay phone' he begged others, imploring them to pray for him; he believed that this was his last resort. Clive realised that he was now, truly, in a hopeless situation. At night, frightened and unable to sleep, with the threat of the imminent ordeal of his treatment looming, he again searched for human comfort and found it with the 'night nurses' who listened sympathetically to his articulated horrors. His description of how he imagined his treatment would affect him was interesting. He almost seemed to be envisaging a situation of male rape, with the hypodermic syringe, charged with toxic liquid, substituting for a penis. He described how he 'could almost feel it at that stage coming into my body, going down, this was coming into me and I was not welcoming it. I was fearing it, pushing it back.' Clive, who until that second diagnosis thought his chief concern lay in other personal problems, was now desperate just to go on living. His disturbed frame of mind had obviously been communicated to the other patients in the ward. He continued:

. . . within that ward there was a . . . friendship which developed among the patients. I remembered one chap, elderly, not very articulate, Jim, but he ministered to me. Every night he came and tucked me in that was almost like an Angel; an Angel of God coming to look after me. That was a beautiful thing.

The social spirit, which had grown between the patients, had extended to embrace Clive in this time of his despair. Earlier, Clive had explained to me that he had previously lived in a family which:

. . . was and still is one of those where you don't talk too much about your feelings, you don't be too emotional, you don't hug. Men are men and women are women. You talk about your work, not about your feelings. This is the Calvinist way I was brought up.

His social group placed value on reserve and maintaining face. They might reasonably have regarded his disturbed reaction to his second diagnosis as threatening their normal mode of behaviour and distanced him from their group. However, so severe was Clive's psychological and physical crisis that they changed their behaviour to allow for his condition.

Clive continued:

My brother actually came and sat down beside me and cried. He is a farmer, a big butch man and he had never showed emotion to me up till then and he fed me drinks through a straw. I thought I was dying, and that particular day I consciously remember struggling and I said, 'If I close my eyes I will just slip away.' I fought it . . . What kept me going? Probably my mother, she slept on a Parker Knoll recliner beside my bed. A big man of 36, with his mother. I don't know what was going on sub-consciously but there must have been a struggle between life and death. All the thoughts of death reoccurred, came into my waking consciousness about coffins, the whole paraphernalia of death. Panic attacks, I was out of bed, in bed, they just sedated me and I was several days unconscious. I remember blurred images of people coming and going. I didn't ever think I would get out of it. I coped with my mother, she was a tower of strength, she was washing, bed bathing me, I had no hair and she massaged my scalp every night. I would always be very conscious of undressing in front of my mother, she brought fresh pyjamas every day, but I didn't care. I was holding on by my fingertips, just holding on, getting through each day.

Clive was right to fear his treatment. His chemotherapy provoked another crisis in his health, resulting in his rapid deterioration. His physical symptoms and psychological deterioration had been so dramatic that they brought about a radical change in family relationships. His brother responded on an emotional level and his elderly mother kept protective and caring station by his bed. Clive had virtually switched his role from that of adult son with dependent mother to one of infant son with nurturing mother. She was his 'tower of strength', and he, barely able to hold 'on by my finger tips' found himself reduced to the level of a dependent child, impotent as a result of his chemotherapy.

Discussion

The conclusion of treatment might appear a time of celebration but it can also, paradoxically, be experienced as a loss. Loss of the psychological security afforded by the knowledge that one is being monitored and treated by experts: loss, too, of the security implicit in a bureaucratically organised schedule of appointments (Weber, 1993). The end of treatment also entails a severing of contact with others, patients and staff, who have, to some extent, shared in experiences. The input made by these others during those times of very real crisis cannot be sufficiently stressed.

The population of patients within a hospital ward is often composed of individuals drawn together by the sharing of symptoms and treatment. Members of that population may, at first, believe they have little else in common. It is interesting that, within what is probably a diverse group, social bonds develop between residents and staff that enable a level of community spirit to exist. The other patients understand directly what it is like to be ill and so extend their care, reaching out psychologically as well as physically to help one another, much in the way that Jim 'ministered' to Clive and Rose would 'sit next to somebody's bed and hold their hand and talk to them'.

My research has highlighted that the time and interest that those who are chronically ill invest in learning more about their own disease results in patients who are themselves, to an extent, experts on their own medical situation. Just as Rose was able to educate a lady who 'was convinced because it had spread to her bones that she had bone cancer', so, too, did Susan feel the need to proffer what she could for others by working with support groups and informing them about what she perceived to be the benefits of the macrobiotic diet. They both took comfort from the fact that they were able to help others in a practical sense.

It might seem then that by 'contributing something' to others, Rose was offering evidence of how the need to be valued can spur the desire to get well. The social interaction which occurs within the ward is of value and benefit to all who participate, either by giving or receiving.

It can also, unfortunately, function to cause distress. Clive told me about some of the patients with whom he shared the ward and seemed to be particularly upset about the sudden and unexpected death of a young boy of seventeen. He said: 'There was always the thought in my mind, "Could I go like that, could it be that quick for me?" The next day I was released, allowed to go home and I celebrated my birthday . . .'

Like Rose's doctor, who in hugging her made her feel 'on a par with him, [like] a human being' and 'the night sister [who] was there the whole night' for Louise on that awful evening before her surgical exploration, Clive's fellow patient, Jim, and Sheila, the nurse who spoke with Clive, made time to listen to his fears and afforded him human dignity. Relating to other individuals on this basic humanitarian level cuts through and beyond the behaviour of strangers and directly contributes to community spirit.

When patients are discharged from hospital, their removal from the physical site of their residential medical treatment results also in expulsion from their newly adopted community. Although many respondents had originally entered the hospital reluctantly, some came to think of it as a sanctuary, a secure place where they could find understanding and safely discharge the strong emotions they experienced in reaction to their illness. However, when their treatment ended, they were expected to return home, like refugees who suffer enforced repatriation to a threatening government. They found their lives once again subject to the rule of well-meaning others. Their family and friends, although their intimates, sometimes did not understand what they were going through and tended to infantilise them. Charmaz considers that if those who are ill: '. . . openly reveal their suffering, show self-pity, guilt, anger or other emotions conventionally believed to be negative, they are likely to further estrange those who still take an interest in them' (1983: 191). This results in a position where, during this remaining precious time in their lives, it seemed as though the respondents had been sentenced to act out two separates lives, where the rules and roles had become reversed. The time and place most suited to airing an honest report of their experiences appeared to be when they were with others, patients like themselves; this inevitably occurred, though, in public places and with short term acquaintances such as support groups. Many respondents' private relationships were now, to an extent, constrained by their attempts to protect others. The fact that their time left was at a premium resulted in it being experienced with greater intensity. This served to increase the burden placed on relationships, already suffering from strain.

This was the broad situation, which many respondents experienced on two fronts. At home, many would appear to have felt the need to protect those for whom they cared from the reality of the disease. In more public areas, their presence sometimes seemed to exercise a disturbing effect as, for example, when acquaintances of Rose crossed the road rather than meet her.

Sontag discusses how, since cancer is, in the public perception, a disease that causes terror and the cause of it remains unknown, it is felt '. . . to be morally, if not literally, contagious. Thus, a surprisingly large number of people with cancer find themselves being shunned by relatives and friends' (1978: 10).

She argues that images of the disease as contagious are exacerbated by the knowledge that it appears to strike individuals arbitrarily and this has led to speculation that there may be 'cancer prone character type[s]'. It does not, then, take much of a leap of the imagination to arrive at the idea that it is the individuals themselves who are in some way culpable and responsible for causing their own cancer (Sontag, 1978). When this attitude is married to Karpf's (1988) 'blame the victim' philosophy, living in mainstream society can, for those with cancer, be quite testing.

It is not surprising, then, that so many experienced some sense of loss on leaving the shelter of the hospital and returning to mainstream society. Although they hoped that the treatments they had received would cure them and wished for life to return to normal, they were astute enough to realise that the legacy of their cancer would colour how others perceived them. By taking direct control of what others would learn about their experiences, some hoped to shape that understanding.

Gerry, it might be remembered, was particularly eager 'to tell everyone I had cancer. I rang my boss because I wanted to shock him.' Susan and Rose too did not seem to mind others knowing. Both were the subjects of documentary films about the way in which people with cancer experience their illness. Following one particularly disturbing scene, filmed live, in which Susan learned from her consultant that her cancer had indeed spread to her liver, she said to camera:

It is everyone's worst nightmare come true. But it is really important for me to tell people that nothing changes in terms of where we go from here. Treatment begins on Wednesday. We are a long way from no hope. There is lots of hope. It is a case of being down, very definitely down, but not out.

Seale (1998) considers the increasing tendency of doctors to make patients who are dying aware of their position. The ensuing existential confrontation may, for many, be their first intimations of mortality and could be responsible for challenging behavioural patterns, which previously were, perhaps, more egocentric. It also might be responsible for encouraging the birth of a more ethical or moral self, which in acknowledging and accepting its own lack, chooses instead to serve the other. Bauman observes that:

> . . . my *life* counts; its termination, its being-no-more, my death, is no more a senseless, absurd, unjustifiable occurrence: not that sinking into the emptiness of non-existence it once was – that vanishing which changes nothing in the world. Through making myself for-the-other, I make myself for-myself, I pour meaning into my being-in-the world. I refuse the world the licence to disdain and dismiss my presence; I force the world to note, and to dread in advance my passing away, and to bewail it when it comes. [his italics] (1992: 202)

Frank (1995) argues that the authors or subjects of illness stories offer 'testimony', which is valuable for three reasons. Doing so enables the storyteller to reorder their individual life story. It also can function as a learning aid to carers, helping them develop their own knowledge of the illness experience, and telling a personal cancer story can serve as example to others who might, one day, experience the same problems. This might explain Susan's need, literally, to broadcast her condition. She wanted to contribute to others; she wanted to make her mark, in some way to make a difference and be useful. She felt an urge to educate the public about the truth of life with cancer. She wanted to lead people out of their complacency by preparing those who are well for this terrible thing that could happen to them. She wanted the film broadcast as text that would serve as evidence of her experience. In making her condition common knowledge, Susan may also have hoped that she would be acknowledged as being in some way different, perhaps admirable, in her stoicism and a person worthy of esteem. If she could make others understand something of herself and the terrible reality of her situation, then their empathy might alleviate some part of her pain. Susan felt she needed to project something of the 'other-within-herself' onto the world, which might register and remember her presence. Perhaps she thought that by contributing to this film she might even ensure her symbolic immortality. She would not settle to become a non-entity, shut away in secrecy to die.

All the respondents were determined that they would survive their cancer. They were delighted to settle into their remission: faith was restored, hope re-established and confidence slowly again placed in their future. However, a resumption of life just as it was prior to their first diagnosis was not always possible. What seemed most important, during this liminal time between treatment and recurrence, was to regain control of their health and their lives. However, a cancer diagnosis tends to be reflected in a shift of identity from one who is healthy to one who is dying (Sontag, 1978). This shift in master status was one that the respondents, now in remission, desperately wanted to redress. Consequently, they made efforts to manage others' impressions of the physical changes that resulted, either directly from the illness or as side-effect of the treatment. Although they had, at times, proved welcome, wigs and walking sticks were particularly eschewed, now only serving to remind them of past physical deficiencies.

The interviewees had changed in response to their experiences and their illness had also led to changes within their social relationships. The shifts in role necessary to maintain normal family life during the crisis points of the illness meant they had surrendered some of their social obligations. Now they hoped they were free from the threat of their illness, they wished to resume those roles. However, those others who had taken up their duties would not always relinquish these responsibilities gracefully, as some found their new roles had afforded them additional power.

Being seen to be recovering well from a life threatening illness is one thing but how that recovery is perceived internally is quite different. All engaged in strategies designed to monitor potential illness indicators. Nearly all were aware of the implications of finding new symptoms. They were, by now, so attuned to the rhythm and appearance of their own bodies that, for most, any sign of potential illness triggered alarm and immediate action. As Susan told me 'You stub your toe and you think you have cancer of the toe, it is the whole idea of living with cancer'. Whenever they grew suspicious of any physical change, which might prove pathological, they were quick to report it to the medical teams, although some, like Susan, felt that they often had to fight to have these indicators taken seriously.

At this stage, the majority were cautiously optimistic of their prognosis. Their emotions were at times conflicting: they fervently hoped they would be cured yet, at the same time, lived in dread that their cancer would return. Becker (1973) might attach this hope to their sense of the heroic, their belief that they were the special one, the one who would overcome the threat of death. Freudians, though, might suggest that this belief in immortality stems from the child's sense of omnipotence, arguing that the child believes itself to be God-like and directly responsible for all that occurs within their world. Some of this is carried into adulthood; hence the sense of guilt when a loved one dies, but also the belief that, should we want something badly enough, we will be able to get it (Roth, 1963).

Susan, who would say to her friends 'I have had it [cancer] and I don't have it any more', clearly had her inner doubts because she never stopped monitoring her body for symptoms. Clive, however, had put his faith in God and never doubted that he had been cured. As a result, he was astounded when he was told that the cancer had returned. Other strategies were also used; Gerry talked about 'it is not a sickness, it is a condition that I have', seeming eager to have his cancer reclassified and downgraded from being potentially life threatening to 'a condition' which, he hoped, was now firmly under his control. Nearly all, however, were to endure the anguish of a second, and for some, even, a third, diagnosis.

There was a qualitative difference in how the interviewees reacted to their first and subsequent diagnoses. Their first diagnosis of cancer was described as 'devastating'. Generally speaking, they entered that first occurrence from a reasonably naive position and felt that some hope lay within the scientific curative regimes suggested to them. That hope, however minimal, was critical to carrying them through the difficult times that lay ahead. The gravity of their later diagnosis lay in the fact that they now, through direct personal experience, had achieved a realistic picture of their own, dismal, prognoses. Living within the cancer culture, attending self-help groups, keeping chemotherapy appointments had resulted in their meeting others with cancer, some of whom were at more advanced stages within their own trajectories. The respondents had seen these others follow that path and knew that many had died. Being told their cancer had returned left them in desperate need of physical, psychological and spiritual support. They had first hand experience of scientific medicine and it had failed them. What hope was left to them now?

The cancer had returned to bodies which, as a result of their initial treatment, were now, like their mind set, substantially weakened. Yet whilst they were in this physically and psychologically reduced position and also shocked from being told that the cancer had recurred, they had to countenance a further onslaught of this, hopefully, beneficial treatment. They had to contend with even more aggressive doses of chemotherapy. Like Clive, 63-year-old Vera did not enjoy this experience at all:

. . . it was terrible treatment this time, it was really hard going. I found it very hard going, I never bounced back quite so much from the chemo. . . . I really got myself in such a state, a pit and I couldn't get out of it. I was not going to live . . . I was not going to come out of it, I wouldn't live till Christmas and I got myself in such a tizwas. I think it possibly was because my blood[count] was low.

Why, then, did they proceed with the medical advice? Rose told me:

... when the pain is at you ... the pain pulls you down, that is when the shock starts, you think, this is severe, I can't cope with this. You think, 'Is this it?' And then you go into shock. I would think, 'Well, don't moan about the treatment, it is going to take a month, three times a week', but you hope it is going to shrink this bugger. You hope it is going to make it smaller, you hope it is going to make it less effective, so let's go for it and that is the frame of mind I used to go in.

Desperate to survive, Louise, who was also enmeshed in a series of other critical family difficulties, allowed herself to be persuaded against her own judgement to take further highly intensive treatment. However, so gruelling was this chemotherapy that 'they then had to reduce the dose. I was very ill with that, lying in bed for a week, not able to eat, looking truly wretched ...'

Not surprisingly, they found withstanding the toxic strength of their second wave of chemotherapy even more difficult than coping with their initial treatment. Their reports suggest that their encounters with others in the cancer culture had informed and educated them as to what they might themselves experience in the future. Earlier, I pointed out how Vera had observed, 'The lady in the bed across at the hospital ... this lady really was ill and I said to myself, what do you do?' Susan, too, had observed that 'another girl in my group had died of cancer ... Siobhan had dealt with the liver before she died.' Rose told me that she, 'had a friend who was really well, perfectly well one day and two days later she was dead. She had an internal bleed ... I have seen so many people die.' The horrifying knowledge of how their journey was likely to develop seemed so intimidating that even considering it became dangerous. Confronting it by talking about it to others, who were not themselves subject to the same mortal danger, proved frustrating. Others just could not appreciate the scale of their fears or the reality of the danger they faced. This apparently resulted in the anxiety becoming repressed; when it inevitably leaked out, it provoked and threatened relationships, which had once been close.

Elias (1985) argues that dying and death in contemporary society have become more informal. He attributes this to the decrease in everyday ritual and the high degree of reserve, which he cites as being part of the civilising process. There is a peculiar embarrassment felt by the healthy when they are around those who are going to die and this unease manifests itself in a lack of communication and affection for those who are most in need. Susan came close to expressing something of this when she said:

Those members of my family who tell me to pull myself together and [say] 'Don't worry, Susan, things will be fine!' when I get weepy. I recognise that and I pull myself together very quickly. What they are saying is 'Please don't do this in front of us, we can't take this.'

This reluctance to engage verbally with those who are dying coupled, perhaps, with a drive to escape physically from the psychological anxiety inherent in the situation, may be responsible for the carer feeling guilty and overcompensating with attention. This is especially a problem when the patient is an adult daughter and the principal carer her mother. The tension becomes manifest in a 'fussing' type of behaviour which can heighten an already stressful situation and result in friction. Louise illustrated this saying:

> My mother and sister are pathological helpers, so when I was feeling well enough to run my own home, they were still here, getting themselves worn out. They were fed up with me, I was fed up with them and that is spilling over in to this very much.

Stress within relationships is also evident, when the patient is one of a partnership. Following an interview with Sue-Ellen who died two months later, I noted of her husband:

> A big, bewildered man in a tiny, pretty cottage. Definitely not his territory. Proportions all wrong. [He comes across as having an] Extreme sense of anger, alienation and aloneness. He is obviously aware of things but does not seem to notice them. He is the one who needs. Everything has changed for him – no longer certain or trusting. [He said of his wife] 'She's cantankerous – I can't even walk across the floor.' He is in a strange role with no comfort. No sleep in a bed largely taken up with a medical mattress. Barely repressed anger. Macmillan nurse commented when we left 'He will kill her then top [kill] himself . . .'

Tension between this married couple had escalated to such an extent that it was being vented in the form of barely repressed hostility, veiled with extreme politeness. Whether the person who is dying ever arrives at the stage of acceptance or not, life continues for the supporters and can at times seem almost impossible. Even sharing accommodation with someone with cancer can be difficult.

In response to this often uneasy atmosphere in the home, the respondents attempted to ease the situation (Goffman, 1963) by playing an heroic role (Seale, 1995). In an attempt to protect their intimates from the harsh reality of their illness (Gyllenskold, 1982), they masked their true emotions. This, however, brought with it the cost of performing emotional work (Hochschild, 1983) for others at a time when they were themselves in very great need.

All the respondents peppered our interviews with comments, which suggested that having cancer had in some way actively enhanced their lives. However, comparison of these comments with other information they provided, indicates that the philosophic version was somewhat removed from reality. Rose had just begun to keep a journal shortly before she died. She did not ever make it clear whether or not these brief writings were intended for publication or were simply a private record of her experiences. In her journal she wrote:

Everyday that I wake up and am able to wash, dress and go downstairs is the most wonderful day of my life. My world is now a truly wonderful place and very, very beautiful . . . even if I die tomorrow, I can say I am truly happy and have faith and happiness way beyond most people's dreams.

The interviews are a testament to how, for the majority of her last year, she faced her imminent death with courage, cheerfulness and acceptance. However, there were moments when she reflected on the bleakness of her predicament. Nonetheless in every interview, Rose remained firm in her conviction that her life was good:

You have to be happy with whatever your lot is and I don't think . . . You can't say, 'Why has this happened to me? Why should I have faith in God if this has happened to me?' That is not where it is at all. You have to thank your lucky stars that you woke up today. After I was ill, the first time I stood at the sink and washed up, I just stood and cried, I was so glad.

Surface analysis might suggest that Rose appears to have conformed with Kubler-Ross's model of the 'good death' and having accepted her illness rejoiced in whatever quality and quantity of life remained to her.

Her stoical philosophy came through during our ten interviews. However, she also had a much more desolate view of her life. During one interview she commented: 'I will not go to bed unless I am absolutely shattered, if I'm not shattered then I am awake all night with the pain.' In another she explained 'you need to have a purpose in life. When you are very ill, just lying there, virtually a vegetable, there is no purpose and it is very, very easy to give up. Very easy . . .' These words though were immediately followed by her saying 'but the thing that kept me . . . The nurses kept me up [her spirits] because they were so sweet . . .' Her strategy was to insert her private feelings between the version she presented for public consumption; it was these more palatable views she tended to stress.

The times when Rose conceded defeat to the reality of her situation occurred only rarely. Rose was aware that the audio tapes of the interviews and her journal were to be made available to her children. These versions of her experience conform to Cornwell's (1984) public account, stressing the non-threatening version of life and minimising much of the painful minutiae. Rose was attempting to protect her children by distracting them from the truth of her experience. How though might others, who have cancer, interpret this 'coffee table book' style of presentation?

People do not exist in vacuums. Empirical evidence garnered, however unconsciously, from physical encounters with others who are more advanced in their dying journey can act as a threat to defence mechanisms, alerting individuals to the hierarchy in the gravity of cancer spread. As a result of contact with others, some respondents realised and appreciated the severity of their situation should their cancer spread to their liver or brain, having witnessed the effect on others. Ben and his wife, Eilish explained to me how Ben had suffered an extreme emotional reaction when told that it was suspected that he had brain secondaries. She said:

. . . he just couldn't take it; he flipped. We was living right by the sea and he just got up out of the chair, without his walking stick . . . and he said, 'That's it, I've finished, I'm gone. I can't go with secondaries on the brain because that is a slow horrible death.'

Ben interrupted, explaining how he had witnessed one of his closest friends suffer a tormented and lingering death from this illness. He said:

. . . and I could see this happening to me and I did flip, I got very angry and I went across the road without looking . . .

Eilish described how he was:

. . . trying to get run over, then he came back and he tried to take all his tablets and whisky because no one would run him over and he started the tablets . . . then he went out again and I couldn't find him. I was running along the sea front and I couldn't find him. I really was panicking and a neighbour saw me . . . and we found him right down by the town and he [Ben] called me all the names of the day.

In his own defence, Ben was only able to say 'I wasn't . . . I couldn't help myself . . .'

Ben's first hand observation of the effects of the spread of cancer to the brain had caused this disturbing and totally uncharacteristic behaviour. Rose, too, felt a heightened fear of her cancer spreading there. When, just three months before her death, I asked her what it would mean if the cancer had spread she said:

Well, it is the beginning of the end, isn't it? Brain tumours . . . You do not last forever. My cousin Catriona . . . She died. The brain tumour killed her eventually. She had exactly the same as I did, she had breast cancer, but she didn't have it for very long, five years.

The film which follows events in Susan's life records live the moment when she is told by her consultant that her cancer has metastasised into her liver. She attended for that, her fourth, cancer diagnosis with two supporters. One, her sister, accompanied her into the consulting room, whilst her mother waited outside supported by a nurse. Susan had already suspected that her cancer had spread to her liver and was aware of the consequences of what she was being told. You will remember that, after she had originally been told that the cancer had not spread to her liver, her friends 'thought I was crazy "She has bone cancer and it is good news?"'

Her specialist began the consultation by observing conventions, asking 'How are you?' to which a, not surprisingly, tense Susan responded, 'Just hurry up . . . I am very nervous.' When he told her that it was now '. . . quite certain that there has been a change in the liver, that there is spread . . .' Susan managed to maintain her equilibrium, holding eye contact with him but began to wring her hands. At this point, her sister Anita reached out to comfort her. Her consultant continued, telling her how he felt '. . . quite confident that we can give you further treatment and hope to get the disease back under control'. At this stage Susan, whose demeanour had been slipping and now appeared totally distraught, interrupted him saying 'Paul, is that why I am in pain? But . . . you cannot have a wee bit of liver cancer.' In reference to his proposed treatment she, who it might be remembered had told him how she would be: 'the captain of the team. I am the All Star and I have to devise the game plan', said: 'I am ready for anything now . . . If I take further treatment . . . I am going to take treatment, no question about that. Will it improve my chances? Are we talking remission?' Her consultant replied using military metaphor 'It is shot down and stable. We can keep it at bay for a good number of months . . .'

Knowledge that their cancer had now returned, or spread, in whatever form, created a crisis in which the respondents said they had actively reconsidered their form of treatment. In their raw need to survive, some were now prepared to challenge the belief that conventional medical treatment alone could conquer their cancer. Susan explained how, although she had changed her diet following her first diagnosis of cancer, she had not been as: 'focused on organic fruit and veg as I have been since I went macrobiotic in July. Now my approach is really focused on real, pure foods. Nothing which has any additives whatsoever. All of my fruit and veg now are organic.' The second diagnosis acted as a dynamic to spur changes that, they frenziedly hoped, would mean the difference between life and death: they were now desperate in their struggle to stay alive.

Like Susan, Louise, too, felt that changing her diet was something that lay within her own control and that might bolster her hopes of survival. She believed her '. . . master plan: The diet is the underpin of the entire thing, so I try to eat a strict diet of fresh organic fruit and vegetables, lots of water and lots of supplements'. This plan, however, was sometimes unfortunately undermined by her mother's well intentioned help. Louise explained how surprised she was when she came:

in from the hospital one night looking for a meal I had cooked, and she [her mother] said, 'I threw that out!' I had cooked it 18 hours previously, full of my organic vegetables, so I said, 'No! I am not having this' . . . My mother stormed out . . . I need this like a hole in the head, but I also need them.

Scrutiny of the respondents' reports suggests interesting differences in the power relationships between patients and doctors. The narratives presented by Susan, Rose and Louise all make reference to social perception of their doctors. Louise specially stressed that 'I love the doctors who look after me.' Susan described how she was teased by others because she was on 'first name terms' with her consultant. Rose too, described how pleased she felt that her specialist 'actually hugs me'. It would appear then that these consultants were all supportive. It should, however, be remembered that Louise, although professing to 'love the doctors' and who told me that 'I worked in the hospital I am being treated in, I am on first name terms with the doctors', felt uncomfortable when her challenge to the doctors regarding her treatment caused them to be '. . . shadier. Start avoiding her'. The consultants apparently felt less comfortable when treating patients who were on a par with them and, therefore, could challenge their judgement.

Susan, reporting on how she took control over her treatment, said she feared that '. . . my immune system will become damaged to the point . . . that when they hit you with something else your body cannot cope and I am not going to allow myself to get into that situation.' Louise said: 'Cancer is a loss of control. The cells have gone wild, control is lost. Do you completely surrender or fight for control back . . . Some are better at surrender but that is not my line of thinking. I want control.' Rose, too, thought along pro-active lines. She said: 'If the cancer is in control then I have lost it . . .' In our next interview, she continued with this theme telling me that she felt:

You can't actually take control of the disease but what you can take control of is your life. I can feel totally exhausted; all I want to do is go to bed, every nerve ending is painful, my bones hurt and my head hurts and I feel as sick as a dog and as if it is all going to end but I will not let it control me. But if I know why I am feeling like that . . . I have to know that I can . . . I can't control the cancer because unfortunately it is a free agent, it can go wherever it wants, that is the worrying part. It is not the bits that you have that you know about, it is where it is going to turn up next. So you can't actually control the cancer but to a certain extent you can control what it stops you doing.

In their endeavour to maintain control, Ben and Eilish made plans for his funeral. They had been troubled by the fact that Ben's religion, Judaism, might prevent him from being buried beside Roman Catholic Eilish. Ben, however, said that they had ultimately found our:

Happy Solution! We were told there was a burial ground, which is multi-denominational. This set our minds talking and we had a chat. . . . We are very relieved; it came through last week, the certificate with the grave number and card, a bit macabre to look at it . . . but it is a relief for both of us. I mean Eilish wants Ave Maria and I want Dies . . . I would like the death prayer for the Jews, I have the words inside . . . I can't think of it off hand. It is a big peace of mind for both of us so it is an ill wind . . . You have to be well organised.

The couple laughed when Ben explained that 'Eilish will always be on top of me' and told me that they would leave details of the plot and the funeral ceremonies with Ben's brother.

Chapter summary

The temporal period between treatment and recurrence seemed in many ways to be as difficult to live through as some of the physical crises of the illness. Respondents were fighting their cancer on three levels: it had struck them hard in almost every aspect of their lives, wreaking havoc in their practical, emotional and social worlds. All had been affected and the effects left them devastated. They had, through no fault of their own, found themselves in a position for which society had not prepared them. Everything, for them now, was changed.

This period following their treatment, which they had hoped would cure them, was a time of flux. All were eager to believe their cancer was now firmly in their past and had to convince not only themselves but, often and with more difficulty, others. They had undergone a massive change in their identity, their master status had become contaminated by their association with cancer. Their problem now lay in trying to effect a reversal in how they were perceived by others. This proved more difficult than most had imagined and was not helped by their own anxiety that the cancer might merely be dormant instead of dead. Although their medical teams had declared them to be 'cancer free', they could not entirely convince themselves.

Their experience with cancer had changed everything. It had injected suspicion into even their most basic element of trust in their bodies. The respondents were bewildered. Once innocent, their previously faithful body had proven treacherous; it had served as safe haven to malignant cells, allowing them access to secret places where they had bred and multiplied in aggressive and invasive swarms. It had conspired to transport those contaminating cells into their most vulnerable and private places, where they were incubated and nurtured. If this could happen in their own bodies, how then could anything be safe? They craved certainty.

In remission, and although allegedly cured, their social and psychological status was now anomalous; they felt that they lacked a clear identity and this insecurity was experienced as fear. To meet this anxiety some erected and maintained psychological barricades of entrenched denial, pinned solely on the evidence of the alleviation of their symptoms, endeavouring to persuade themselves that this respite heralded permanent cure. Although they presented sophisticated arguments to that effect to others, they found it difficult to be convincing.

In response to their need for assurance many, by now enlightened as to what might happen, exercised a heightened awareness of potential symptoms in an attempt to pre-empt their cancer's return. Many proactively engaged in attempts to bolster their body's own immune system, researching and educating themselves on the potential value of life style changes such as diet and exercise.

When there was a recurrence, their despair was more profound than at their first diagnosis. Their hope in medical science had proven barren and they were now desperate for any solution, which might affect the miracle of extending life. For the most part, they did not want to burden their intimates with knowledge of such profound gravity. Many struggled alone, repressing their heightened emotions in an endeavour to secure and maintain domestic harmony in what little time remained to them. This knowledge though was not easily repressed.

Lifetime relationships were, as a result, suddenly proving difficult. Family and friends, individuals who had, over time, come to be trusted and loved, now seemed somehow, distanced, unable fully to understand and relate to just how exacting the experience had been, how alarming the fear of death. These close relationships proved especially testing on two fronts. First, because sometimes what was meant by the carer to be close, well intentioned ministering, was experienced as unwarranted intrusion and second, because the respondents often felt constrained by the need to protect their family and carers from the harsh realities of their own situation.

All the respondents really enjoyed the opportunity to re-enter mainstream life by sharing in the mundane details of the ordinary world. However, the psychological adjustment and stark physical realities involved in living with a chronic dying trajectory entailed a shift away from the concerns of normal everyday life towards coming to terms with their new role.

When the Health Service provider's aim of encouraging patients towards the ideal state of acceptance appeared to be realised, then these patients responded by complying with expectations and beginning to make physical and psychological preparations for death. The participants had all, to varying extents, considered contributing ideas for their own funerals and disposal and two, both mothers, spoke to me of the arrangements they had made to provide for their children.

Their cancer exercised not only a devastating corporeal impact but also had the effect of placing them at a remove from the mainstream society into which they had been socialised.

5   Stage Four – Destination

The deaths

Thanks to the interventions of modern medical science, many individuals survive their encounter with cancer and go on to live out their lives in a full and productive way. However, the respondents you have met in this book, with one exception, were drawn from a population of individuals who had been reported to me as dying, they all volunteered to help in this research, because they felt that their contributions would help others.

These respondents lived through many, sometimes prolonged, periods of remission; during this time, many began to place their trust in this respite, hoping it would prove permanent. For the majority, when their period of remission ended, they had to face again the horror of their prognosis and, consequently, endure bouts of extreme frustration and bewilderment. This confrontation with their fears led to discussion and efforts at resolution between patients and their carers and often concerned practical issues, such as the physical site where death would occur. For some, such discussions freed them from previously internalised anxieties. Decisions, once articulated and arrived at, allowed their wishes to be met.

In agreement with Kubler-Ross (1995), all the respondents interviewed, as well as many of those patients studied during my periods of participant observation in the hospices, had, at some stage, tempered their attitudes to their imminent deaths. This change in outlook resulted in a philosophic shift away from fighting to stay alive towards an acknowledgement of their impending death. Though this acceptance of death was assumed, to varying degrees, by all my interviewees, it should be noted that I observed some other patients (whom I did not interview) in the hospices, who, whilst in a conscious state, raged against their ultimate fate. They had clearly not arrived at that stage of acceptance.

Residential hospices in the United Kingdom function to meet three key needs; first they offer accommodation to individuals who are dying, to give their family or carers a period of temporary respite from their caring role; second, they offer residential care to people who are dying, who require clinical monitoring during a change in their drug regime and third, they also offer a sanctuary in which death can actually take place.

Lawton's description of hospices being places of '. . . deterioration, decline and death' (2000: 75) runs counter to my observations and experiences. Although hospices are, indisputably, places where people die, my experience of working there was of participating within an actively caring community. The remit of the, for the most part, sensitive and compassionate staff and volunteers who worked there was to nurse the patients competently through the end-stage of their lives and into their deaths. This was usually done with, when appropriate, a warm and ready smile. This positive but realistic service symbolised hospice care to me and certainly seemed to be appreciated by those patients who were conscious and lucid. Yet, because mainstream public opinion usually associates hospice care with immediate death, there can be a resistance by some patients and their carers to using their facilities.

In spite of the accelerated growth in the development and application of palliative care (Maddocks, 1996) dying is still, as may be expected, an unpleasant business. Those who are dying of some forms of cancer are forced to live through their own bodily breakdown. Appetite, already confused by taste-altering drugs, dissipates and, when it is possible for food to be taken, it is often thrown up before it can be digested. Double incontinence is frequent and, with vomiting, is, for many, the greatest fear. Noises and smells from an exhausted, leaking body not only affect the patient, who may experience a total surrender of dignity, but also penetrate and permeate the spatial boundaries of the accommodation, intruding into and threatening to rupture others' sense of bodily territory (Lawton, 2000). The patients I observed in hospices were usually aware of their body's impact on others and, if able, would take any steps they could to alleviate the stench, cloaking themselves in strong smelling perfumes and encouraging the staff to light scented candles around their beds.

Lawton (2000) argues that hospices protect the public from the reality of dying and it is true that dirt, decay, disintegration and smell are not even openly discussed as part of hospice promotion (Froggatt, 1997). The public usually witness only the more positive aspects of dying, such as the development of a philosophic attitude and increased wisdom, as they are sheltered from the truth of the sometimes harrowing experience.

Not surprisingly, the respondents attempted to measure the acceleration of their deterioration and most of them tended to use pain as a benchmark. Hospice and hospital patients were subjected to a routine of pain control. This should have prevented, or significantly reduced their pain, but this was not always the case. Patients suffered; their pain, whether real or imagined, physical or psychological, became manifest in distress that transmitted itself to others who were present, causing some of them in turn to become disturbed. The contagion of this unease was threatening to one of the principal canons of Good Death, as it presented the possibility of jeopardising the emotional stability of other individuals who were present.

Rose's narrative

The last time I saw Rose was on the 6th December, just five days before she died. It was freezing, an overcast day, which threatened snow, and she, as usual, was dressed in the same faded pink, fleecy tracksuit that she had worn when I first met her. Although she haltingly managed the few steps from the front door to the living room she was clearly exhausted and seemed very unwell. As ever, in spite of the proximity of the oxygen cylinder that had appeared one month earlier, Rose smoked steadily away; she had, after all, said in our third interview that she smoked: 'more when I have more pain. If I am pain free I actually go without any cigarettes at all. I smoke more when I am bad [feeling pain] but I would rather do that than take the pain killers which tend to make my whole system go all at once.' Finding comfort in such a bleak situation cannot have been easy. However, Rose's inclination to indulge in smoking supports Graham, who considers smoking to be '. . . a necessity when material and human resources are stretched . . . In a lifestyle stripped of new clothes, make-up, hairdressing, travel by bus and evenings out, smoking can become an important symbol of one's participation in an adult consumer culture' (1987: 55).

When I asked how she had been she said:

Not too well! I have been back in hospital. They don't really know quite why, what went wrong but I think I had an embolism . . . and they are not at all sure because they can't find it. The trouble is that my lungs are so badly scarred from the cancer that, if it dropped into the lung, they couldn't see it anyway. And the fact that I haven't recovered yet, I am still quite . . . my breathing is still very bad, would point to an embolism to me.

On the 30th [November] I was taken in [to hospital] by ambulance. I had gone into the kitchen, it was about 2 [pm], to get a glass of water or something and I went dizzy, started to see stars. Marie [her daughter] was in here [the living room] then, just suddenly I couldn't breathe. I felt as if I had been kicked in the chest by a mule, the floor came up, the ceiling went down, the room went round and I just couldn't catch my breath at all. Marie phoned for the Doctor . . . I was heaving for breath, I was making terrible noises . . . and they got an ambulance to us quite quickly and they kept saying to me, 'Don't panic, don't panic.' Well I was not panicking, I just couldn't breathe! And they kept saying 'Calm down.' I was calm, I just couldn't breathe. They took me in. I was on oxygen the whole time, then slowly I came off it but . . . I haven't really been with it and I have had so much pain and discomfort in my stomach. I have had radiotherapy in both hips, which has burnt all my insides, so the pain in my gut is really quite severe and I now have a urinary tract infection, which is due again to being burnt and that is making me feel quite sick. [At this point Rose became quite short of breath, requiring oxygen, so we took a short break.]

I will see Dr. T on the 18th, so I will speak to him. It is a bit unpredictable, because the way I feel at the moment . . . I am very worn down, I am very low, I don't normally get low, it takes a lot to bring me down but it has been a long time now and I have had a lot of radiotherapy treatment. I have not been well . . . I am just hoping to stay away from the radiotherapy long enough to recover, because it does take a while to come back [to normal health] especially when you have had a lot [of radiotherapy] in a short period of time and it does tend to knock me for six. I will just hope now that everything that is going wrong will just settle down and I will start to pick up.

The oscillation between acceptance and denial, remission and recurrence, hope and despair continued even, it seemed, until the moment of death. Rose was still in an optimistic frame of mind in which she believed that her health would settle and she would 'start to pick up'. Her hope still seemed buoyant, sufficient for her to assume that her 'feeling well' may indicate that she was once again 'on the mend'. This notion was, however, confounded by her being 'slap back down' again within a twenty-four hour period and subject to the attention of an ambulance crew, people she did not know and who, although trained in emergency procedures, misunderstood her, despite her protestations. She was frustrated by her own physical helplessness.

However, she was full of the promise of future events, telling me that although she was looking forward to going back to her native Greece, the trip there was:

. . . not actually important for me, but certainly the baby [her grandchild who was due to be born shortly after Christmas] is. I just hope I will be able to be there for Marie, there is no point in my being like this, so I need to get up off my butt . . . but I don't know if I can manage it just yet. [laughter] Maybe if my gut would settle I would feel better, because I can't stand up straight, it is very painful and I don't seem able to do anything. I have chronic diarrhoea and there is nothing I can do about it till the burns [a side-effect of radiotherapy] go . . . and when it starts to heal I shall feel better but I would not have thought it would have kept up for this long. They said to me [the after-effects would last for] about three or four days, but they lied, because it is eight days now, so they are obviously trying to . . . they do this a lot with the chemo routine. They will tell you lots of fibs; they are good fibs but if someone tells you it will take three weeks it will take four, if someone tells you it will take three days and it takes three weeks, well you are just unlucky. But rather than psych you up for three weeks of feeling ill, they will say to you, 'It will take three or four days', though they are really expecting it to take a couple of weeks.

Rose, although suffering cruelly from the side effects of her treatment, was still insistent on presenting an optimistic view of her position. She was clearly very much alive, to the extent that she was envisaging herself in a future, which would include her grandchild and potential trips back to her homeland of Greece. It was the promise of these social events which stimulated her drive to go on living and caused her to censure what she implied was her own idle behaviour and minimise the reports of her pain. Indeed, so loath was she to appear to be malingering that she cited some of her individual problems which, when articulated, formed a veritable litany of validating symptoms. It seemed also that she had grown sceptical of medical promises but, rather than appear cynical or jaded by this, she instead trivialised it and relegated it to the childish level of telling 'fibs'.

She was, however, a much harsher judge of her own role, guiltily rebuking herself in the fear that her illness had affected her ability as a mother. She said:

I can't do that much really, I feel I have let them [her children] down a bit. Not that there is a lot that I can do but I just feel that now they needed me and now I am not available, so that is something I can't help. I have no control over it . . .

She did take heart from the close relationship which her children shared, telling me:

. . . they are very loving to each other, they don't argue . . . but in a nice way they tease each other and both usually end up laughing. I know they are there for each other, if I pop off [die], which is comforting. My mum has got to do something practical in order to feel that she is helping. She said to me, 'Let me know what you want', when I came out of hospital. 'Anything! I'll come and sit with you all day if you want.' But there is nothing more that I do not want. I love my mum but I can't sit with her all day! I need my own space and I don't think my mum understands that. She is having difficulties in accepting that I will die; in fact she has said that I am not going to die, I am going to go with her [die together], [laughing] we will go together when we go!

Typically, she minimised the awful threat of her impending death and softened the expression of the frustration she endured as a result of her mother's behaviour by tempering it with an expression of love. It was, though, her role as mother of two teenagers, which caused her most concern. It should be noted that, at this time her daughter, Marie, was heavily pregnant and also about to celebrate her birthday in just ten days. Her much loved son, Tony, was away from home, training for a career as a pilot at a flying school in Florida and was due to return home in a few weeks for the Christmas holiday. Rose had a lot to look forward to.

She continued and, in these, her last words to me, summed up the key themes of this book. Unconsciously, she referred to the framework of time, typically drew on heroic themes and also made reference to how things practical and social entered into and affected her emotional experience. Her words to me were forward looking:

I'm really looking forward to seeing my son. I don't think I'm going to be that well, this is going to be a slow process. I think this will take me into the New Year; still the main thing is I get back on my feet at some time but I'm not going to be . . . I know I'm not because I know how ill I am and I know that I won't be that well, even if I want to be, but it will come. I will just have to wait and see . . . I have always got an aim, I couldn't ever be aimless, there is just too many things going on, even though I am just sitting here looking and not doing. There is an awful lot I don't want to give up and I'm certainly not ready to die yet. There is just no way; I am not ready yet. Not until I see my son at least settled in a job, if not settled with a family. I expect a lot less and I do get a lot more out of it. I think our fate is mapped out for us, you can't say, well this has happened it is not very fair because I don't think there is any such thing as fair. I think it is a case of hit and miss, whatever we do in life, it is all a chance. We don't ever know what any outcome in life will be. It is a case of you pay your money and take your chance.

Rose's death – 'Bye darlings, love you all!'

Marie telephoned me, five days later, the evening her mother died. A few days later we met in her mother's home. I found the occasion emotionally difficult, as Marie, who bore a close resemblance to her mother, sat where Rose would have done. The room had been stripped of the familiar medical aids and oxygen cylinder. She explained that even 'the medicine cupboard is empty, the Macmillan nurse came and took it all away'. It seemed that not only was her home bereft of her mother's tangible presence but also her symbolic presence, her pharmaceutical drugs, had also been removed. I asked Marie what happened around the time of her mother's death. She said:

She was fine over the weekend. You know she had problems with her breathing? Sunday, she really wasn't feeling too good all day and Monday . . . down and a bit poorly . . . not normal. Monday night she had a breathing attack and I gave her everything I possibly could, I couldn't do any more. I phoned an ambulance and they took her to the hospital and stabilised her overnight. She couldn't talk because she was so out of breath, just the odd few words but she seemed alright . . . She seemed as if she was going to recover but she couldn't really talk. She was making sense, telling me to go home and get her some bits that she wanted, 'Don't sit here, go home and eat your dinner.' Tuesday morning, she had a relapse and then another one. Her breathing was really bad and she could only say a few words at a time. I visited her on Tuesday, during the day and she

was a lot worse and they moved her from on the actual ward to a single room
and the nurse said they had given her more drugs to combat the pain. She was
alright while I was there, falling asleep and waking up but she was quite with it.
Then she said, 'You may as well go, I'm just going to fall asleep, there is no point
in your being there.' So I said, 'Alright then', because I could see she wanted me
to go. I came back later but she asked me to leave again because she was falling
asleep.

Then about 11[pm], the hospital phoned and said she had had a third relapse
and her breathing was really chronic. 'Can you come to the hospital, because we
do not think your Mum is going to make it through the night?' I got Nan [her
grandmother], we went to the hospital. Nan was very upset already. On Tuesday
afternoon when we were there, the doctor took us into a little room and he said,
'Look, I really don't think your Mum's going to be here at Christmas; it is that
bad. I don't know how long, I can't give you a time limit.' I was devastated but,
at the same time, I had been told that before [during Rose's other crises]. I broke
down in tears and so did Nan but I cleared myself up and went to see Mum. The
following night, when they phoned, my first thought was 'Oh my God! Tony [her
brother in Florida] is not here.' I feel guilty about the way I felt, because when
Mum was first ill before and they said, 'She has less than ten days', something in
the back of my mind, something . . . I wouldn't believe it, I was upset, I cried,
I was very upset . . . but for some reason I knew she wasn't going to go. I knew
she wouldn't leave me and I was so blasé about it, I kept going to see her and she
was alright. They said, 'She has only got until Christmas' and I believed it and I
have never felt like that before.

Tuesday night, we stayed in the hospital. I went for a couple of hours and slept
in a different room. Mum kept asking what we were doing here, I said, 'Oh, we
have come to visit you' and she kept saying, 'It is the middle of the night!' and
I said, 'No, it is just early in the morning.' She asked why I was there when it
was early and I said, 'I have an ante-natal appointment at ten o'clock, I thought
I would see you first.' I don't think she was quite aware but she knew something
was a bit . . . she wasn't with it enough to . . . she couldn't see the clock but
she knew it was silly hours . . . and at 5 [am] my grandmother came in and said,
'Quick come in, your Mum has stopped breathing.'

She had actually stopped breathing for about a minute and a half and she started
breathing again, it was just like . . . Oh . . . ! She was conscious, she was talking to
us. She kept telling me that she loved me, she loved Tony, she loved Del [Marie's
boyfriend], just silly little things like that. She kept blowing me kisses. She asked
for water. That was Tuesday night and in the morning, she remembered I had been
there. I told her I had gone home in between and she said 'Rubbish!' Wednesday,
she perked up, was more with it, more awake. She couldn't say much, only a couple
of words, but she was actually moving whereas on Tuesday, the nurses were
turning her because she couldn't. Then I saw her Wednesday morning and I
knew that was the beginning of the end.

This account of the time leading up to her mother's death provides further
evidence of the difficult physical and psychological swings which mark

the dying journey. From being 'fine over the weekend', Rose's health had deteriorated to such an extent that she was largely moribund with only brief periods of lucidity. Not surprisingly, her worsening condition alerted her daughter to the gravity of her position. Although content to be at home with her daughter when she felt physically in control, she was probably pleased to be brought to the hospital when she had the critical breathing attack. Rose had said she wanted to die in hospital because as she had told me, 'If you are ill and you are on the way out, the last thing you want is panic. Also, if you are in hospital, you know that there is more pain control and the care is there that you would need.' On another occasion she commented: 'if I have got to die, then I would like to die in hospital, don't want to go to the hospice, don't want to die at home. I don't want the children to see me dying.' More than anything else, Rose's urge was to protect her children from her dying, so it was possibly in a bid to distract Marie that she sent her off to do something practical, 'get her some bits'.

Rose was subject to cruel swings in her physical condition, which changed dramatically, veering alarmingly from stable to critical. Rose may have found those times of crisis most frustrating as her breathing made it difficult to make herself understood. Although heavily sedated and dying, I would be surprised if Rose was not aware of the implications of being moved 'from on the actual ward to a single room' and capable of discerning that her daughter's recall to the hospital at such an anti-social hour signalled her impending death. Visiting patients in hospital is usually an activity conducted during social hours but being summoned to appear at night suggests a situation of utmost crisis such as imminent or actual death. Consequently, Marie and her grandmother rushed to be by Rose's side fearing this would be their final opportunity to see her alive. They had, remember, at the behest of the medical staff, already been removed from Rose's company and taken to another 'little room' where the imminence of Rose's death was made clear when her doctor said 'I really don't think your mum is going to be here at Christmas.' Whilst a surface reading of their separation from the activity in the ward may suggest it was the medical team trying to respect their privacy, a deeper analysis may instead suggest it was an attempt to preserve the moral order that prevailed in the ward. How may the others there, staff and patients, have reacted to Marie and her Nan, if they had broken down? It is, also, particularly interesting to recall how, during our final interview, Rose said that the doctors 'will tell you lots of fibs. They are good fibs, but if someone tells you it will take three weeks it will take four weeks.' This is effectively the same technique being applied in reverse, the gradual dismantling of hope, which the doctor applied when breaking the news.

These events took place on the 10th December but the doctor's suggestion focused the family's mind on the death not actually occurring until
around Christmas time, the 25th when it actually occurred on the 11th.

What was most critical to Rose during this difficult time was her need
to convey her love to her family. Marie continued, telling me that it was
'Because I have seen it happen before with so many other people' that
she realised her mother was dying. She continued:

> . . . [Rose] perked up, she was really happy to see us, she wasn't talking much but
> she was ok. I went to my ante-natal appointment and came back and Mum said,
> 'It wore me out having you here last night because I couldn't sleep properly' so
> I said, 'Alright then, we will not stay, we will go home and see you tomorrow.'
> She said . . . Mum just sat there and cried and held my hand and I thought, 'Oh
> dear!' I said, 'That is just what you need!' [laughter]. We sat and I said, 'This
> is great conversation isn't it?' and she said 'Yes!' I said 'We are a right pair of
> boring old farts!' and she said, 'Aren't we just . . .' She was having a laugh and
> she started dozing off at 11.30 am, dozing and wakening and she said, 'Go, I am
> going to fall asleep.' I said 'Ok then' but I had to wait for Nan to come back. I
> went in the other room and I said 'Ok I will see you later', gave her a kiss and
> said, 'I love you' and she blew me a kiss, she said, 'Bye'. She waved to me.

> I went downstairs to get a magazine and just before 1 o'clock a nurse came in
> and said, 'I think your mum has passed away.' So I went into her. I put on her
> necklaces and stuff, which I still have on and waited for Nan to get back and we
> told her. She was very, very distraught, I was trying to get her to calm down a bit.
> She was crying her eyes out. I gave her a big hug and said, 'We were expecting
> it' and she said, 'No we weren't, no, we weren't expecting it! It was not going
> to come now!' and I said 'Well, it has been coming for the last five or six years;
> it is not unexpected.' She said, 'No, no, no, we didn't know!' I said, 'But the
> doctor called us in yesterday and told us that she was not going to be here at
> Christmas. How can you say you didn't expect it to happen?' Even now she still
> won't accept that Mum was ill before. She kept saying, 'We have lost our love, we
> have lost our love!' I don't know what she meant by that, she was very, very upset,
> and I tried to comfort her, I said, 'You have still got me, Tony, there is a new
> baby on the way, we have the rest of the family.' All she could say was, 'It's not
> enough . . .'

Rose was able to gather what strength remained to her and use it in one
last desperate bid to prolong her relationship with her family. Slipping
in and out of consciousness, when lucid, she still endeavoured, in an
heroic attempt, to shield her daughter from the reality of her death. It
is interesting, therefore, to speculate on the motives which lay behind
her comment, 'It wore me out having you both here last night because
I couldn't sleep properly'. I argue that this mild rebuke was actually an
attempt to divert her daughter from witnessing her death. It is not surprising that Rose, during these last few moments of her life, which she

was well aware was quietly and quickly escaping, 'just sat there and cried';
she knew that she was dying and she was aware of the pain it would cause
her family.

How, though, does one behave when dying? What is permissible? What
may one say? At this time of dramatic and heightened tension, humour
was used, perhaps in an attempt to ease the pressure and lift something
of the emotional angst. Still, Rose remained entrenched in her need, as
mother, to protect her child. She finally died, much as she had wished, in
hospital, in a virtual re-enactment of the scenario she had envisaged four
months before when, in telling me how she wished to die, she stressed
that she did not want her family to witness her death and said: 'I'd rather
say "Bye darlings, love you all" and that is it . . .'

Gita's death – 'She just drifted away . . .'

You may remember that Ash's 41-year-old wife, Gita, who had delayed in
presenting the lump in her breast for medical treatment for over two years,
had died in the local hospice just a few weeks prior to our interview. I
interviewed him, his two sons, and his mother-in-law in the elegant living
room of their modern family home. He explained that he felt: 'The last
three weeks of her life was just sheer hell, she must have walked through
hell, the pain and everything was just very uncomfortable.' He continued,
telling me that he had given 'permission for her to die'. When I asked
him if he felt that that had made it easier for her, he replied:

Yes, it did because the last two or three weeks, she had been fighting [to continue
living]; she realised it herself. This is a no win situation, she is going to go anyway.
I said, 'Look if you think you are not going to make it, don't fight, let go. You have
done your bit.' And she said, 'Yes, I have done everything I can, I don't think I
can survive.' I said, 'Yes, don't worry about it; I know you are worried about the
two children but I will make sure that they are looked after. Don't fight, let it go
because you have done what you have done, there is no way out.' And she said,
'Yes, I agree with you.'

Gita's role as mother dominated her perception of life. Having delayed
too long in reporting her symptoms, she now appreciated the inevitability
of her death and struggled to come to terms with the loss she knew her
children would experience. She did not want to leave them nor to be
responsible for causing them pain. As Ash said:

. . . her main worry was Dalraj [her 8-year-old son]. [Gita said] 'How will we
cope?' Like all mums with young children . . . 'How we will cope? What will
happen? What will happen to him?' And we discussed it privately and I said
'Look [this] is something which, if you are to go [die] you are not going to do

anything about it.' It is just . . . we have to take it from there. There is no point in worrying about it but then again, it is a mum and any mum would worry about her children.

In spite of her overwhelming desire to stay with her children, the futility of her struggle was clear and she reluctantly accepted her sad prognosis and allowed herself to die. This was, however, only after she had gained her husband's assurance that he would 'make sure that they [the children] are looked after'.

I asked Ash if, after that conversation, her dying had been easier; and he said:

Yes, when I came then they [her medical team] said that they were going to put her to sleep, rest the whole body, unwind the whole thing and I realised that was it. There was no way out now. They said, she would just drift away, which she wanted. She just wanted to go peacefully, which she did. That was a prayer answered. It could have happened this week, or next week, but I think everybody knew it was just around the corner. I think Sunday was her deadline.

Ash finally realised that, in spite of his wife's determined struggle to survive, her death was inescapable and, having confronted the reality of this and accepted that 'There was no way out', was comforted by the team's reassurance that she would die peacefully. For him it was 'a prayer answered'. Yes, she would die, and the psychological pain of that could not be denied but at least the fact of her death would be easier to bear in the knowledge that it had been physically painless. Gita may have sensed the strength he had drawn from this coming to terms, because her behaviour changed; Ash said:

. . . her last three weeks were just hell for us . . . And for her . . . I mean more her than us . . . Because she couldn't stand . . . She just wanted to just literally go . . . because she was just fed up . . . She just wanted to call it a day now . . . and I said to her 'Just don't fight now but just let go.' I mean no one wants to see their loved one lost but nobody wants to see their loved one to suffer. I said 'Don't fight now, just let it go because I don't think you know this is something for you to call it a day now.' And she said 'Yes, I think you are right, I've done everything I could for the children.' She said 'I'm fed up and I just want to go . . .' The last week was just literally, you know, complete torture . . . Dr. X and Sister Y told her what they were going to do . . . They would put a syringe driver with a high dose of morphine and just rest the whole body. They say there is nothing to be done about it, just let the whole body rest and she will drift away, which is very good because . . . she just drifted away.

In view of the fact that her life was 'hell', it may be surprising that Gita was so determined to cling on, regardless of her own pain. She, after all, 'wanted to call it a day', but still insisted on maintaining her hold on a life in which she lived in 'complete torture' so that she could be close to her young sons. Ultimately, though, her pain tested her endurance, until she reluctantly acquiesced to her husband's suggestion and decided that she would 'just let go'.

The family went on to talk of how Gita had been transferred into a single room within the hospice, three days before she died. Ash explained how this had helped them all: 'I slept one night with her in that room you know but Saturday I couldn't sleep. I just frozen myself completely, don't know why, but I just couldn't do it.' Dalraj assumed control of the conversation, saying: 'She kept on asking me "What will you do when I've gone, when Mum's gone?" She kept on asking that . . . and I said "I'll stay with daddy!"' Ash said: 'Wednesday night we all had a conversation with her – we all went to the hospice and had a conversation with her . . .' The older of the two, Vikram, a 14-year-old, interrupted him to clarify how his mother had been conscious, saying: 'She was talking that day . . .' Ash nodded his head in agreement and said: 'Yes she was talking . . .' At this moment, Saldu, Gita's mother, who had remained silent until then commented: 'The only thing is that she was talking too much that day . . .'

The family sat in silent contemplation for a few moments; this was eventually broken when Vikram, talking as much to the others as to me, said:

I think she knew what was happening. She knew she was dying and that talking she did . . . She was talking away about, 'This is my last time I'm going to talk to the kids, my mum and my husband . . .' and when we came back on Thursday she was, as Dad said, semi-conscious . . . And that is when I felt really shocked . . . That is when I first cried, except when she was first diagnosed. When I came on Thursday that is when it hit me hard and it hit my family as well . . . On Friday . . . that is, like, when I was really taking my temper out, having a go at everyone I saw. Anyone who stepped in the way of my path, I pushed about and Friday I came back to the hospice . . . and . . . I knew it, then, that it was today, tomorrow or the next day . . . It was at that stage that she said 'Good bye . . .' And that was the last words . . .

Ash interrupted him saying:

Yes, Saturday morning I gave her a glass of water, early morning, about half past six . . . There was no response. She was just literally sleeping, you know, and her body was completely . . . It was just because of her brain and her heart was keep going. Everything else was, you know, just gone because her digestive system had packed up . . . and it just literally took its course on Sunday. She just wanted to be free with what she was going through. She wanted to go peacefully and quietly . . . She just stopped breathing . . . She just drifted away.

When I asked if anyone was with her when she died, Ash said:

Yes, I was there, I just went out of the room . . . I stayed there the whole evening. I went into the M&S room to sleep [A family room whose furnishings were donated by Marks and Spencer]. That night, I just couldn't just keep my eyes open, I don't know why . . . and, at 11.50 [pm], she passed on. They just came and gave me a call and I went back [to her room]. But then again, if I was there or not, it wouldn't have made any difference in such a way for nothing could be done about it. It just make sure she was nice and peaceful. I don't think she knew what was going on around her. She was just completely unconscious anyway.

Although Gita was unconscious at the time she died, Ash felt:

She did die well because that is what she wanted, you know? She did, because she went completely peacefully, she just drifted away. That is what she wanted. I couldn't ask more than that. It is what we were hoping for and praying for. That she didn't have to suffer any more . . .

John's death – 'Dying as an everyday thing'

When I met Mary, she proudly said that she was 76 years old. Since the death of her husband and son, both within a six-month period, she lived alone in her semi-detached, rural cottage but was often visited by her surviving son and daughter. She said she was a regular attendant at the local Anglican church. I saw her three times, during which she discussed the deaths of her 47-year-old son, which occurred at home, and the hospital death of her husband. Sadly, since I finished my fieldwork, Mary herself has died.

Her son, John, died from cancer of the bowel. He had never married and lived with his mother. She explained how, although he saw his doctor on three different occasions, 'he was told that he had indigestion and given medicine to sort it out'. His physical condition, however, suddenly deteriorated alarmingly, leading to emergency surgery and his being put on a course of chemotherapy. However, he received only two doses, since the treatment was so severe that it resulted in an emergency admission to hospital. There, his doctor told Mary that his:

. . . liver had stopped working and I said to the doctor, 'You won't tell him his liver has stopped working will you?' And the doctor said, 'Well I won't tell him but, if he asks, I shall tell him.' Well, then he [John] says to the doctor, 'What happens about my chemotherapy – have I still got to have it today?' and he [the doctor] said, 'No, we're not going to give it to you any more because we find that it's not working. And now your liver has packed up.' And straight away John said, 'There is no need for me to stop in here, I can go home' but the doctor had already said that they were not going to let him go home because they thought I couldn't cope [because of her age and bad health]. John said, 'I'm not going to have any more chemotherapy, I'm going to come home . . .'

John knew the grievous implications of having a non-functioning liver. Being informed that he would no longer receive chemotherapy had alerted him to the severity of his condition. Suddenly made aware he would not have long to live, he focused his thoughts on finding comfort and voiced his wish to return home, a place where his friends had gathered previously to cheer him through the rigours of recovering from his surgery: a safe place to die. Mary remembered how he had enjoyed it, when:

. . . he first came out of hospital, before he got bad, he would sit in the chair there and all his mates used to come, even from work and from where he worked before . . . He knew he was going to die at the end of the year. . . . He was determined and they couldn't believe it that someone that knew . . . he was going to die . . . could act like he could but he did. He wasn't miserable, or nothing, he used to laugh with them.

John was determined to maintain his controlled front and rebelled against the precepts of the traditional sick role, by keeping in as close contact as he could with his friends in mainstream society and refusing to go to bed. His established circle of friends, 'mates even from work and from where he worked before', offered him their support and the opportunity to forget his fears and lose himself in their company. It was to this support and, perhaps, to that time, that, realising that he was dying, he now wished to return.

Mary continued telling me of John's disposition then:

He was so cheerful all the time, right until when he came in [from hospital] that Saturday and he was so ill and I think he knew then that he only had so long. I think he knew then that he was dying but he still wasn't letting on to me, if you know what I mean. I knew it and he knew it but it was something he didn't come out with and I thought well, if he wants me to think that he's going to get better then I shall live that with him, which I did do.

Mary intuited, and respected, her son's unspoken desire not to discuss or acknowledge his impending death. This is an almost classic example of Glaser and Strauss's (1965) 'mutual pretence' category in which, although the concerned individuals are well aware of the reality of the impending death, both refuse to acknowledge it openly.

Mary continued, telling me that, as a result of his sudden decision to discharge himself from hospital, coupled with a clerical error which allowed that to happen, John's return home to die was badly managed, resulting in anxiety for both his family and the medics involved. She explained, at length, how physically weak John was and how both she and her other son, Tom, had struggled just to get John into the house. She wondered how she would manage the practical problems involved in nursing him at home:

> . . . So, Saturday morning, Tom went in the car to get him and he [John] was really ill then . . . I had already said to Tom, 'He won't be able to go upstairs no more.' I did not feel that I wanted to make a bedroom down here for him to come home to without asking him, I wanted him to say it his-self. I . . . said, 'I have been thinking, do you think it is a good idea to bring your bed down, in there? Just for a couple of nights, till your legs get stronger?' and he said, 'Yes, I've been thinking that myself for I shall never go upstairs.'

In situating his physical decline within a temporal framework and suggesting that the proposed changes to the layout of the house were only for 'a couple of nights', Mary was effectively colluding with her son, in their mutual pretence, maintaining and bolstering the charade that his condition was merely temporary and that he would recover. She had recognised his struggle to acknowledge his situation openly and this had prompted her discreet and sensitive management. John, not surprisingly, was quick to seize the opportunity that his mother offered him.

In spite of her efforts, John's installation back into his home environment did not function as smoothly as Mary had wished. Other family members had met the challenge initiated by John's sudden return, by converting an area of the tiny downstairs accommodation into what she described to me as 'John's new place'. His bed was brought downstairs and a delegation sent into town to make what purchases they believed necessary to secure his comfort and privacy. She told me how shocked the district nurse was when, by chance, she learned that John had returned home to die. The nurse knew that John was now in extremis and without the medical input to which he was entitled and which he urgently needed. Mary said that:

> . . . she [the district nurse] couldn't believe it. She had not had a letter . . . did not know nothing. She said, 'I'll be back this afternoon.' She said he needed a urine bottle, a special mattress, a commode and she couldn't get anything, she said it was all shut [it being the weekend]. She was so upset, so my grand-daughter took me back into town in the afternoon and we tried in the chemist for some of the things the nurse had mentioned . . . and then the nurse came back and said he [John] needed 24-hour nursing but she had not been notified [and so could not provide this service]. Sunday night, he was sick all night . . . he had this thing that feeds in the morphine [a syringe driver] but when he left the hospital they had taken it off, so therefore, he wasn't taking nothing, and the nurse was in a proper state because she could not get hold of a doctor. And all Sunday afternoon, she said, 'I have to get hold of a doctor because if anything should happen to John tonight, you are going to be in queer street.' And she was phoning around here

and everywhere for a good hour and eventually she got hold of one of the doctors. Then a doctor came on Monday and put the thing on him for his morphine and the nurse said he had not very long. She said they would get another nurse in for tonight – she was very nice, a very nice person.

How may John have experienced these events? I would imagine that, in spite of his pain and sickness, he probably felt relieved at being able to return home and his mother's diplomatic handling of the practical and psychological problems caused by his physical incapacity may have encouraged this relief. I doubt that he had any conception of the practical crisis that his homecoming had provoked both within his family home and, also, in the community medical and social support teams. Seventy-six-year-old Mary had, after all, been absorbed in psychologically filtering and physically handling, as best she could, the fact of John's impulsive return home. Through a combination of lack of notice and lack of familiarity with such circumstances, she had, though, not been able to assemble the fundamentals the district nurse deemed essential to his basic nursing care. When alerted to the need for such equipment, Mary's attempts to find it, although enthusiastically supported by her family, were thwarted by the fact that she lived in a small town, where the pharmacy did not find a reason to stock such specialist equipment. At this, the end-stage of his illness, and without adequately prescribed and administered pharmaceutical drugs, John was probably drifting in and out of consciousness. When medical help was finally found, it is possible that the relief this brought to his mother, Mary, was communicated to John.

Mary continued telling me how his death occurred, remembering how one of the nurses, who had been positioned on shift to care for him, told her:

You can talk to him, because although he's going [dying] the last thing that will go on him will be his brain, he knows what you are talking about . . . And I think John was like me, he lived a lie at the end, he didn't want me to know, and I thought, well if he wants it like that – I'm like that. But . . . when I stood there talking to him Tuesday morning all the tears come down his face . . . I can understand that . . . It felt as if . . . he just didn't want to go . . . but there . . . he really didn't suffer.

Mary was determined that her son would die exactly as he wished. She did not want him to spend his last few moments knowing the extent of the pain that his dying was causing her and so she fought to contain her own emotions. She went on to tell me that:

. . . it was only when I was talking to him on that Tuesday morning, because they used to call me a proper old fuss pot, and I said to him, 'Oh your old fuss pot is still here, fussing you', and he didn't actually cry but the tears just kept rolling down his face, I had to keep wiping the tears off . . . Since Charlie [her husband] died, he [John] was all for me. We were not like mother and son, we were like pals.

Although the relationship between mother and son had always been close, since her husband's death, just six months before, Mary and John had developed a special bond, which had helped ease the mourning for her husband. Now that it was time for John, too, to die, Mary desperately wanted to return some of the support John had shown her when she had needed it. When I interviewed her, her grief for her son was still raw but still she took time to seek out and draw comfort from the fact that she did not:

. . . think he was afraid of dying, I think that because he . . . because the tears just run down his face, that he didn't want to go because he was going to leave me all by myself. Apart from that he took dying as an everyday thing. I mean, I do myself; you can't prevent it. I'm just thankful . . . I'm glad that he didn't find out beforehand. He would have had to live on tablets . . . but he was able to live his life.

Steve's death – 'He just died well'

I met divorced, 37-year-old Sophie, who said she had only recently returned to work as a nurse following the death of her three-year-old son, Steve. She explained that she was currently in a relationship but now lived in her smart semi-detached bungalow with only her other son, seven-year-old Dean. Her wider family were physically and emotionally close. Sophie said that, though she was not then a regular attendant, she thought of herself as being Church of England. I saw her twice, when we discussed her son's death, which had occurred at home.

Steve's condition had initially been detected approximately six months before his death. It had been discovered during a medical check, which arose as a result of having 'a playful dig' from a friend. Following his participation in a clinical drugs trial, which had involved ten doses of intensive chemotherapy and an operation to remove his left kidney, Steve seemed to recover well, so much so that, at one stage, she hoped that he was cured. During his last summer:

We did lots of things, we went out, the carnival . . . did all the things. Things that you would normally do, because he was well enough. At the end of August, my Mum and I took Dean and Steve up to Norfolk for a long weekend . . . and while we were there Steve wouldn't eat. Then he began to complain of a tummy ache . . .

Desperate to persuade herself as much as others that Steve had recovered from his cancer, Sophie and Steve lived as normal a life as was possible. However, confronted with his returning symptoms, Sophie, not surprisingly, feared the worst and returned for medical opinion, ending up, eventually, at one of the senior London children's hospitals:

They did all the tests again . . . and the 6th September . . . they called us in. . . . It was a total nightmare; she [Steve's consultant] just said, 'I'm sorry to have to tell you this, but we can't cure him.' I felt angry, very angry. Angry at . . . them, they couldn't do anything . . . Surely, there must be something they can do? But they said, 'No'. You can't go higher than the consultant paediatrician on the oncology ward at that hospital . . . There is nobody else, you know? You just had to accept that they can't . . . And I did accept it . . . It's not easy . . .

Her reaction to being told that a cure was not possible was instantly to offer one of her own kidneys for Steve. Her behaviour conforms to the classic Kubler-Ross (1995) theory, with anger, denial and bargaining vying together for dominance. She was, however, able to put her emotions to the side as she explained:

. . . at that point the foremost thing in my mind was making sure that Steve was comfortable and not in pain but whether that is my nursing background I don't know. Whether I'm being . . . I'm sure the fact that I'm a nurse helped me cope . . . Then when Michael [local Macmillan nurse] came around and we discussed pain relief . . . we discussed giving something to calm him [Steve]. I could talk about it on a professional level rather than just being a mum but at other times I wanted him [Michael] not to talk to me about that, I mean it was killing me . . .

The only way she could deal with the awful situation in which she, as a single parent, found herself was to attempt to distance her maternal and emotional reactions to Steve's treatment and behave in her practical role as professional nurse. She fought for the right to take Steve home, telling me:

I'm glad that I did all that, because I was really taking part in trying to get him better, rather than just sitting on the sofa and watching . . . I really feel that although we were so hell bent on getting him well, we weren't going to let this thing beat us. My son wasn't going to die, no way. I think deep down, the seeds of possibly losing him must have been there.

Sophie's instinct compelled her to take Steve home; back to his brother, surroundings and food, which were familiar and comforting to him, and where she felt more confident and able to participate in his care. She was quite determined to do all within her power to boost any remaining chance for his survival and she steadfastly clung to that hope. To this end, she endeavoured to keep home life going, much as it had before Steve's condition deteriorated and so encouraged friends whom he knew well to visit. She said how she 'tried to make it as normal as possible, there was familiar voices, faces, sounds around him. He was just laid on the settee during the day.'

At this difficult time, Sophie, as well as Steve, were able to benefit from the goodwill generated from her social group, whose ready presence challenged traditional images of the solemnity of the deathbed scene. She said these were:

. . . people who had been around all the while he was dying, they had all probably got used to being at ease with the situation. I mean Michael [the Macmillan Nurse] will tell you, that he would come around and I would have a few of my girl friends there and we would all have a laugh and a joke together and I wanted that because Steve was used to it. I am quite outspoken and outgoing and I like a laugh and my friends are like that. And he [Steve] could hear all that. I wanted his last ten days to be normal. I didn't want us all to be sitting there looking at him, not saying a word. It just seemed right at the time. We weren't laughing at what was happening, we were laughing in the face of adversity? Is that the right word?

Sophie felt that Steve would respond more positively to the domestic atmosphere of his home rather than that of a hospital. She felt that the ambience was more intimate and therefore, perhaps, relaxing and that this may somehow bolster his strength. It may be that the laughter generated by the presence of her friends served as a defence mechanism, countering her heightened emotions and tension of developing events.

In spite of her best efforts, however, Steve:

. . . went down very quickly. Because the way he was then. I wouldn't have wanted . . . If he had been up and running around, I would have asked Him [God] for as long as I could have had him [Steve], but the way he was . . . I couldn't take it much more. Maybe that is being selfish, saying I couldn't take much more, but, I couldn't sit and watch him lying there, it was tearing me apart seeing him . . . lying there, just waiting to die.

She explained her anxiety:

I would fetch him in [to bed] with me at night, I was just so frightened all the time that he was going to die when I was not there. I mean, I was there, but suppose I was in the loo or at night if I went to sleep . . . ? I didn't sleep all that much. One girl in particular, Eve, she is a staff nurse from the hospital, who I got friends with, she said 'He won't die without letting you know that it's time' [she knew that] through her experience with children. I now know that they don't. But I didn't really believe her . . . till it happened.

Sophie was so frightened to leave Steve even for a few moments, lest he die alone, that she kept him with her at all times. She desperately needed to be there for him and lived in fear that she may, through no fault of her own, let him down. She was, however, able to gain hope, by taking counsel from a well-experienced friend, that Steve may somehow let her know when he was ready to die.

She explained that she:

. . . didn't really sit and cuddle him but that particular evening on the sofa, we had people in. My dad had been to work. I was in the kitchen getting something to eat. I walked in to ask my dad something. [I asked what time this was at] Six in the evening? And, as I walked into the lounge, Steve saw me and put his arms up to me . . . just like that . . . It was the first time he'd done that for such a long time, it made me think that he wanted me to pick him up, so I did. And I don't know . . . I went around and held him . . . I don't know, just something said that it was very close, that tonight was going to be it. I mean, the night before, we had had an awful time because he vomited awful black gunge . . . And it was fortunate that Eve [her nurse friend] was there and kind of took control. And it was just awful because we had some friends there and I thought, if this happens when he goes out [dies] it will be in everybody's memory that that is how he'd died, you know, this awful vomit. But he rallied round. Anyway, so I sat there with him . . .

Striving to maintain a level of normality in a home where a child is dying cannot have been easy and so, naturally, Sophie found it difficult to quell her angst. Her reaction to Steve's spontaneous gesture of holding out his arms was instinctive, she 'held him' realising that in his need for maternal comfort, Steve was possibly signalling to her that his death 'was very close' and she was now prepared and ready to face and help her son to his death. She wanted it to be a good death, calm and peaceful and was fearful that the physical mess of dying may intrude on memories of the occasion. She sat holding her young boy, sharing his last few precious moments and felt relieved that her parents were there to support her.

Sophie continued, telling me how her parents and she:

. . . just sat there talking quietly. I could tell that Steve's breathing was becoming more laboured, which meant it was going to happen. I was aware that I was tickling him with my hand, here [indicates the head]. I felt at that point that I was holding everyone else together. My mother was in an awful state by then, I was being the strong one at that point; whether it was my profession, I don't know. My mum and dad were quite aware it was happening. It was quiet, just mum and dad, it was just right, it was completely the way I would . . . It was just like he fell asleep.

Attuned to even the least change in Steve's physical condition, Sophie hesitatingly awaited her son's death. At this most fragile time, the last few minutes of her baby son's life, she was, however, distracted by her own mother's distress and attempted to calm her. This was a time, one would imagine, when she should be receiving comfort; instead she offered it to others, thereby helping herself.

After his last breath:

[Steve's] . . . face just drained away all the . . . He had a very puffy face by then, his little eyes . . . He looked horrible, really, but I thought he looked lovely, he was mother's boy, and so . . . It just drained away, all the puffiness. He had a tube that he had his drugs through, and I said, 'I'm just going to take that out now' and he was just Steve again. It was so peaceful, it was just alright, I couldn't have wanted it any . . . He just died well.

We just sat for a while, crying obviously, I wouldn't let anyone take him off me. They didn't try to. I wouldn't have him prised out of my arms . . .

Hospice case studies

Jean – 'Just closed her eyes and died'

Jean lay in bed wearing a peach turban, with her eyes closed and a multi-coloured, crocheted blanket round her. It was difficult to know how old she was. Her body was wizened and she seemed very poorly and weak. She was well enough, however, to joke that she dances and drinks when I leave the room. She was visited by her son. After he left, she haltingly came for a cigarette into the kitchenette, where tea is prepared for the visitors and which doubles as a smoking area. She explained to me that she had been ill for two years with leukaemia, that she was a widow and lived with one of her two sons and his dog in his flat. She worried that, although she 'used to skip up and down the stairs like a young one' she feared that she 'won't be quite so mobile when I go home' but then she said, very casually, 'I may not be.' We had quite a long conversation with the relative of another patient, who came to get some water, and that really seemed to brighten Jean's mood. We talked about all sorts of things, including holidays and Jean said that she would like to go to Cornwall. Jean asked many questions of the relative, about how the man she was visiting was feeling. After the relative went, Jean told me how she said, 'No', when she was asked, in hospital, if she wished to be resuscitated should her heart fail. She said her mum and dad and husband would be waiting for her 'upstairs' [in heaven] but that she was not ready to go just yet. Almost every comment she made was punctuated by her saying, 'not to worry!' (Field-notes – three days to death)

At this stage of her illness, Jean complied quite unconsciously with the practical expectations of her role as good patient. She was in bed and wore a turban to conceal her bald head, which may have, however unintentionally, alarmed visitors. Although weak, she was able to draw benefit from, as well as contribute to, what social world remained to her. She was, at that time, able to sustain her dominant social identity of mother and seemed to enjoy and meet well the social and practical responsibilities of that role during her son's visit. However, the main reason for her admission to the hospice may have been practical, as it could have been difficult for her working, unmarried son to manage her death alone in his apartment.

Jean really enjoyed visiting the kitchenette; it enabled her to maintain her link with the wider social world and she used humour with both me and the visitor in her heroic attempt to distract us from the realities of her harsh plight. During her visit to the tearoom, when she sought the comfort of a cigarette, our chat enabled me to learn more about her frame of mind. It would seem that she did not conform to Kubler-Ross's (1995) stage model of dying, as she swung radically between the stages of denial of her impending death to accepting that she may not recover. Even whilst speaking of proposed holidays in Cornwall and worrying about her mobility when she returned home, thereby indicating that she still maintained a sense of self in a projected future, she also realised that she may die during this admission to the hospice. It was interesting, too, that when asked about her willingness to be resuscitated should her heart fail, she had responded negatively. In telling me that she had refused to accept resuscitation, she was, effectively, letting me know that she no longer wished to live. This may be explained by her belief in an afterlife, where she was looking forward to a reunion with her mother, father and husband who were 'upstairs'. Jean believed that, although physically dead, her parents and husband were very much socially alive.

Jean's condition had noticeably deteriorated; she remained in bed for the duration of my shift. She appeared to be incredibly weak and did not smoke, although she still had time to joke that as tomorrow, Thursday, is her 63rd birthday, she had arranged for the Chippendales [male striptease artists] to come in! She had several birthday cards up beside her bed but said that she had no plans to celebrate her birthday, 'What can you do in here?' she asked. She also said that her daughter-in-law was due to give birth shortly. Again, she was visited by her son and, when I entered her room to offer him tea, she was being violently ill but typically said 'not to worry!' and that she really was ok. She made jokes about her being sick because she had drunk too much brandy and champagne together! I was told by the nurses that she does not sleep. (Field-notes – two days to death)

Although Jean seemed a lot weaker than she had been the day before, she still endeavoured to maintain her social self, again using humour, which challenged conventional modes of behaviour. What was important to her was her forthcoming birthday and she certainly felt proud of the support implicit in her many birthday cards but this event seemed overshadowed by some indication of depression. It may be that she was aware of her imminent death and this threatened her so much that it affected her physically and kept her awake. Dein and George use Kubler-Ross's (1995) stage model theory of dying to account for how the time of death may be determined psychologically, allowing individuals to '. . . live in order to witness a specific event . . .' (2001: 205). Kubler-Ross defined the stage of bargaining as one when patients attempt to negotiate an extension of their lives with God. Frequently, individuals desire to live to see a specific event: for Jean this was her birthday and also the birth of her first grandchild. She may have perceived the joint occurrence of these two events as being sufficiently significant to motivate her flagging will to go on living long enough to reach them. It should also be noted that, in accepting her position as patient, Jean had surrendered most of her rights to privacy, which was evident in how even I, only a volunteer working in the hospice, could find her in the intimate position of being sick. The role of hero came readily to Jean, even at this late stage in her illness as, although clearly most ill, she did not complain but rather seemed intent on minimising any possible problems her difficulties may cause to others.

Jean was really most unwell. Surrounded by birthday cards, she was not wearing her turban and her head was almost completely bald, with only a few strands of hair on top of her head. It was her birthday and although she had no visitors, she showed me a gift of toiletries she had received. I had been told by staff that her new grandson, Jack, was born that morning too. She said that it had been a really long day and kept asking what time it was and then seeming surprised that it was so early. She was confused, asking me to take a frozen chicken from her handbag. When Jean tried to put the small, pudding bowl sized, sick bowl on her head confusing it with her turban, I realised the extent to which her condition had worsened. One of the nurses said that this confusion was tied to the breakdown of her kidneys. The nurse also said that Jean had had another sleepless night. As the evening wore on, one of the nurses said that she smelt smoke and Jean was found to have lit up a cigarette in bed in her, strictly no-smoking, room. Eventually she was brought out in a wheelchair to the tea-making area, where she managed to smoke part of a cigarette. We chatted together and laughed during a brief singsong; Frank Sinatra and Doris Day. I tried to warm her feet, which she said were freezing. All the time she shivered and said that she felt ice cold. She said that she felt like she had flu and thought that she was going to faint. Telling me again that she did not think she would leave the hospice, clearly in great discomfort, she asked to be moved back into bed; however, the nurses were having tea and said to tell her they would be there in fifteen minutes. Jean was living from minute to minute and it was very difficult to watch her distress. One of the nurses said that she hoped Jean could see her grandson really quickly because, she thought, only then could she die in peace. (Field-notes – one day to death)

Jean's condition had deteriorated to such an extent that she was now dipping in and out of her quickly evaporating periods of lucidity. She had lived to see her birthday and learn of the birth of her new grandson and now focused on attempting to survive long enough to see him. Her anxiety to know the time may have arisen, in part, from her attempting to estimate how well she was doing as regards that pressing necessity, as well as from her requirement to maintain her social self, by displaying behaviour appropriate to the time of day. She wanted to retain her public front. Her choice of songs, which we playfully sang together, also fixed her temporally in the past as she had selected music that would have been popular when she was younger and in better health. It is, however, most important to observe how Jean suffered as a result of the difference in how time was perceived by her and by the medical team. Although the edge of her pain had been cloaked by her palliative drugs, she was still feeling most unwell. She was feeling as though she was freezing cold and 'felt like she had flu and thought that she was going to faint'.

I have previously noted how individuals are socialised into their perceptions of time, highlighting the disparity between individuals, who as patients are assimilated into hospital time, and clinicians who adhere to the rigid bureaucratic timetables, without which the hospitals would not be able to function. The nursing staff are allocated specific periods of private time within their shift, in which they are, quite reasonably, entitled to refresh themselves. As healthy individuals they probably tend to exist in a present, which is substantially experienced with the future in mind; for example, making a bed knowing that they will within moments help their patient back into it. I noted earlier how time appears to slow when intense or heightened emotions are experienced (Flaherty, 1987; Denzin, 1984; Charmaz, 1991; Prichard, 1992). What, to a clock-oriented nurse, is just a few moments can, for a patient in immense physical discomfort, living moment by moment and focusing on survival, being sick or choking, feel like a lifetime. I suggest then, that the nurse's instruction for me to tell Jean that '. . . they would be there in fifteen minutes . . .' was framed within their professional, future-orientated view of time, which, sadly, bore little relation to Jean's temporal experience.

So confused and physically ill was she that any concerns she may have had with vanity had now gone and, at the beginning of my shift, she was not wearing her turban. She must, though, have noticed this lack as she tried to find it and, in her confusion, mistook her sick bowl for her turban. This confusion escalated to the point where she became a practical danger, both to herself and others, by lighting her cigarette whilst clearly not in control of all her faculties. Nonetheless, she was still, with only hours left to live, seeking comfort from smoking cigarettes and the opportunity to relive happier and healthier times through the songs we sang. This was a dying woman, who felt so intimidated by the prospect of her death that she was unable to sleep. Although she did not receive visitors, possibly because they were preoccupied with the birth of her new grandson, she still related to her social group through her birthday cards and gifts.

As I signed on at reception for duty I was told that there were 'not many people up there'; that lots of them had died. I immediately asked if Jean had and I was told, 'Yes'. It transpired that when her family arrived with her new grandson, Jack, she had held him for a few minutes, handed him back over, closed her eyes and died. (Field-notes – Jean's death)

The ability to postpone death briefly until a meaningful event has occurred has been well documented (Phillips and King, 1988; Phillips and Smith, 1990) and it would seem that this is what Jean achieved. So great was her emotional need to see her first grandchild, tangible evidence that her line would continue, that she was able to temporarily hold off her death until she saw the baby.

Janet – 'A shame she had not waited to die on another day'

As I went up the stairs to go on duty, I met the husband and two young children of one of the patients, Lisa. They said that there was a new lady, sharing with their mother and that, as she had just been moved there today, she was very tired and would appreciate quietness. The new lady, Janet, has three children, two of whom go to primary school with my youngest pair and the oldest, who goes to secondary school with my oldest. Although her children were very polite and pleased to talk about school their mother was almost completely silent and did not move much. When her family left she underwent a short medical procedure in which she had a syringe driver put into her arm. (Field-notes – four days to death)

Hospice protocol respects and encourages, especially new, patients to rest. In deference to this practical and social etiquette, Lisa's family left to allow her new roommate to settle in, in the company of her husband and three children. What was significant was that, in spite of being surrounded by her family and obviously cognisant of where she was and what was happening, Janet, who was propped up in bed by pillows, was almost completely withdrawn, showing almost no interest in her family's presence. I assumed this distancing of herself from the social to be a measure of her understanding of the seriousness of her condition. This assumption was verified when I learned that the syringe driver, a device which feeds medication on demand, had been fitted. In the context of a patient with cancer, this is usually a signal of imminent death, with morphine being delivered. Prichard (1992) observed that, although individuals are aware that they will ultimately die, they spend most of their lives attempting to ignore their mortality and all moments seem open-ended. However,

Living and Dying with Cancer

to those who are aware of the immediacy of their impending death, time becomes a closed and finite dimension and is experienced as running out. Although it might be thought that this would add to the appreciation of life, when time is spent in pain or is experienced as something just to be got through, life becomes devalued (Prichard, 1992).

Janet was not visited by her children who, her husband said, had school commitments. He was with her for about an hour and they talked quietly together. After he left, she asked, in a surprisingly strong voice, for a bacon sandwich, which she only picked at. Other than that request she did not speak but stood silently looking from her window.

When I woke this morning, having met her for the first time last night, it occurred to me that her expression and demeanour was one of fear. (Field-notes – three days to death)

Janet appeared to be more attuned than previously to the life going on around her in the ward. The fact that her children were not there allowed the couple time to confer privately and I hesitated to intrude upon them at such a difficult meeting. They were working together, negotiating how life would continue for the family after her death. Janet's concerns lay in the future, with how her family would manage. When her husband left, she returned to her introspection, refusing my offer to read to her or to put on the radio or television. It was as though, in looking out from her window, she was unwittingly using it as metaphor, in which she, trapped within her dying body, could only look out on, but not actively participate in, the social world outside. She seemed totally lost in her own thoughts and, other than her conversation with her husband and her practical request for food, made no demands of, nor contribution to, the outside world.

As I drove up to the hospice, Janet's husband Paul was walking up the drive. He said that their children would not be visiting tonight. Early in the evening the couple were joined by a Roman Catholic priest, who stayed for almost an hour. While he was there, Lisa [who shared the room] and her husband went to sit downstairs. When Paul left, I was surprised to have a brief chat with Janet, who I found lost in thought, and again, looking through the window. She said that she believed that she can no longer eat solid food. She explained that she has ovarian cancer and, although the children are aware of everything, she fears for the oldest, a girl, who, she thinks, is bottling up her feelings. She said that she is in severe pain and that, having spoken with her husband, they have decided not to have visitors, so that she can conserve her strength. Other than this brief conversation, Janet was as silent as ever. (Field-notes – two days to death)

At this difficult time, so acutely aware of her need to save energy that she would not see even family or friends, Janet and Paul turned to their religion for support. Their local priest came to share these moments with them, in an effort to bolster their spiritual strength. In recognition of this, Lisa, Janet's roommate, took her husband to another, more public, area to allow them privacy. It seems that Lisa recognised Janet's condition was sufficiently grave to accord her a higher priority of need and privacy. Respecting Janet's obvious closeness to death and her unspoken but clear wish to be left undisturbed, I had desisted from attempting to engage her in conversation, so, not unnaturally, I was quite surprised when she spontaneously chose to confide her worries to me. I would attribute this to the fact that she needed to talk to someone of a similar age and that we both had children who attended the same schools. Our brief relationship was based solely on these elementary commonalities. Our connection seemed primarily to stem from our shared role as mother but her lack of communication served to screen her off. It was the knowledge of her family, her social unit, which built a bridge allowing empathy between us to become established, albeit for a minimal duration. They were her link away from her withdrawn physical self, back into the mainstream world. It may be argued that a person who is totally incommunicado and does not communicate with any other form of life, for example a hermit, is quite simply a biological entity. If knowledge of that person's social role can be established, then relationships can be built on a sense of shared identification. Janet recognised that her increasing pain, which now could only be handled by a constant feed of morphine, and her lack of appetite were signals of her impending death. It was, though, her role as mother which took dominance in shaping her attitudes to her death, as she was aware of the pain her death would cause her children.

When I began my shift, Janet was sitting on the side of her bed surrounded by her family. She looked visibly better and was talking quite animatedly. She told me about her young daughter's success in playing basketball for the county and, rubbing her hair, said how proud she was of her. The atmosphere was so much more relaxed and her husband told me that Masses were being said for her all over the country. Janet's daughter laughingly said that her mother had had scrambled egg and bacon for breakfast that morning! When he was leaving, Janet's husband said that he had brought his brother up earlier in the day having prepared him for the worst and had been embarrassed to find Janet looking and feeling so much better than she had done. (Field-notes – one day to death)

Janet had managed to gather what strength she had left and, reminiscent of a swan song, used it to ensure that her children would remember her smiling. This was the first time that I had seen her meet her social role as a mother and she rose to the occasion with aplomb. She showed excitement and pride in the achievements of her children and appeared humble and grateful that her social circle was responding to her plight in the way she hoped by offering prayers. It seemed that part of the excitement had been generated by the return of her appetite and this fact, which appeared to be attributed to the prayers, caused much speculation that, even at this late stage, she may recover.

Before reporting to the nurses' station for instruction, I checked in to see how Janet was faring. I felt awful when I saw another woman in Janet's bed and asked one of the nurses if she had died. She said that, 'Yes, after spending a really bad night Janet's family were called in' and that 'her social worker had even organised for the family dog to be there'. Although, when she died she was in bed surrounded by her family, she had, I was told, retained such a tight grip on her own left wrist that, when it was ultimately removed after death, extensive bruising was revealed. The nurse said that it was Janet's oldest daughter's 14th birthday and that it was a shame she had not waited to die on another day. (Field-notes – Janet's death)

Janet had been fully aware of the reality of her situation. Knowing that she could not avert or escape her own death, she had, with the assistance of the priest, managed to find some degree of psychological and spiritual peace. Having found this, and content in the knowledge that she had done her best to convey her love to her family, Janet began to slip toward death. She wrestled physically with her impending death during her troubled night and felt so frightened that, presumably in an attempt to still her terrified body lest her family see her shaking, physically restrained herself on and through the time of her death. It is possible that Janet struggled to live on to be with her daughter on her birthday and, having met this goal, she died.

Geoff – 'He's gone, he's at peace now'

There is a new patient in the front room. Looking as though he was in his mid-sixties, he was dressed and lay on top of his bed. A woman, who was sitting by his bed and who may have been his wife, was obviously upset. She appeared to have been there all day. She was very smartly dressed and there were lots of ruby wedding presents around. They were joined by an older woman and ultimately another couple. Later a girl visited, perhaps his daughter, and someone who, I assumed, was her husband or boyfriend. The girl became very upset and came into the kitchenette to cry. Although my initial reaction was to comfort her, I hesitated, wondering if it would be more helpful to leave her alone. Instinct won out and I put my arm around her. She said that they are her parents and that she is worried for her mother because, when her father, Geoff, dies, she will be left alone. She asked me if her father will leave the hospice alive. (Field-notes – three days to death)

I can only speculate as to why Geoff, who had been admitted to the hospice much earlier in the day, remained dressed and on the bed. It could be that he realised that being in bed may be interpreted as a tacit acceptance of his admission into the hospice and perhaps he, however unconsciously, was struggling to resist this. Still communicative, he fidgeted constantly as though trying to position himself more comfortably. The remnants of what seemed to have been a small party, much finger-printed wine glasses and plates with icing left on them, were still around the bed. It was the couple's wedding anniversary, an event which most couples look forward to and anticipate celebrating. An occasion redolent with symbolism, Geoff may have felt it sufficiently significant to have lived on to see. It paid homage to an enduring partnership, which was now on the verge of dissolving. During the evening the couple were joined by other members of their social group, who had come, ostensibly to offer congratulations but, perhaps more realistically, to offer support to the family at this difficult time when the two events of death and celebration seemed oddly juxtaposed.

Geoff was again surrounded by family. His wife all the while sipped herbal tea and fingered an alternative health book, which lay on her lap. His son, daughter and a friend were in attendance and, at one stage, the group was joined by two teenagers. Geoff had deteriorated immensely and appeared to be suffering greatly. It was distressing to watch his discomfort. He did not seem able to get comfortable and he sat, bent double on the bed, wearing just underpants. His family worked really hard to try to make him comfortable, his daughter came into the kitchen to get iced water for his parched lips. Various family members stroked or held his hands. They took turn to cry, although at times I could hear, in a hushed way, the younger ones giggling about unfunny jokes. 'His double-chin means double-trouble.' Geoff was clearly most poorly. He kept shouting 'Help me!' and pulling off his incontinence pads. He sipped water and soft drinks and was obviously feeling most uncomfortable. His pillow was soiled with his faeces. (Field-notes – two days to death)

In these, the last few hours of his life, his family kept bedside vigil. They worked as a team and, although they endeavoured to distract him from his dismal situation, their joint efforts appeared to ease more their own psychological pain than to calm his. The tension and emotion emanating from the group was, though, so great that, at times, when it threatened to reach crisis point, the younger members attempted to dissipate it by employing diversionary tactics, such as the use of humour. I found it difficult to assess Geoff's frame of mind. Uncomfortable, if not in actual pain, Geoff was clearly distressed and the fact that he cried for help suggests that, to some extent, he was lucid though confused; he was aware of the truth. Such was the severity of his physical and psychological plight that, although conscious and the focus of his group, he was clearly at a remove from mainstream activity, his confusion actually seeming to protect him from the fact that he was dying. His pain had removed

him so far from the social that he was unembarrassed by his own loss of
dignity.

Geoff had managed to cling on through the night. When I began my shift, I was
told that he was dying and that it was very slow. All of his family were there,
gathered behind the closed curtains. I was told that he had calmed down a lot
since last night. Several times when I was in the room I heard muffled sobs. At
7.35 pm, I was told that 'He has gone' and there was a lot of rushing around and
gestures from the nurses. The birds still sang outside, other visitors continued
to laugh and the kettle came to the boil. The curtains remained drawn around
his bed. Lots of movement. His daughter dashed, sobbing, past me on the stairs,
followed by her husband. She went into the cloakroom and her husband sat
outside and cried. He said, 'He really was ok.' I passed his wife on the stairs and
she said 'He's gone, he's at peace now.' She was followed by one of the younger
visitors. Eventually, the family gathered in the garden for coffee, while his body
was being prepared. His daughter and her husband sat together, while his wife
moved around. There was a lot of to-ing and fro-ing from the nurses into and out
of his cubicle. Sheets in disposable bags being brought out and then a tray with
empty coffee cups. When I left at 8.30 pm, his body still had not been brought
down to the mortuary. (Field-notes – Geoff's death)

As death approached, Geoff's mania abated. However, his peaceful
demeanour probably had more to do with the fact that he was now heavily sedated than with his acceptance of death. It would seem that, even
when individuals are actually dying and in a hospice, whose philosophy
is after all to enable people to die as they wish, there is still a requirement
to comply with society's prescribed behaviour. Deaths that threaten to
breach the emotional tenor of the hospice are frowned upon by those in
authority. Field considers that:

Although hospices are committed to allow and enable people to die in the way
they want to, it is difficult to die an overtly angry death in a hospice as the 'hospice
smile' can be very constraining to those who want to rage against the dying of the
light. (1996: 260)

Clustered together, in their need to be both physically and psychologically
close to him and enclosed behind the curtains around his bed, Geoff's
family kept their death watch. His final movement into death itself was
not, however, as wild as his behaviour of the previous day. His distraught
body had been stilled and he lay, rendered unconscious by medication,
awaiting his death. His artificially contrived, tranquil passing initiated a
flurry of urgent action. Tension had escalated as a result of the efforts
of both staff and relatives to present an appropriately serene stage for
Geoff's dying. Immediately after his death occurred, it was as though
a dam had burst and the emotional and physical vitality, which had, in

the presence of his dying, been repressed, flooded forth. His daughter dashed past me releasing her pent up physical and psychic energy and the nurses sprang into action determined to fulfil the last duties due to their patient. Although this activity appeared, at times, chaotic, there was an underlying method to it. Whilst the staff attended to the practicalities, his family struggled to express their turbulent emotions.

Discussion

Walter considers that: 'The catch phrases of the neo-modern death are expression of emotion, personal growth, sharing, autonomy and informed choice, while the most heinous sins are social isolation and psychological denial' (1994: 59). Reports from the respondents and those who cared for them appear to support this. The contemporary tendency to sanction autonomy to individuals was evident in how, although they could not consider how they died, the respondents were enabled to choose the place of their death, be it home, hospital or hospice and, for some, even the time when it would occur. It should, however, be noted that the ability to exercise autonomy presupposes that the individual is capable of expressing and enjoying individual choice and was not an option for children such as three-year-old Steve.

The duration and shape of the dying trajectory exercised a significant influence on how the imminent death was perceived by patients and their carers. Rose had lived with her cancer for seventeen years before her eventual death. She had survived three critical bouts of ill health during each of which she had been given ten days to live. At the time of her final crisis, her daughter found it difficult to believe that her mother would die as she had been told this before and her mother had survived. This may account for her feelings of guilt because she now:

. . . feel[s] guilty about the way I felt, because when mum was ill before and they said to us she has less than ten days . . . I was so blasé about it and I kept going to see her and she was all right . . . [This time] they said, 'She has only got until Christmas' and I believed it and I have never felt like that before.

Rose's elongated trajectory, which included prolonged periods of remission punctuated by severe crises, influenced how her condition was perceived by her social group. This may go some way to explaining why Rose's mother reacted so strongly to her death. When, immediately after the death, Marie questioned her grandmother's extreme emotional reaction by saying, 'We were expecting it . . .' her grandmother responded by saying, 'No we weren't! No, we weren't expecting it, it was not going to come now!' Rose's death, although long anticipated, had occurred relatively rapidly. The duration of her life with cancer had been seventeen years: a substantial period of time, in fact a veritable lifetime, almost as long as her 18-year-old son had lived. The line of her dying trajectory, though, had dramatically and unpredictably plummeted from the position she was in when I last saw her, just five days before she died, when she had been coherent and relatively mobile, to her total collapse in her kitchen. Her family, though, had become so accustomed to her living as an invalid and surviving near fatal crises that it seems they had, however unconsciously, credited her with having achieved the impossible feat of transcending death. Although aware, on a cognitive level, that Rose's health had deteriorated dangerously, they had still managed to keep up a substantial level of hope, which had probably been transmitted to Rose and helped her to cope.

This contrasts markedly with Gita's experience. Gita had been diagnosed with her cancer just fourteen months before she died but had lived through 'complete torture' for three weeks. Her actual death then appeared to have occurred relatively slowly: as Ash, her husband, pointed out, on 'Wednesday night we had a conversation with her' till the Saturday night when '. . . she just stopped breathing . . .'

Sixty-three-year-old Vera, who had been desperate to win what had been a long and hard fought battle with both her cancer and 'this terrible, terrible chemo', had an accelerated end-stage dying trajectory. Her psychological and physical condition had shifted rapidly, from a position where she felt that she owed 'it to my husband who I love very, very dearly and I have two kids and three grandchildren. I owe it to them to have a fight' to one where, en-route to the hospital she told Albert, her husband, that she:

. . . wanted to go because she was in pain, couldn't stick no more. She said in the ambulance she wanted to die. That night . . . I never seen her face so bad, twisted in pain. Her eyes were rolling, teeth grinding in pain . . . When they took her out of the house, she was making this awful noise with pain.

A range of factors combine to influence the way in which the dying condition is perceived by the social groups. Rose's family's anticipation of her recovery flourished, almost pathologically, as a result of her ability to overcome regular crises, although her end-stage dying was relatively accelerated when compared to her protracted dying trajectory. In contrast, although the families of Steve, John, Gita and Vera had, throughout the course of their illness, maintained the hope that they would survive, that hope was gradually dimmed by the obvious and rapid deterioration in their health. Others, like the families of Jean, Janet and Geoff, whom I observed in the hospice, were in no doubt that their relatives were soon to die. Although all three had been ambulant and lucid until the immediate period before death, the families realised their admission into the hospice was evidence of imminent death.

Becker (1973) argues that we throw up culture as a defence against the psychological awareness of our mortality in an attempt to evade the 'sure and certain knowledge of our deaths'. Culture is, in part, concerned with social niceties, for example, when and with whom one can appear naked, awareness of the dignity of the physical self in dress and manners. As death closes in and the physical self declines, cultural affectations are dropped, there as a regression to our animal instincts devoting whatever energy remains to pure survival. This may account for why Louise 'didn't give a damn about the children' and Clive 'didn't care' and Geoff, who had maintained his dignity by remaining fully dressed on the day of his admission to the hospice, in his death throes became oblivious that he was semi-naked. This radical change in behaviour may have accelerated their families' awareness that death was looming.

It is interesting to explore how and why choices are made about the place of death. It would be wrong to generalise from the results of such a small sample but all the female respondents died either in hospice or hospital. This may be because, as women, they were likely to be the primary carers within their domestic units (Hochschild, 1983) and thus, when they themselves became dependent, the others available to care lacked sufficient confidence in their ability to perform the caring role.

Three-year-old Steve was subject to the wishes of his principal carer, his mother, who decided that he should die at home, where she could nurse him herself. John, Mary's adult son, succeeded in his wish to return home to die. I have already commented on how some respondents, like Clive, said how it was the 'working staff' in the hospital whom he considered to be his family and how he perceived the hospital as a place of sanctuary. Others, however, especially during their initial admissions, experienced it as alien in both culture and temporal pace.

Rose achieved her wish to die in hospital. She had, in this final crisis, been removed from her home by ambulance and taken, not to a hospice but to a hospital, an institution which may have fuelled within her optimistic family the flames of hope and the expectation of recovery. Her daughter's decision to send her mother there, though, may have arisen, in part, as her defining her mother's sudden turn as an acute emergency requiring immediate medical attention, rather than her respecting her mother's wishes not to be admitted to a hospice.

Ben was more concerned with how he, as a (non-practising) Jew, would fit into his local hospice, whose ethos was Christian. He explained:

When I was going downhill . . . the Macmillan nurse said, 'Would you consider going into the hospice?', and I said, 'Yes . . .' and of course it is very Christian orientated there. And I found a lot of comfort in that, strangely enough . . .

It is also interesting to learn in which specific zone within those chosen locations the deaths occurred. As the deaths approached, Gita who was in a hospice and Rose who was in hospital, were moved from their original positions on public wards, into smaller, single rooms. However, Geoff, whose dying had, at times, been quite turbulent, maintained his position in a hospice room, which he shared with three others. Forty-seven-year-old John and three-year-old Steve had died, not as I expected in upstairs bedrooms, but, somewhat ironically, in the living room areas of their homes. Although John's desire to die at home could have sprung from his need for comfort, he may also have felt the need for the familiar. Young and Cullen observe that:

In the hospital you had little more than a toothbrush to call your own. At home it was all yours. You could shut the front door and only open it to let in the people you actually wanted to see instead of those who wanted to see you. Medication permitting, you could wake up and get up in accord with the routine you wanted instead of when the nurses wanted . . . (1996: 95)

Like John, three-year-old Steve was also to die at home, although this was at the behest of his mother Sophie, whose training as a nurse had given her the confidence and ability necessary for the management of a dying child at home.

Coming to terms with, or accepting, impending death was not just the concern of the person who was about to die. As social beings, their experiences influenced and were, in turn, shaped by others within their social groups. Their carers were especially involved, as their close participation and understanding of what was happening enabled them to form attitudes, which may, in turn, have directly shaped and influenced how they responded to the imminent deaths of their patient. Sophie attributed her ability to perform the difficult task of nursing Steve at home as being in part due to the fact that, when she was speaking with the professionals dealing with Steve's illness, she 'could talk about it on a professional level rather than just being a mum'. This strategy of switching roles from mother to medic was also, it may be remembered, employed by ex-GP Louise, when she, herself dying from breast cancer and with a husband who was chronically disabled, had to deal with the management of their four-year-old daughter Laura's leukaemia. Referring to the consultations

she had had with Laura's specialists, they, recognising her medical exper-
tise, had felt somewhat awkward and, in response treated her as though
she were her daughter's GP, instead of her mother.

Both Louise and Sophie clearly recognised that, when dealing directly
with health professionals about the care of their children, their best tactic was to temporarily discard their social persona as mother and adopt
instead their professional medical role. It cannot have been easy for them
suddenly to effect this change as it probably required them having to
suppress their maternal feelings, which may, not surprisingly, have been
heightened at such a difficult time. This ability to switch role was not
easily accomplished. Sophie, just days before Steve died, had found it
difficult to discuss a change in his medication with Michael, the nurse.
She said, 'I wanted him [Michael] not to talk to me about that, I mean it
was killing me.'

Featherstone's consideration of the hero is also equally applicable to
the carers. His definition of the hero is, as noted earlier, '. . . one who
excels at the performance of a necessary social role' (1992: 168). In drop-
ping their social role as mother at this testing time and assuming instead
their professional roles, both Louise and Sophie were responding to what
they, health professionals themselves, recognised as an inequity in the
doctor/patient/carer relationship. Louise, who had been a doctor herself,
felt sorry for the non-medical out-patients whom she would encounter
whilst waiting for her treatment and who she could 'see with results and
[not understanding the implications, remain] still smiling'. Both had
worked in the health system and were all too clearly aware of how the
professionals dealt with patients and their carers. It was the desire for
further knowledge about their children's situation, which they believed
may inform and enhance how they managed their children's care that
motivated this switch in role. Like 76-year-old Mary, who colluded with
her adult son, John, in a mutual pretence about his state of health, they felt
compelled to do all that was within their power to protect their children
for as long as possible.

I have already discussed how living with a chronic and life threatening
illness can, sometimes, result in an escalation of tension within close social
groups. For example, Louise likened her mother to 'a volcano which will
not erupt' and Susan's mother 'spent 12 weeks here [at home, post-
surgery] which drove me crazy'. Rose, too, had problems; once, even
having to have her mother removed from the hospital.

The frame of mind of those who were close to the respondents influenced the dynamics of the interaction and exercised a significant effect on
how the various individuals died. Ash believed that Gita, his dying wife,
had heard and interpreted his words, 'Look if you think you are not going

to make it, don't fight, let go. You have done your bit' and she replied, 'Yes, I have done everything I can, I don't think I can survive . . .' Gita interpreted these words as her husband virtually giving her permission to die and it would seem that this directly affected her attitude and the mode and temporal pace of her dying.

Although nearly all of the respondents illustrated something of the problems created by their relatives, they also took time to tell me how they valued their efforts. The degree of emotional work and physical labour undertaken by carers cannot be adequately stressed. Seventy-six-year-old Mary had said how she even 'had to keep wiping the tears off' her dying son's face. Sophie who sat with three-year-old Steve said that she 'was aware that I was tickling him with my hand' and Rose's daughter, who minutes before she called the emergency services to order an ambulance for her mother's final crisis 'gave her [mother] everything I possibly could, I couldn't do any more'. Albert, Vera's 73-year-old husband also explained how his wife: 'was never any trouble to me, I used to take her out of bed, put her in the bath and wash her, change her twice daily. I don't mind, I told her.' Nothing was too much trouble. This sympathetic spirit would probably have been transmitted to the patients who, as social beings, would have appreciated it and responded.

Immediately before she described how she had to have her mother removed from the ward, Rose had said that 'My mother, now my mother is brilliant. I can't cook or shop and things like that, so mamma does that for us. She actually cooks our dinner and brings it over. She is gorgeous. I don't know where I would be without her. She has been so supportive.' On one occasion Louise, who was ill herself and trying to cope with her disabled husband and sick daughter, surprised me by balancing her witty but nevertheless harsh condemnation of her mother by saying 'She is a good woman, she is a nice woman but she is away for a week and it is bliss, heaven.' Bob, too, it may be remembered, appreciated how his family had helped him out of his post-diagnostic depression. He said that:

. . . my wife said she was going to get the kids . . . very good, very loving, and . . . we had a good, old fashioned chat. I started to come alive again, because I got a good talking to from the family.

This supports my argument that the attitudes and perceptions of the carers contributed significantly to the way in which the interviewees lived throughout their dying.

The respondents' social roles also played a critical part in how they died. The role of parent particularly affected those mothers and fathers who were themselves dying. Young and Cullen consider how: 'The person who dies in peace, with acceptance rather than bitterness, bestows a gift upon the survivors, which lasts for them, and can quieten their own fears' (1996). Although aware that their own lives would shortly come to an end, the respondents still concerned themselves with the future of those for whom they cared. Rose did not wish her daughter to see her die and told her 'Don't sit here, go home and eat your dinner.' Gita, who was tortured by the 'sheer hell' of her pain, fretted about her sons, asking eight-year-old Dalraj what he would 'do when I've gone, when mum's gone?' Louise too, tormented herself feeling 'unbelievable sadness for my children, what are they going to do?' Gerry, whose wife Claire gave birth the day following his diagnosis, also said how he 'could not stand the thought of that wee child [his older daughter Diana aged 4] crying for her daddy'. Although aware their own life would shortly come to an end, the concern of the respondents lay in the future: the future as it would be experienced by those for whom they cared. Their lives may have been drawing to an end but they needed to ensure that everything that could be done would be done to help those they would leave behind.

These parents and spouses had worked to ensure that some of the pain caused by their dying would be alleviated by preparations that they themselves could make. Rose had realised that she 'needed to make a will and . . . to pay for my funeral because I did not want to leave my mother and my children with financial problems'. Louise had made an arrangement with a 'sister who was . . . going to come up [from the country] and rear my wains [children]' and Jewish Ben and his Roman Catholic wife had worked jointly, researching burial plots before they finally decided on one that conformed to their disparate religious creeds. Since then, they felt 'very relieved . . . with our "Happy solution"!'

Langley-Evans and Payne (1997) argue that humour is sometimes used as a device by those who are dying in an attempt to open up what is, after all, a distressing subject, whilst at the same time enabling the patient to remain comfortably distanced from its reality. This device was also used by those within their social groups to help dissipate the extreme emotional tension generated by the imminent death. Rose's teenage daughter, keeping watch by her mother's deathbed, cut through what was surely an uncharacteristic and heavily emotional silence between them and laughingly said 'We are a right pair of boring old farts!' to which her dying mother responded 'Aren't we just . . .' 76-year-old Mary, who tended devotedly to her dying son, disparagingly told him 'Oh, your old fuss pot is still here, fussing you' and Geoff's grandchildren giggled about how 'His double-chin means double trouble.' Sophie wanted three-year-old Steve to be in an atmosphere where 'we would all have a laugh and a joke together' and Jean laughingly attributed her violent vomiting to the result of drinking 'too much brandy and champagne together!' It may not have been possible to conquer death but these individuals attempted, through humour, to disarm it of its sting.

Charmaz (1989, 1991) argues that when present life is lived with no sense of future, the self becomes devalued and life becomes untenable. Escaping to a reconstructed and idealised past offers release. This tendency to live in the past is enacted by those with low self-esteem and is situated in the need to assume an improved sense of value. This is because the past appears to be a time when the self was more active and consequently valued, life was controlled and offered promise; the retreat to better times bolsters the self and adds the strength necessary to deal with the risky present. Present realities and how we choose to define or interpret events remould our past experiences (Maines *et al.*, 1983).

A significant proportion of patients in the hospice, before succumbing to death, lived in the past, considering events, which happened often as long as 70 years previously, to be as valid and fresh today as they were then. In his study on the effect that temporal perspectives have on concepts of selfhood among Japanese youth, Lifton (1967) identified one approach, which he calls a 'mode of restoration'. In this, the individual deals with what is perceived as an impure present, by returning to the idealised past. These restorationists view themselves as being organically united with the past, defining themselves in symbols derived from a sacred past. I have observed 90-year-old women displaying dog-eared photographs of long dead mothers and fathers and fondly touching the photographed images of dresses and suits long discarded telling me 'It cost much too much but I didn't half look good in it!' I have also observed elderly men, who when asked for their opinion of the World Cup, can only relate to it through talking of past Cup Finals and matches fought and won fifty years previously.

The prospect of living on to see a significant event can also influence, to an extent, the timing of a death. My research substantiates that of Dein and George (2001: 206) who indicate how dying can sometimes be tempered by Kubler-Ross's (1995) stage of Bargaining. They report how the *Daily Mail* (10/1/00) pointed out that in the first week of January 2000 in Britain there was a 65 per cent increase in deaths from natural causes compared to the last week in December. Having lived to see and hold her newborn grandchild, Jean died. Geoff, too, saw through his ruby wedding anniversary and, although she did not survive the course of the full day, Janet lived long enough to wish her daughter a happy birthday. This ability many dying people have to live to see a specific event was illustrated to me time after time during my observances in hospices. One patient even held on till the last set was played in the men's finals at Wimbledon, so she died knowing who had won. It could be for this reason that so many respondents said that they feared sleep, believing that, quite literally, the only thing that keeps them alive is their own will-power and feeling that, should they surrender to sleep, they will die. Like Jean, who would not sleep, Rose explained to me that she had:

> ... two or three very dear friends who have been as ill as me and they never went to bed either . . . because they were too frightened to go to sleep in case they didn't wake up again. . . . I just couldn't bring myself to go to bed and in the hospital, I actually slept on the couch in the day room and in the end the nurses brought my pillows, sheets and blankets down to the couch; I just wouldn't go to sleep. You go into overdrive and the mind takes over and you know subconsciously that you are on the way out, there is no two ways about it, you do know and everything goes weak and then you think to yourself, 'Well, I am so weak, if I go to sleep I may not wake up.' So, if I lay on the couch, I will cat nap, I won't sleep.

Roberts (1986) considers the plight of individuals who are dying and argues that they adopt one of two strategies to cope with the horror of their situation, flight or freezing. Janet, towards the end of her dying journey had almost completely surrendered linguistic communication and conveyed the stark terror of the awful present in which she found herself by using non-verbal language. She remained almost exclusively silent and spent many of her last mobile hours staring from a window. Flight may best be illustrated by describing Peter, a young man who was totally unable or unwilling to still his body and who spent his last hours before his final sedated death rampaging breathlessly around and on top of his bed. A more extreme case than Geoff, Peter shifted his position constantly and this agitated movement had a disturbing and unsettling effect not only on his family, gathered helplessly close by, but also on the staff who attempted the impossible feat of trying to prevent the communication of his distress to other patients in his ward.

However, not all responded in such a disturbing way. Richard, who was 28 years old, had a cancer of the mouth. He was usually to be found sitting up in bed, playing Game Boy [a computerised game] while he waited for his cancer to eat its way through his carotid artery. Surrounded by dark towels to absorb the blood, and unable to speak, he would write scribbled notes to his devoted parents who kept station.

The earnest attention of staff and visitors to those who are dying in a hospice ensures that both social and biological life endure as long as possible (Walter, 1994) but, although in this world, many of the patients were no longer of it. As the dying trajectory escalates, many patients move in and out of coma and experience the drifting time of loss of consciousness. Charmaz (1991) argues that time appears to drift when action remains limited. For these end-stage patients then, time appears to just slip away with each movement into coma, bringing them closer to death. The dying, dipping in and out of awareness, become more and more withdrawn until they ultimately die.

Chapter summary

Encounters with those who are dying are not commonplace within the present day United Kingdom. Unless our work is specifically involved with people who are ill, or is in the emergency services, it is likely that the only people we will witness dying are those to whom we are close. This unfamiliarity with dying, coupled with the heightened emotions from all concerned that may reasonably attend it, results in the time of death being perceived by all to be a unique and significant occasion.

When the reality of an impending death can no longer be avoided, practical plans for how it will occur can be drawn up by the individuals most involved. Decisions are made, either by the dying person, or their carers, on practical issues, such as where the death will occur. Factors which influence this choice may involve gender and social role, since the mothers and the wives who had, presumably, filled the role of primary carer within their family (Ungerson, 1987) died not at home but in institutions providing professional care.

As the time of death looms closer, the individual is moved physically into the location where the death is planned, whether home, hospice or hospital, and it would seem that then the actual end-stage of the death begins. The fact of the impending death is usually, by this stage at least, acknowledged if not accepted by the person who is dying and by those who care for them. As a result, no effort is spared by the supporters to ensure the physical and psychological comfort of the dying individual.

Those close to the patient recognise that the opportunity to be with them is increasingly becoming limited. Their time together is now at a premium; a scarce and precious commodity that is to be valued. These last days and hours of the person who is dying are usually reserved for those closest, although the dying person and their families, by association, appear to become the focus of their wider social group, who offer support by showing that they are attuned to the event and prepared to do what they can to help. The physical deterioration, experienced as part of the dying process, often means that, by this stage, they are totally dependent on other members of their social groups for even their most rudimentary physical needs such as eating. Even at this time though, many of the respondents and those whom I observed still insisted on minimising the extent of their pain or discomfort in an effort to shield family and friends. As their condition continues to deteriorate, many of the basic social observances, such as the need for modesty, are abandoned as what energy remains is channelled into simply remaining alive. It is at this time, too, that relationships are affirmed, emotions are declared and wishes for the future made known.

Although dying within an institution such as hospice or hospital can, to an extent, liberate the individual from burdening their social group with the full responsibility for their care, on balance this choice can act to constrain their behavioural autonomy. Hospitals and hospices are, after all, public spaces, which serve groups of people.

Last words

The shift in mass attitudes to dying and death from post-war times to the present day came about because of the integration of strands of the combined innovative work of Kubler-Ross, Glaser and Strauss and Saunders. These significant changes in the management of individuals who are dying has directly shaped how the people you have met in this book experienced their illness. The consequent growth in research about dying and the subsequent interventions designed to facilitate an enhanced quality of life for those who are dying, such as the revival of the hospice, has generally allowed for an increase in the choices available.

Patients who, because of Glaser and Strauss's work, are kept honestly informed about their actual condition, move into a psychological situation that allows them to consider the reality of their position and so might, to use Kubler-Ross's language, move into acceptance of their imminent death. As their physical condition deteriorates, their psychological awareness of their position may help in enabling them to make an informed decision on the optimum conditions for their impending death. Some of my respondents preferred to die at home, others considered a hospice or hospital death preferable.

Writing in the United States of 1969, Kubler-Ross explored something of what it was to die, depicting it as a painful but enriching time that affords the final growth stage of life. I have approached the subject from an alternative perspective, as I felt that the many changes wrought in society over the time that has elapsed between her work and my own fieldwork, completed in 2002, needed to be addressed.

The changes since Kubler-Ross developed her model are significant. On the one hand, advances in medical science have resulted in the temporal period intervening between initial diagnosis of cancer and death being dramatically increased (Young and Cullen, 1996): there are now more people who are terminally ill but still alive than ever before. On the other hand, the work of Glaser and Strauss (1965) has done much to encourage clinicians to make patients aware of their prognosis and so, because of this knowledge, individuals who are diagnosed with cancer live through this time with a heightened awareness of their own mortality.

Living in the light of this knowledge, allows individuals who are dying the opportunity to be perceived, by both themselves and others, as being heroic (Seale, 1998). The role of the hero is a status that is contingent on cultural and temporal factors. It might be useful therefore to explore something of the essence of that position. Reflection suggests two forms of hero: The first conforms to traditional ideals and ranges from those who voluntarily risk their lives, for example in order to climb a previously unconquered mountain, to an individual who unquestioningly puts their own life at risk to save, perhaps, a child or weaker individual who is in peril. The second form of hero is the one with which this book is concerned: the individual who 'lives up' to a role into which they find themselves thrust. Featherstone observes:

Yet while the hero is one who lives within a fragile world in which he [sic] is vulnerable to fate and death and can display courage in face of his destiny, he is effectively seeking to live up to an ideal of excellence which is a social role. Hence in heroic societies, the heroic person is one who excels at the performance of a necessary social role. (Featherstone, 1992: 168)

Individuals who are dying are expected to live up to specific social roles to maintain the moral order and my respondents were no different. However, the significance of truth telling (Glaser and Strauss, 1965) and the consequent open awareness it engenders is well expressed by Seale, who observes that 'Awareness determines whether dying can be written into a heroic, self-defining narrative where the individual is depicted as rising above mundane concerns' (1995: 598). Seale's argument is that, nowadays, those facing death encounter many of the challenges faced by the traditional hero. Their confrontation with their own mortality has alerted them to the grievous physical danger they are now in and, in an endeavour to counter this, many choose to pursue what becomes a gruelling search for 'the truth', overcoming a host of obstacles along their way.

This contemporary hero is a character whose survival is exacerbated by the fact that their life is pitched within an ambiguous framework, lacking even the certainty of a fixed timeframe. As I have previously noted, individuals with cancer, for the most part, do not die suddenly but rather tend to experience prolonged illness trajectories. This has resulted in the situation where some individuals, once confronted with the truth of their own mortality at diagnosis, go on to live out what is left of their lives, buffeted by recurring health crises which keep the terror of imminent death at the forefront of their minds. These present-day, ordinary, heroes display a consistency in conducting what remains of their lives with courage and self-sacrifice in the face of pain and adversity. The respondents displayed not only classic heroic behaviour in showing fortitude in the face of their struggle against difficult, if not impossible, odds but also employed the, once perceived to be feminine, quality of emotional labour (Hochschild, 1983; Seale, 1995) in their attempts to protect those for whom they cared from the pain of their suffering. The respondents were, effectively, living up to the contemporary ideals of dying.

By virtue of the dying role, the respondents' behaviour met the heroic criteria as specified by Featherstone (1992) and Seale, who observed how:

> Characterising the 'stiff upper lip' of the traditional hero as 'denial', professional expertise now offers the dying individual and his/her 'carer' a heroism involving emotional expression and self-sacrifice. (Seale, 1995: 599)

Behaviour such as this, challenging for short time spans, can be, as a result of elongated dying trajectories, even more arduous. This book has also examined the part played by the length of the dying trajectory and how it exerted a significant influence over how the death was perceived. For example, although Rose was originally diagnosed some seventeen years before her eventual death, when she did ultimately enter the 'end-stage' of her trajectory, the events appeared, especially to her mother, to have accelerated quite rapidly in proportion to her prolonged dying trajectory.

The end-act of dying can only be fully grasped when it is framed within the events leading up to it; death is an event that is only one component of an often complex dying trajectory. All of the three stages I have described leading up to the fourth stage of death – from detection of the initial symptoms to acknowledgement that the condition is no longer respond-ing to treatment – contribute vitally to how the death is experienced. Just as an adequate grasp of the plot of *Romeo and Juliet* cannot be achieved by confining reading to the final act, so too can only an incomplete under-standing of what it is to die be learned from isolating and studying the 'end stage', separate from the entire trajectory.

Loss of ability, both physical and psychological, was a gradual process and it entailed respondents coming to terms with an increasing depen-dence on others. This relinquishing of responsibility was, however, all too often experienced as problematic and, at times, became defined by all concerned as a crisis. The perception of others proved critical, too, in influencing the respondents' sense of self-identity, significantly affecting how they managed and presented themselves in the wider social world.

Just as the respondents had, prior to their diagnosis, formed opinions of how cancer impacts on individuals, so too had their supporters. Sup-porters' expectations of how performance might be affected by the illness sometimes did not reflect reality and this shortfall, as we have learned, often resulted in an escalation of tension. It would seem that in their efforts to be of service, the well-intended help of some supporters unwittingly provoked feelings of frustration and impotence within those for whom they were caring at what they considered to be overly intrusive and smothering behaviour. The converse proved also just as difficult for respondents to endure; for example, Rose was badgered by her mother when she was in 'agony with the pain' of her tumour. They all struggled in their attempts to maintain social and domestic equilibrium. Failures in communication were, unfortunately, not helped by the respondents' tendency to endeavour to protect even their most enthusiastically involved supporters from the full extent of their difficulties.

Although devastating in its effect, an illness such as cancer is often seen to strike arbitrarily and, unfortunately, did not excuse the individuals unlucky enough to have it from having to bear their share of other hardships. Frequently, the respondents found themselves struggling to manage not only their own illness but also addressing other problems that arose. Gerry, for example, had to balance the social demands attendant to the birth of his daughter with the medical routines necessary to his recent diagnosis with cancer. Louise, whose active treatment had been halted, lived with her severely disabled husband and mid-way through our series of interviews learned that her four-year-old daughter had leukaemia.

Being physically unable to meet their social responsibilities did not prevent the respondents' interest in those for whom they cared. No matter to what extent they were physically unable to participate within their social groups, they were still firmly anchored there psychologically. In turn, concerns expressed by their supporters were taken as an indication of their continued participation within these social groups.

Just as relationships could prove stressful so, too, did they sometimes function to ameliorate something of the problems inherent in a chronic cancer trajectory. Respondents benefited from the knowledge that, to whatever extent, they were still useful members of their new society, that of the ill, and enjoyed opportunities to assist or educate others about their illness. Input from supporters, healthy and ill, proved in turn to be beneficial to the respondents, for example, when they faltered both physically and emotionally, by encouraging them to seek medical counsel on detection of symptoms, as well as by being tangibly present at other difficult moments, such as diagnosis or prior to, or when coping with, treatment.

More ambiguous though were the relationships formed by respondents with their medical teams. At this difficult time, when they felt their very lives to be under immediate threat, they had to negotiate what they believed to be their only chance for continued survival in a way of life, which was, for the majority, very different from that with which they were familiar. As all had placed their trust in traditional medical science, most of their encounters with their clinicians took place within hospitals, terrain for the most part not only entirely unfamiliar to many of them but also populated by a host of individuals with whom they were previously unacquainted. Because medicine is a specialist discipline, hierarchies of power also exist where the jargon employed to expedite treatment may, however innocently, serve to endorse the subordinate status which some felt when dealing with the staff. The stress that these difficult times placed on all the respondents involved was immense and often resulted in outbursts of uncharacteristic anger directed at their supporters, which, in turn placed those relationships under extreme strain.

Not surprisingly, the sudden switch into the medical realm resulted in the respondents feeling confused. The shock, which they experienced on learning their diagnosis, turned to fear as they realised that the future which they had envisaged was now in jeopardy and they mourned for the losses which this curtailed future would mean. It was their own bodies that had betrayed them and they felt anger and frustration at their own ignorance of how such an insidious, sly growth could have been nurtured unknowingly within.

This book also highlights the sudden and dramatic swings experienced by individuals with cancer as they dared to hope that they might recover but feared that they might not. These fluctuations in thought and feelings were especially difficult to endure both in the build up to learning the results of tests and whilst living through periods of often prolonged remission. When reporting their emotional reactions to the difficult events that they were enduring, respondents adopted an almost 'confessional' tone to me. They actually felt guilty, embarrassed and ashamed to admit to these feelings towards those who cared for them, particularly feelings of anger and jealousy.

To exacerbate their difficult situation further, the respondents also had to learn to adapt to the practical problems they would encounter, such as having to fit into the rigid time regime that hospitals operate in their endeavour to maximise efficiency.

Amongst the problems that can occur whilst dealing with so many specialist professionals, for example surgeons, oncologists and radiographers, are difficulties caused by breakdowns between multi-disciplinary teams. We have learnt how Ben was upset by the difficult relationship that existed between his oncologist and his consultant radiologist and how he suffered from the lack of communication between the two specialist teams.

It should be stressed again that all of this is happening at a time when individuals are attempting to learn how to cope with the, often worrying and difficult, physical problems that their symptoms have brought about, such as reduced mobility and pain, as well as learning to manage their new treatment routines.

The intensive contact I had with the respondents educated me about some of the many trials they were forced to endure as their dying journey drew progressively closer to its destination. My respect for these individuals increased as my relationship with them deepened and they, in turn, drew closer to me, offering me their confidence as our bond developed. At this most difficult time in their lives, when they were confronted with the multiple losses which they knew their deaths would cause, they found that even the extent to which they could continue to maintain their powers of self governance were subject to negotiation with others who were sometimes more interested in appropriating that power rather than sharing it.

The adjective 'dying' evokes certain images. It is perceived as a negative. Those I met, however, were very far from negative. Although Sudnow (1967) is right to observe how some, for example the elderly, die socially before their final biological death, those individuals I interviewed and who, it should be noted, had been classified and described to me as dying, were vital in their drive to exhaust every opportunity which came to them in what remained of their lives. By dint of their illness, the respondents had been removed from mainstream society; however, this abstraction from what is accepted as conventional life brought them an alternative perspective. Although they did not appreciate being physically restricted, they rose psychologically above these limitations, making the most of what they could do and particularly valuing their ability to continue engaging with their social bonds.

They were desperate to stay alive in order to maintain contact with those who they loved. In contemplating what dying meant to them, they did not rue the relinquishing of things practical or ever complain about the intensity of their emotions, which at times threatened to overwhelm them. Rather, they pined for the social losses, which they knew their death would bring. These were individuals who, altruistically, worked up till their last breath to protect those for whom they cared. They were individuals who lived up to their deaths.

Bibliography

Ariès, P. (1974) *Western Attitudes Toward Death: From the Middle Ages to the Present*, Baltimore: Johns Hopkins University Press.

Ariès, P. (1981) *The Hour of Our Death*, London: Allen Lane.

Armstrong-Coster, A. (2001) 'In Morte Media Jubilate: an empirical study of cancer-related documentary film', *Mortality*, 6(3), 287–305.

Bauman, Z. (1992) *Mortality, Immortality and Other Life Strategies*, Oxford: Polity.

Becker, E. (1973) *The Denial Of Death*, New York: Free Press.

Bertman, S. (1991) *Facing Death: Images, Insights, and Interventions*, Bristol, USA: Taylor & Francis.

Blauner, R. (1996) 'Death and social structure', *Psychiatry*, 24, 378–94.

Bourdieu, P. (1990) 'Time perspectives of the Kabyle' in J. Hassard (ed.) *The Sociology of Time*, London: The Macmillan Press Ltd.

Bowlby, J. (1961) 'Processes of mourning', *International Journal of Psychoanalysis*, 42.

Brown, R. and Kulik, J. (1977) 'Flashbulb memories', *Cognition*, 5.

Bury, M. (1982) 'Chronic illness as biographical disruption', *Sociology of Health and Illness*, 4 (2), 167–82.

Busfield, J. (2000) *Health and Health Care in Modern Britain*, Oxford University Press.

Charmaz, K. (1983) 'Loss of self: a fundamental form of suffering in the chronically ill', *Sociology of Health and Illness*, 5 (2), 168–91.

Charmaz, K. (1989) 'The self in time', *Studies in Symbolic Interaction*, 10, 127–41.

Charmaz, K. (1991) *Good Days, Bad Days: The Self in Chronic Illness and Time*, New Jersey: Rutgers University Press.

Christakis, N. (1999) *Death Foretold: Prophecy and Prognosis in Medical Care*, London: University of Chicago Press.

Clark, D. (1999) 'Cradled to the grave? Terminal care in the United Kingdom, 1948–67', *Mortality*, 4 (3), 225–47.

Cornwell, J. (1984) *Hard-Earned Lives*, London: Tavistock Publications.

Coser, R. L. (1961) 'Insulation from observability and types of social conformity', *American Sociological Review*, 26, 28–39.

Costain Schou, K. and Hewison, J. (1999) *Experiencing Cancer: Quality of Life in Treatment*, Buckingham: Open University Press.

Craib, I. (1994) *The Importance of Disappointment*, London: Routledge.

Davis, F. (1959) 'The cabdriver and his fare: facets of a fleeting relationship', *American Journal of Sociology*, 65, 158–65.

Dein, S. and George, R. (2001) 'The time to die: symbolic factors relating to the time of death', *Mortality*, 6(2), 203–11.

Del Vecchio, M. J., Good, M., Munakata, T., Kobayashi, Y., Mattingly, C. and Good, B. J. (1994) 'Oncology and narrative time', *Social Science and Medicine*, 38(6), 855–62.

Denzin, N. K. (1984) *On Understanding Emotion*, San Francisco: Jossey-Bass Publishers.

Diamond, J. (1999) *C: Because Cowards Get Cancer Too*, London: Vermilion.

Doka, K. J. (1993) *Living with Life-threatening Illness: A Guide for Patients, Families and Caregivers*, Lexington, MA: Lexington Books.

Donne, J. (1624) *Devotions upon Emergent Occasions*.

Douglas, M. (1984) *Purity and Danger: An Analysis of Concepts of Pollution and Taboo*, London: Ark Paperbacks.

Duclow, D. F. (1981) 'Dying on Broadway: Contemporary Drama', *Soundings*, Summer, 64 (2), 197–216.

Elias, N. (1985) *The Loneliness of the Dying*, Bath: Pitman Press.

Exley, C. E. (1998) 'Living with Cancer, Living with Dying: The Individual's Experience' (Unpublished PhD Thesis), Coventry University.

Featherstone, M. (1992) 'The heroic life and everyday life', *Theory, Culture and Society*, 9, 159–82.

Feifel, H. (1959) (ed.) *The Meaning of Death*, New York: McGraw-Hill.

Field, D. (1984) 'Formal instruction in United Kingdom medical schools about death and dying', *Medical Education*, 18, 429–34.

Field, D. (1996) 'Awareness and modern dying', *Mortality*, 1(3), 255–65.

Field, D., Hockey, J. and Small, N. (1997) *Death, Gender and Ethnicity*, London: Routledge.

Flaherty, M. (1987) 'Multiple realities and the experience of duration', *The Sociological Quarterly*, 28(3), 313–26.

Frank, A. (1991) *At the Will of the Body: Reflections on Illness*. Boston: Houghton Mifflin.

Frank, A. (1995) *The Wounded Story Teller: Body, Illness, and Ethics*, London: University of Chicago Press.

Frankenberg, R. (1988) '"Your time or mine?" An anthropological view of the tragic temporal contradictions of biomedical practice' in M. Young and T. Schuller (eds.) *The Rhythms of Society*, London: Routledge.

Frankenberg, R. (1992) *Time, Health and Medicine*, London: Sage Publications.

Freimuth, V. S., Stein, J. A. and Kean, J. (1989) *Searching for Health Information: The Cancer Information Service Model*. Philadelphia: University of Pennsylvania Press.

Freud, S. (1959) *Mourning and Melancholia: The Standard Edition of the Complete Works of Sigmund Freud, Vol. 14*, London: Hogarth Press.

Froggatt, K. (1997) 'Rites of Passage and the Hospice Culture', *Mortality*, 2(2), 123–36.

Gergen, K. J. (1991) *The Saturated Self: Dilemmas of Identity in Contemporary Life*, New York: Basic Books.

Germain, C. P. (1980) 'Nursing the dying: implications of the Kubler-Ross staging theory', in R. Fox (ed.) *The Annals of the American Academy of Political and Social Science* Vol. 447 (46–58).

Glaser, B. G. and Strauss, A. L. (1964) 'Awareness contexts and social interaction', *American Sociological Review*, 29, 669–79.

Glaser, B. G. and Strauss, A. L. (1965) *Awareness of Dying*, Chicago: Aldine.

Goffman, E. (1963) *Stigma: Notes on the Management of Spoiled Identity*, Harmondsworth: Penguin.

Gorer, G. (1965) *Death, Grief and Mourning in Contemporary Britain*, London: Cresset.

Graham, H. (1987) 'Women's smoking and family health', *Social Science and Medicine*, 25(1).

Guthke, K. S. (1999) *The Gender of Death: A Cultural History in Art and Literature*, Cambridge University Press.

Gyllenskold, K. (1982) *Breast Cancer: The Psychological Effects of the Disease and Its Treatment*, Patricia Crompton (trans.), London: Tavistock.

Hammersley, J. and Atkinson, M. (1996) *Ethnography: Principles in Practice*, London: Routledge.

Hart, B., Sainsbury, P. and Short, S. (1998) 'Whose dying? A sociological critique of the "good death"', *Mortality*, 3(1), 65–77.

Hassard, J. (1990) (ed.) *The Sociology of Time*, Basingstoke: Macmillan.

Herman, J. (1992) *Trauma and Recovery*, New York: Basic Books.

Hochschild, A. R. (1983) *The Managed Heart: Commercialisation of Human Feeling*, London: University of California Press.

Howarth, G. and Leamon, O. (eds.) *The Encyclopaedia of Death and Dying*, London: Routledge.

Illich, I. (1976) *Medical Nemesis*, New York: Random House Inc.

Karpf, A. (1988) *Doctoring the Media: the Reporting of Health and Medicine*, London: Routledge.

Kellehear, A. (1984) 'Are we a "Death Denying" Society? A Sociological Review', *Social Science and Medicine*, 18(9).

Kfir, N. and Slevin, M. (1991) *Challenging Cancer: From Chaos to Control*, London: Routledge.

Kubler-Ross, E. (1995) *On Death and Dying*, London: Routledge.

Langley-Evans, A. and Payne, S. (1997) 'Light-hearted death talk in a palliative day care context', *Journal of Advanced Nursing*, 26, 1091–7.

Laslett, B. and Rapoport, R. (1975) 'Collaborative Interviewing and Interactive Research', *Journal of Marriage and the Family*, 37, 968–77.

Laurer, R. H. (1981) *Temporal Man*, New York: Praeger Publishers.

Lawton, J. (2000) *The Dying Process: Patients' Experiences of Palliative Care*, London: Routledge.

Leak, W. N. (1948) 'The care of the dying', *The Practitioner*, 161, 80–7.

Lewin, K. (1936) *Principles of Topological Psychology*, New York: McGraw-Hill.

Lichter, I. (1987) *Communication in Cancer Care*, Edinburgh: Churchill Livingstone.

Lifton, J. (1967) *Death in Life: Survivors of Hiroshima*, New York: Simon and Schuster.

Lofland, L. H. (1978) *The Craft Of Dying: The Modern Face of Death*, London: Sage.

Lutfey, K. and Maynard, D. (1998) 'Bad news in oncology: how physician and patient talk about death and dying without using those words', *Social Psychology Quarterly*, 61(4), 321–41.

Maddocks, I. (1996) 'Hope in dying: palliative care and a good death' in J. Morgan, *An Easeful Death – Perspectives on Death, Dying and Euthanasia*, Sydney: Federation Press.

Maines, D. R., Sugrue, N. M. and Katovich, M. A. (1983) 'Sociological Import of G. H. Mead's Theory of the Past', *American Social Review*, 48, 161–73.

Mamo, L. (1999) 'Death and dying: confluences of emotion and awareness', *Sociology of Health and Illness*, 21(1), 13–36.

McKeown, T. (1976) *The Modern Rise of Population*, London: Edward Arnold.

McNamara, B., Waddell, C. and Colvin, M. (1994) 'The institutionalisation of the good death', *Social Science and Medicine*, 39:11, 1501–8.

Melbin, M. (1987) *Night as Frontier: Colonizing the World After Dark*, New York: McMillan Free Press.

Mellor, P. A. (1993) 'Death in High Modernity' in D. Clarke (ed.) *The Sociology of Death*, Oxford: Blackwell.

Neilson-Chapman, B. (1997) *Sand and Water*, London: WEA Records.

Nekolaichuk, C. L. and Bruera, E. (1998) 'On the nature of hope in palliative care', *Journal of Palliative Care*, 14(1), 36–42.

Nettleton, S. (1995) *The Sociology of Health and Illness*, Cambridge: Polity Press.

Nowotny, H. (1994) *Time: the Modern and Postmodern Experience*, Cambridge: Polity Press.

Parkes, C. M. (1972) *Bereavement: Studies of Grief in Adult Life*, London: Tavistock.

Parkes, C. M., Laungani, P. and Young, B. (1997) (eds.) *Death and Bereavement Across Cultures*, London: Routledge.

Parsons, T. (1951) *The Social System*, London: Routledge & Kegan Paul.

Parsons, T. (1978) 'Death in the Western world' in T. Parsons (ed.) *Action Theory and the Human Condition*, New York: Free Press.

Parsons, T. and Lidz, V. (1967) 'Death in American society' in E. Shneidman (ed.) *Essays in Self-Destruction*, New York: Science House.

Phillips, D. and King, E. W. (1988) 'Death takes a holiday: mortality surrounding major social occasions', *Lancet*, 2, 728–32.

Phillips, D. and Smith, D. (1990) 'Postponement of death until symbolically meaningful occasions', *Journal of the American Medical Association*, 263, 1947–51.

Platt, J. R. (1966) *The Step to Man*, New York: Wiley.

Prichard, P. (1992) 'Doctors, patients and time' in R. Frankenberg (ed.) *Time, Health and Medicine*, London: Sage Publications.

Radley, A. (1999) 'The aesthetics of illness: narrative, horror and the sublime', *Sociology of Health and Illness*, 21(6), 778–96.

Roberts, S. L. (1986) *Behavioral Concepts and the Critically Ill Patient*, Norwalk, Connecticut: Appleton-Century-Crofts.

Roth, J. A. (1963) *Timetables: Structuring the Passage of Time in Hospital Treatment and Other Careers*, New York: Bobbs-Merrill.

Saunders, C. and Baines, M. (1983) *Living with Dying: The Management of Terminal Disease*, Oxford University Press.

Seale, C. (1995) 'Heroic Death', *Sociology*, 29 (4), 597–613.

Seale, C. (1998) *Constructing Death: The Sociology of Dying and Bereavement*, Cambridge University Press.

Simmel, G. (1964) *The Sociology of Georg Simmel*, K. H. Wolff (ed.), New York: Free Press.

Small, N. and Rhodes, P. (2000) *Too Ill to Talk?* London: Routledge.

Sontag, S. (1978) *Illness as Metaphor*, New York: Farrar, Straus and Giroux.

Spradley, J. P. and Phillips, M. (1972) 'Culture and stress: a quantitative analysis', *American Anthropologist*, June, 518–42.

Stacey, J. (1997) *Teratologies: A Cultural Study of Cancer*, London: Routledge.

Sudnow, D. (1967) *Passing On: the Social Organisation of Dying*, Englewood Cliffs: Prentice Hall.

Thomas, L. (1980) 'Dying as failure', *Annals of the American Academy of Political and Social Science*, 447, 1–4.

Tuchman, G. (1973) 'Making news by doing work: routinizing the unexpected', *American Journal of Sociology*, 79(1), 110–31.

Ungerson, C. (1987) *Policy is Personal: Sex, Gender and Informal Care*, London: Tavistock.

Walter, T. (1991) 'Modern death – taboo or not taboo?' *Sociology*, 25(2), 293–310.

Walter, T. (1994) *The Revival of Death*, London: Routledge.

Weber, M. (1993) *From Max Weber: Essays in Sociology*, London: Routledge.

Weisman, A. (1980) 'Thanatology' in H. Kaplan, A. Freeman and B. Sadock (eds.) *Comprehensive Textbook of Psychiatry II*, Maryland.

Wolff, K. H. (1964) (ed.) *The Sociology of Georg Simmel*, New York: The Free Press.

Young, E., Bury, M. and Elston, M. A. (1999) '"Live and/or let die": modes of social dying among women and their friends', *Mortality*, 4(3), 27–42.

Young, M. and Cullen, L. A. (1996) *A Good Death: Conversations with East Londoners*, London: Routledge.

Zborowski, M. (1952) 'Cultural components in responses to pain', *Journal of Social Issues*, 4:16–30.

Zerubavel, E. (1981) *Hidden Rhythms: Schedules and Calendars in Social Life*, University of Chicago Press.

Zerubavel, E. (1982) 'Personal information and social life', *Symbolic Interaction*, 5, 97–109.

Zola, I. K. (1972) 'Medicine as an institute of social control', *Sociological Review*, 20.

Zola, I. K. (1973) 'Pathways to the doctor – from person to patient', *Social Science and Medicine*, 7, 677–89.

Index